Simón Bolívar

BOLÍVAR

A Contribution to the Study of his Political Ideas

By

C. PARRA-PEREZ

Translated by

N. ANDREW N. CLEVEN, Ph. D.
Professor of History, University of Pittsburgh

GREENWOOD PRESS, PUBLISHERS
WESTPORT, CONNECTICUT

Library of Congress Cataloging in Publication Data
Parra-Perez, Caracciolo, 1888-1963.
  Bolívar : a contribution to the study of his political
ideas.

  Reprint of the 1928 ed. published by Editions
Excelsior, Paris.
  Includes bibliographical references.
  1. Bolívar, Simón, 1783-1830. 2. South America--
History--Wars of Independence, 1806-1830.
F2235.3.P2513 1975   980'.02'0924   74-12756
ISBN 0-8371-7754-5

Originally published in 1928 by Editions Excelsior, Paris

Reprinted in 1975 by Greenwood Press,
a division of Williamhouse-Regency Inc.

Library of Congress Catalog Card Number 74-12756

ISBN 0-8371-7754-5

Printed in the United States of America

To

Doctor Pedro Itriago Chacin
an honor to Venezuelan Politics
and to the Venezuelan Bar
this book is cordially
dedicated

Translator's Introductory Note

This translation of Doctor C. Parra Perez's work is intended to serve a double purpose. First, to give a larger circulation to the political ideas of Simón Bolívar. Secondly, to serve as an act of homage, however modest and informal, to the memory of the immortal Liberator. During the century that comes to an end on December 17, this year, since the death of the Liberator, his star has been in the ascendancy, until he has become the Liberator *par excellence*. The present work is not a biography as such. It is, however, a discussion of one of the most important, if not *the* most important phase of the activities of Bolívar. As an analysis of the *political ideas* of the Liberator this work should have a large appeal for the political unrest and commotion in several of the Spanish American Republics at the present time should lend an added emphasis to any analysis of the political ideology of the leaders of those countries.

It has not been the purpose of the translator to offer a commentary upon either the work of Doctor Parra Perez or upon the political ideas of Bolívar. The translator has confined himself wholly to the task of clothing the contents of the work in English as faithfully as possible. He craves the kind indulgence of the reader for the task was performed under great pressure and in a rather hurried fashion. The reader is asked to look for the elements of greatness in Bolívar and for the essence of his political views. He will find therein an illuminating exposition of many of the characteristics of the Spanish American *caudillo* and *caudillismo*, a subject which constantly presents itself to the student of the peoples and countries of Hispanic America. Some day the present translator may venture forth with a study of the political philosophy of Bolívar: but until he shall have completed the study of the political organization of Bolivia, as Research Associate in History of the Carnegie Institution of Washington, nothing will be done, save that of gathering information for such a work.

The translator is under obligation to Doctor L. S. Rowe and Doctor E. Gil Borges, Director General and Assistant Director respectively of the Pan American Union. Both of these distinguished men approved the idea of a translation of Doctor Parra Perez's work at this time. Neither of them is, however, in the slightest degree, responsible for the character of the translation, or for the manner of its publication. The translator is under an especially peculiar obligation to Mr. David A. Buerger, a rising attorney of our city. It is an obligation which comes about through the relationship of instructor and student in academic life. Mr. Buerger made, as a graduate student in a course in the *Political Theories and Practices of Hispanic America,* conducted by the undersigned, a rough translation of the work of Doctor Para Perez. The present translation is, however, the work of the undersigned, and for any defects therein he alone must bear the responsibility. Appreciation of the assistance rendered by Mr. Buerger is hereby publically expressed. To the Pittsburgh Printing Company, publishers of the work, kindly thanks are offered for the excellence of printing and binding. Thanks are also due to my good wife, Hilma Willd Cleven, whose patience and good will at all times have made the present work possible.

N. Andrew N. Cleven

The University of Pittsburgh
Pittsburgh, Pa.
August, 1930.

TABLE OF CONTENTS

Foreword

THIS book was written during the years 1914 to 1916, which fact should explain, to the hostile critic, most of the defects and shortcomings of the work, although that fact should not justify them. The most important of the defects are the profusion of literal citations from Bolívar, and the absence of unpublished documents which, many claim, give value to an historical work. As for the citations, the reader may find consolation in the fact that it is better to have the exact words of a great man in order to understand him, than it is to have a commentary on what he said or wrote. Such a commentary is also likely to be quite irrelevant, most of the time, to the object in hand. As regards documentation and a bibliographv, we may say that we used what we had at hand, and that we undertook the preparation of the work without any other object than that of killing time in peaceful Burdeos during the first weeks of the European War. On our return to Paris, absorbed in official duties and in the excitement of that formidable cataclysm, we had no real opportunity to add to our store of information, or to secure anything new bearing on the general theme.

The majority of these chapters, which are, in a way, separate studies of the different episodes in the life of Bolívar, have been published in Latin American reviews and other periodicals. We have decided to publish this volume in order to bring the history of these episodes to the attention of those to whom a series of articles would not be attractive; and for the purposes of criticism and reference. If we were to write or revise this work today, it is likely that we should adopt a different method, and so modify our interpretation of some of Bolívar's ideas. These new studies might reveal the imperfections of our work much after the manner of the mischievous mirror which reveals silver threads in a head of black hair. But sentiments easily understood impels us to reproduce some of the chapters as originally published and to add others without any appreciable variation from the original. A few notes, presented later, give explanations or additional data that seemed necessary. One of these indicates, at the end of chapter eight, the omission of paragraphs dealing with a certain dispute which historical propriety demands should remain unrecorded, and which it is useless to consider now.

In our eyes, Bolívar was not a monarch, nor did he ever aspire to a crown. Unqualified approval, which does not constitute in itself a title of greatness for him, does not prove his personal disinterestedness, nor predetermine the wisdom of his beliefs. In politics, words have lost much of the magical power which the past century gave them. Our contemporaries prefer, instead, deeds and realities. Immortal principles alone have enjoyed academic immortality, while the literature which gave them form has given place to other principles and other writings no less immortal or ephemeral. In every case, the question of the theoretical form of government holds only a secondary place, while the place of primary importance is given to the social problem. The French revolutionists, Siéyes and Robespierre, for example, so considered it in the moments of their greatest vision. If we examine Bolívar basically, we shall find how much the social aspects of the theory of politics meant to him.

The form of government which the Liberator considered the best may be found through a study of existing data; but, to those who prefer the actual texts, the best method is a study of the Constitution of 1826, or the Bolivian, which seems to suggest the form which he believed to be the best for the countries which owe their liberation to him. The exercise of autocratic power, on the other hand, also attracted Bolívar, at first because of his personal temperament, and later because of political necessity. In addition to this, there are the sources of his views. The Liberator found in Voltaire, Rousseau, and in all the encylopedists arguments favoring his views, for the political literature of the eighteenth century was favorable to the régime of an enlightened despotism. History proves that there never existed, except in small and humble societies, a form of government that merited the name of democracy. History proves that the State, as a matter of fact, always finds itself in the hands of a man or group of men who form an all-powerful oligarchy (aristocracy in Rome of the early centuries, aristocracy and plutocracy in Venice and England, and pure plutocracy in Carthage and the United States of North America), although the oligarchy rarely consents to be known by that name or to acknowledge frankly its real character.

But Bolívar was subject to influences of every kind which, by virtue of their force and diversity, tend to obscure his own originality. His case is similar to that of Mirabeau. Barthou, among others, has shown the influences working on the great orator: the ancients, Voltaire, Buffon, Rousseau, all of whom at last made Mirabeau. This man Mirabeau did not take, however, as gospel, the ideas of the Social Contract, and so we see him, for example, attacking the doctrine of the presumed state of nature, which he called dangerous to the progress and civilization of humanity. We can affirm that the process of assimilation of ideas through reading was the same in Bolívar, and likewise in all persons of the epoch, reflecting the singular influence of Miranda. Contradictions are inevitable, we should say necessary, among men who have been educated in a certain manner, and the genius, who is popularly appreciated but who has himself but little popular feeling, is a contradiction, or seems to be so, to the majority of people.

The author of this book broke away completely ten years ago from the ideas of Jules Mancini concerning the intellectual development of Bolívar: imbued by Jean-Jacques, Mancini saw his master alone on every side. We have not, for a moment, attributed to the methods and personal counsels of Simón Rodríguez the influence which some consider decisive in the education of the Liberator, and which the Liberator himself, kindly and graciously, proclaims in his radiant writings. The genius of Rodríguez is comparable to the redoubtable Henri Rousseau, whose accounts declare in extravagant terms the movements which the Venezuelans call posthumously *delpinismo*. Imagine what Bolívar would have been as a disciple of Don Simón Rodríguez! The *delpinistas* of the history of Venezuela bury, with a jovial farce, a plate of irony in the grave face of the epopee.

Bolívar, from 1810 to 1812, conversed with Miranda, followed his ideas, and received directly the famous sacred zeal. In London he read the correspondence and political tracts of the illustrious agitator; in Caracas he was one of the noble supporters of Miranda in the struggle of the Patriotic Society against the vacillating Congress. The constitutional theories of the Liberator, for example, on the force and vigor of the executive power, essentials in his sytem, are identical with those which Miranda proposed in 1795 in the treatise on the evils which afflicted France and their possible remedies. Some one spoke to me of the interest which he would have in determining, in the ideas which we call Bolivarian, which were common to the men of the time, those of Miranda and those of Bolívar. A study of these ideas which are more or less elaborate would determine the contribution of the latter to the general movement of human politics, and would exalt his originality more than a hymn of praise such as the fabulous hozanas sung to the praise of Alexander.

However, Bolívar is not a doctrinarian as was Miranda, and herein lies the great difference between them. The Precursor believed, at that time, in the Constitution as the panacea for all public calamities. The Liberator was always sceptical as to the virtue of all legal precepts. For Bolívar there was not one constitution, but many, as many as there are states and nations. He was an opportunist after the manner of Solon:

"Which is the best constitution?"

"For whom and at what time?"

Admirable political philosophy this for all times, the product of the judgment of humanity and not of its science. It was called positivism in the works of August Comte, and which was signalized as characteristic of the conduct of Bolívar by Venezuelan authors long before it was presented to us as a new revelation in strange words which confused in strange language the criticism of past deeds and the expression of new thoughts.

Bolívar believed that the important thing that matters was to insure liberty to the citizens, and did not believe in seeking to perform miracles with the word Liberty even when written with a capital letter.   Unfortunately, the Goddess of Liberty caused great disasters in Hispanic America because the Revolution destroyed the vital cells of future states in destroying the colonial municipalities, which were organs of true civil and administrative liberties. The Peruvian writer Beláunde recently expressed the thought that the Liberator did not escape this sad error. The author of the present lines, referring to this particular point, observed, in 1925, in a letter to the historian Pouget de Saint-André, that the sponsors of Independence did not know how to utilize the solid foundations which the Spanish régime bequethed to its children.

Some of our conclusions coincide with those of brilliant scholars who, in America and elsewhere, in recent essays, have written on the work of Bolívar. And as this book is primarily based upon the ideas of two or three masters of Venezuelan and American history, these coincidences deserve to be dealt with since they tend to prove that the test of any work lies in the same field, and tends to be purged of impure elements in the complicated process of definite evaluation. As we contemplate the numerous works now devoted to Bolívar, we recall with pleasure how twenty years ago, when we were scarcely of age, we heard the words of our national Eloy González ring out with fiery eloquence, in his book *On the Margin of the Epogee*,[1] which marks an epoch in the rebirth of historical studies in Venezuela.

General Juan Vicente Gómez, President of the Republic, has kindly ordered this edition to be published at government expense, desiring to further, according to his laudable custom, the forces designed to increase the knowledge of our glorious countries. May his benevolent Excellency here find testimony of our sincere gratitude and most respectful loyalty.

C. P. P.

Rome: February, 1928.

---

[1]*Al Margin de la Epopeya.*

The Manifesto of Cartagena

BOLÍVAR, escaping the reprisals of the royalists in Caracas for the surrender of Miranda, and after having spent some time in Curaçao, went to Cartagena, where Torices received him kindly, and soon entrusted him with the command of a detachment stationed at Barrancas.

The disastrous failure of the first Republic of Venezuela at the hands of the Generalissimo and the experiences of the two years of political and military activity profoundly impressed the young colonel, purifying his patriotism and developing his iron will. Bolívar, like many another of that age, could not renounce liberty. With full knowledge of the conditions of his countrymen he judged it important to explain, in a public document, the basic causes of the loss of Caracas. He did this in order to awaken the ardor and the confidence of the patriots who had been terrified by the catastrophe and the vengence of the Spaniards. The *Manifesto to the People of New Granada*,[1] which he issued, accordingly began the series of writings, proclamations, discourses, letters, and messages with which, for eighteen years, the Liberator electrified America with an eloquence, prudence, and moral value equalled only by his energy and strength of arm. Muncini declared that these writings of Bolívar stirred the governing classes in New Granada profoundly, and that they prepared a path by which he was to realize his ambitions. The protection given him be President Torices, and the support of the handful of soldiers by which Cartegena had been won, thus became the means by which he was to realize many of his ideals.

Among the causes of the disasters which had befallen the patriot movement, up to that time, which Bolívar dealt with in the *Manifesto*, the elements of constitutional order are very important. The other matters dealt with were also important, because a knowledge of them will help us to understand his political theories. The moderate character of these theories is noteworthy. Even when experience caused him to modify them, this moderation still characterized his political philosophy during this period. I certainly am not able to understand why certain authors will insist upon calling Bolívar fickle. A study of his writings and activities of this period is sufficient to prove that he followed a well defined policy. The views of these authors can only result in a deplorable confusion of the principles of Bolívar's political philosophy, or of his views on constitutional order in general. And while the studies of these authors may give the reader a

---

[1]*Documents Dealing with the Public Life of the Liberator* (*Documentos para la vida pública del Libertador*) IV, 119

certain amount of new materials, they do not contribute to a clarification of his principles.[1]

The Liberator never ceased to denounce, as a grave danger to society, the turbulent systems of government born of a demagogic idealism which incites to Revolution. He saw the abyss of ignorance into which our people had been plunged, the lack of any ethnic cohesion, the struggle of races for freedom through war and incessant propoganda, the lack of culture among the people and the absence of any desire for culture in the Spanish lands of northern South America. He saw clearly, too, the need of establishing a powerful but temperate rule before there could be a union of these peoples. For such a rule is essential, in the creator and educator alike, to the exercise of liberty. Bolívar had just witnessed in Venezuela, reconquered by an adventurer, in the resignation of Miranda, late generalissimo of the patriots, to what ends a desire for imitation and the picturesque literature of ideologists might lead a people. An energetic authority, without needless laws, was all that Bolívar wanted to make war and to prepare the country for war. After the country had been reduced to peace and order, the State could be organized to preserve the national customs, modes of life, and the social conditions of the new groups. Considered in this light, it becomes plain that a definite, continuous, systematic purpose guided the political activities of the Liberator through his triumphs and through his defeats; and that this purpose remained uppermost in his mind in the hours of hope at Cartagena and during the period of disaster in Haiti, no less than during the glorious days in Lima and Bogotá.

The Congress of Venezuela declared that the country did not need any soldiers, for, in the case of an attack, all the citizens would rise to defend their country. With this ingenious formula they had lost the Republic. Bolívar ordered the organization of an army, and declined to be influenced by the flowery eloquence of demagogic strategists. He declared:

> Education and practical military science are indispensible to us. As reagrds the political doctrines which have prevailed to this day, they are incompatible with our present social status. We citizens have not yet learned the virtues which characterize true republicans. . . . . The codes of law which our magistrates consulted were not those which could teach us the practical science of government, but those which were formed by certain well-meaning visionaries who, imagining fantastic republics, have sought to obtain political perfection, presupposing the perfection of the human race.

Bolívar critized the weakness of the independent government, its tolerance and its good nature; condemned the degeneration of public fortunes and the reactionary influence of the clergy; and attacked the federal system, adopted by the Constitutional

---

[1]Lauteano Valle-Nilla-Lanz declared:

"It is impossible to find in any leader or any revolutionary chief the moderation in the statement of ideas and principles more nearly perfect than in Simón Bolívar."

Convention of 1811, as the plaything of future dreamers and greedy politicians. In this connection he expressed himself in this wise:

> "But what most weakened the Government of Venezuela was the federal form which it adopted, which, following the wildest exaggerations of the rights of man, ordered that it might rule itself for itself alone, broke social laws and threw nations into anarchy. . . . The federal system, although it may be the most perfect and the most capable of adjusting human happiness in society, is notwithstanding the most opposed to the interests of our new-born States. Generally speaking, our citizens are not capable of exercising their rights fully themselves because they lack the political virtues which characterize the true republican, virtues which are not acquired under an absolute government where there is so much difference between the rights and obligations of the citizens. . . . It is necessary that the government identify itself, as it were, with the character of the circumstances of the times and of the men it rules. . . .I am of the opinion that if we do not centralize our American governments our enemies will gain the most complete advantages: we shall be plunged hopelessly into the horrors of civil dissensions and vilely conquered by this group of bandits which infests our coasts."

The flow of ideas from France and of the constitutional principles from England and the Americans of the North deluged our intellectuals with an extraordinary profusion of words and notions which were readily accepted in many circles. Many of these ideas were, however, insufficiently understood by the neophytes, and for one reason or another could not be assimilated under our social conditions. These conditions could not support our own more advanced systems with the result that these new ideas brought about a confusion of doctrines and a falsification of concepts. The Liberator himself, when he speaks of the federal system, does not seem to distinguish clearly between political theory and administration. He exalted the excellencies of the federative principle as established in the United States, and praised the advantages of its federal system. He probably did this to flatter the supporters of the federal system, which he imagined implied complete individual liberty, and the full exercise of all the rights of the citizen, which are the final stage in political evolution. He even conceded a virtue which does not exist in any other institutions, and which, if they existed, would convert the federal states into political parasites. The Liberator believed, with Rousseau, that the republic is a type of free government. This is a false assumption; and Bolívar himself held that it was impossible to apply the principle of federation to America. The philosopher of Geneva, whose ideal it was, considered the federal, in the final analysis, a system suitable only for small city republics, able to defend, through union, their common independence. The federal system may, accordingly, not be a question of politics at all, but a system of administration with defects and advantages like all other systems.

The Liberator's criticism of the application of the federal system to our countries was, in another way, well founded. Among peoples who have a considerable number that are undeveloped politically, and among whom a minority, capable of exercising all the political rights which the citizens of a democracy enjoy, barely exists, it was, without doubt, folly to attempt to implant principles which, in the minds of our chiefs, were inherently bound up with the idea of the free and absolute exercise of the rights of the individual. The complex administration of the federal system further weakened by the inconveniences of the physical conditions of those countries and by the lack of the necessary preparation. "Popular elections," declared the Liberator, "carried out by country farmers and intriguing city-dwellers, add a great obstacle to our use of federation, because the former are so ignorant that they vote foolishly and the latter so ambitious that everything is in the hands of factions, so that free and honest voting in Venezuela is impossible." Another inconvenience, a most important one, lies in the weakness that establishes the system. A federal government may be and is, fatally, weak, because the great part of the administration and political activity is discharged by the autonomous provinces. It is the inability of the provinces to live their own life that has demanded in Hispanic-America a vigorous central government, and which has shown the essential fallacy of the principles of federation. The example of various American countries who, in the course of the century, have adopted federal forms and ultraliberal charters, but whose political customs have not varied sensibly with the application of this panacea, is a categorical reproach to the theorists who would divert our society from the slow but sure path towards perfecting their institutions. I should not wish to attribute to a man, or group of men, the responsibility of a national disaster, because I do not prefer to explain an inevitable series of sociological phenomena in the light manner of our professional political reformers. But I do feel that the premature propoganda, and the application of principles which are obviously inopportune, have contributed greatly to complicate the process of constitutional evolution in America. The excess of theoretical liberalism has caused the ruin of these countries, and in them, as in no other, the political principle that peoples lose more through bad methods of progress than through absence of reform, receives full confirmation. It cannot be repeated too often that it is not enough to proclaim right, liberty, and justice to have them come into being and to have them survive.

The results of the federalism of 1811 and of the democratic canons of the first Constitution gave no promise of success. It was not by such means, certainly, that the renovation of that anarchical and enfeebled society was to be achieved. The lack of authority, the small divisions, and the ceaseless liberal babble of the patriots were substituted for the vigor, the unity, and the actions which the circumstances demanded. Bolívar explained, in January, 1815, in an address before the Congress of the

Garanadian Union, the deep and basic causes of our inability to pass suddenly from oppressive tyranny to the enjoyment of the rights of citizens, as follows:

> The New World, created under the fatal power of the mob, has not been able to break its chains without maiming its members, the inevitable consequences of the vices of slavery and the errors of ignorance, so much the more lasting, as it is the more fanatical daughter of a superstition that has covered mankind with disgrace. Tyranny and the Inquisition have degraded the Americans and the children of the conquerors, who introduced these deplorable vices, to the class of brutes. Hence, what good reason, what political virtue, what pure principle can we find among ourselves to end the reign of oppression, and quickly substitute that of laws, which should establish rights, and impose obligations on the citizens of the new republic? The habit of blind obedience has so stultified our spirit that it is not possible for us to discover truth or to find the good. To submit to force was always our only duty; the great crime was to seek justice and to know the laws of nature and of men. To study the sciences, to consider the useful, and practice the virtuous, were offenses almost of treason, easier to commit than to obtain pardon for. Incarceration, exile, and death frequently followed the creation of means, which the talents of the unfortunates devised, for their own ruin, notwithstanding the numerous obstacles interposed by the masters of this hemisphere.

And Bolívar concluded with a very fine phrase:

> We were not even allowed to be the instruments of our own oppression.

In September of the same year, he wrote from Kingston:[1]

> The position of the inhabitants of the American hemisphere has been, for centuries, purely passive. The political life has been practically nill; we are in a position slightly higher than slaves, and, at the same time, in a more difficult condition to enable us to enjoy our liberty. . . . America was deprived not only of her liberty, but also of active and dominant tyranny. . . . We were, as I have explained, isolated, and I may say, deprived of all knowledge of the science of government and administration of the State. . . . The Americans have suddenly risen without previous knowledge of, and, what is more important, without experience in public affairs, to play a part in the world of eminent dignitaries as legislators, magistrates, financial administrators, diplomats, generals, and all authorities of the administration of a regularly organized State. . . . If we had at least managed our own domestic affairs, our internal administration, we should have known the nature and operation of public affairs. We should also have enjoyed what is so necessary to conserve, during revolutions, a certain mechanical respect for personal consideration in the eyes of the people.

It was a country without preparation and without ideals whose condition the Liberator described with exactness, where the parliamentarians of the Eleventh Year aspired to perpetuate the rule of the Constitution, which was[2]

> for dignity, clarity, logic, and perfection of its text, a model of its kind.

Bolívar does not forego an opportunity to critisize the system and the principles which, with the general notion which he considered inherent in them, are applied to the Indo-Spanish continent. An active and restless spirit, half warrior, half apostle, expelled from Venezuela by hostile arms, he visioned, with his

---

[1]*Letter to an English Gentleman*, September 6, 1815.
[2]Mancini, *Bolívar and the Emancipation of the Spanish Colonies*, p. 365.

pen, in the free land of Jamaica, the new religion, and indicated the means of emancipating enslaved America. A reform in the institutions adopted by the independents seemed to him indispensible. He wrote:[1]

All the new governments signalized their first movements by the creation of popular juntas. These promptly provided rules for the convocation of congresses, which made important alterations. Venezuela established a democratic federal government, having first adopted the rights of man; maintained a balance of powers and enacting laws in favor of civil liberty, the press, and other matters; finally, constituting itself an independent government. New Granada followed the example of Venezuela, adopting similar political practices and reforms, and taking for the fundamental basis of its constitution the most exaggerated federal system that ever existed. It has recently somewhat improved in respect to the executive power, having given it certain necessary attributes. Buenos Aires and Chile have, as I understand it, followed the same line of operations . .

Thus is may be said that:

"the experience of the continent has proved that pure representative institutions are not suitable to our character, customs, and present conditions. In Caracas, the party spirit found its origin in the societies, assemblies, and popular elections, and these parties forced us back into slavery. Venezuela which has been the American Republic which has advanced most in its political institutions, is also the best example of the inefficiency of the democratic and federal form for our new States. In New Granada, the excessive powers of the provincial governors and the general absence of centralization of power have led that poor country to the condition in which we find it reduced today. For that reason, its weak enemies have maintained themselves despite everything.
So long as our compatriots do not develop the talents and political virtues which distinguish our brothers of the North, the entire popular system, far from being suitable to our conditions, may, I fear, be our ruin. Unfortunately, these qualities seem not to be developed in us to the extent necessary; and, on the contrary, we are dominated by vices which, developed under the guidance of a nation like Spain, become weighted with ferocity, ambition, vengeance, and cupidity."

Bolívar, after having considered the need of institutions based on justice, liberty, and equality, asked:

Shall we be able to maintain in its true proportions the heavy load of a republic? Is it possible that a people, recently freed, can seize the star of liberty without having its wings melt, as it did with Icarus, and fall away into the abyss? Such a thing is inconceivable, never experienced. Therefore, there is no good reason why we should believe such a condition possible.

Accordingly, in order to conduct the war, the Liberator proclaimed that dictatorial power would suffice to give peace to America. He indicated in three lines the ideal formula for the institutions needed by America when it shall have been emancipated from foreign domination:

"The American States need the care of a paternal government to cure the wounds and sores of despotism and war."

It is the prayer of Pisistratus, the good despot, the educator of democracy, for the advent of which Bolívar dreamed in the vision of his America, consigned, without remedy, to demagogic furors and military tyranny. He explained again his views:[2]

---

[1]*Letter to an English Gentleman.* This is the letter of September 6, 1815.
[2]*Letter to an English Gentleman,* September 6, 1815.

"I do not agree with the federal system, as compared with the popular and the representative, for it is too perfect, and requires virtues and talents in politics very superior to ours. For the same reason, I condemn monarchy composed of aristocracy and democracy that England has developed with such fortune and splendor. If it is not possible to select some other form than that of the most perfect and completely developed republics and monarchies, we shall inevitably have to fall into demagogic anarchies or plutocratic tyrannies. Let us seek a medium between the opposite extremes that would lead us to the same reefs of unhappiness and dishonor."

Ten years later, the Liberator wrote the Constitution of Bolivia.

The Second Republic

FIFTEEN days sufficed for Colonel Simón Bolívar to go from Barrancas to Ocaña, where he arrived on January 7, 1818, with five hundred soldiers, after a strenuous campaign. He had, declared Mancini, dispersed the enemy, ten times superior in numbers, and had freed a province. When the troops of Correa were defeated at San Cayetano, Bolívar requested the Congress of the Granadian Union, assembled at Tunja, for authority to carry the war into Venezuela, then almost wholly occupied by the royalists. The jealousy of Castillo hampered for a considerable time the large forces under Camilo Torres. Later, when the Congress had given permission for the advance up to the provinces of Médira and Trujillo, Torres found many excuses for delaying the march of his troops. In case Venezuela should recover her independence, Bolívar was to try to have her adopt the federal form of government.

During the first fifteen days of May, the army of the Liberator crossed the Táchira River, and had begun the Great Campaign. Four months earlier, at the other extreme of the country, Mariño and the heroes of Chacachare, who had sworn, on their honor as gentlemen, taking for witnesses God and their swords, to die for liberty, began the liberation of the eastern provinces.[1]

In Mérida, Bolívar, acclaimed Liberator, increased his forces by six hundred men, who were to immortalize themselves at Campó Elías. Rivas Dávila. and the Picóns enlisted. A fiery proclamation informed the inhabitants at Mérida, who were "again citizens of the federal republic", that the war which was about to begin was to be a war to the death that our land might be "purged of the monsters that infest it". On June 15, Bolívar signed, in Trujillo, the most frightful document in all history:

Spaniards and Canary Islanders: Count on death although you may be indifferent to it; Americans: Count on life although you may be culpable.

The declaration of war to the death has been a question widely debated. Men of highly cultured minds, like Juan Vicente González and José Gil Fortoul, have severely critized it. Galindo and Mancini declared that, for this and other acts, Bolívar was lacking in piety. Larrazábal, on the other hand, qualified his censure with imprudence. The decree of Trujillo, frightful though it was, really only legalized a method of warfare deliberately employed by the Spaniards from the beginning of the Revolution. Dr. Antonio Nicolás Briceño, a fanatic, had, earlier, proclaimed in Cartagena in the Indies, the atrocious system of bounties, declaring:

---

[1]Mancini, *op. cit.*, *Doc.* IV, p. 468.

22

To earn pay or promotion, it will be sufficient to present the heads of a certain number of Canary Islanders: the soldier who presents twenty will be made a standard-bearer, thirty a lieutenant, fifty a captain, etc.

Bolívar had tried to justify the execution of prisoners through Captain Alcántara, alleging the crimes of the Spaniards.[1] The Liberator thought it necessary to turn to this terrible method, declared Restrepo,[2]

not through cruelty or hardness of heart, but through a system formed, after thoroughly considering the character of his compatriots, and the deeds which the Spaniards had already committed, or were then committing round about him in Venezuela.

In truth, the temperament of Bolívar had a great deal to do with it. Gil Fortoul observed:[3]

If his body were, above all, Spanish, the impulse of his soul was, likewise, so. In 1812, the defeat of Puerto Cabello exasperated him, and, on arriving at La Guaira, blinded with rage, he wanted to take vengeance on Miranda, in the manner of the barbarians, for a disaster for which all were equally responsible. When he began the campaign of 1813, his words and his acts seemed to imitate the vehemence and cruelty of the conquerors of the sixteenth century; in 1814, he did not hesitate to resort to the barbarism of Boves, by ordering Arismendi and Palacio to sacrifice eight hundred prisoners from Caracas and La Guaira. . . The Hispanic arrogance of the classic periods permeated all his proclamations.

However, Bolívar was not cruel. The presence of the prisoners mentioned proved that the decree received, at his hands, considerable provocation. A manifesto signed by Muñoz Tébar, Secretary of State, attempted to justify, before the world, the execution of the enemies.[4] The Liberator always practiced reprisals with repugnance. In December, 1814, in spite of his threats, he freed men, detained in Santa Fé; and in the proclamation of the Year 16, he declared that he was willing to end the war to the death. O'Leary told us of the "kindness of his heart, which prosperity had not been able to corrupt." "I know your heart, and I know that your soul is generous and compassionate," General Santander wrote to him after the massacre of September. Bolívar himself declared to the commander of the Spanish troops at Pampatar:[5]

The true warrior glories only in conquering his enemies, not in destroying them.

I feel that posterity will blame me for the blood that has flowed in Venezuela and New Granada, but I am consoled by leaving authentic documents of my philanthropy, and I trust that the blame will be placed where it properly belongs, on the European Spaniards.

"Bolívar was always great and noble even in the days of his errors," wrote General Posada Gutíerrez.[6]

---

[1]Restrepo, *History of Colombia*, I, 313.
[2]*Ibid.*, II, 142.
[3]*Constitutional History of Colombia*, I, 330.   [4]Larrazábal, *History of Bolívar*, I, 285.   [5]May 17, 1816.
[6]*Historical-Political Memoirs* (*Memorías Histórico-Politicas*), I, 78.

One should not attribute to the decree of Trujillo the ferocity that characterizes the struggle in Venezuela and New Granada. The Spaniards began the methodical killing, and even after the new regulations, Morales continued beheading Americans. In the spirit of the realists, an attempt was made to annihilate the white element on the continent in the hope of destroying with it the ideas of independence. This attempt to annihilate the white element is the most serious charge that can be made against the proclamation of war to the death: it contributed toward the depopulation of the country, by depriving it of a large number of men of the white race, and brought on a preponderance of half-breeds. It may also be observed, that all other civilizations have often presented the spectacle of real barbarism, just as frightful as that which took place in the American struggle.

A campaign worthy of Bonaparte brought the Liberator to Caracas, where, having restored, at least in form, the federative Constitution, in the provinces of Mérida and Trujillo, he hastened to organize a provisional government. At least this was the account given in the records of Sanz and Ustáriz. Bolívar assumed the position of the head of the government thus organized. He established three secretaryships for the conduct of public affairs; the first, of State, Foreign Relations, and the Treasury (Muñoz Tébar); the second, of War and Navy (Tómas Montilla); and the third, of Justice and Police (Rafael Diego Mérida). He appointed a civil and military governor for each province, and local heads for the districts or cantons. He also centralized the administration of the national taxation. Cristóbal Mendoza was appointed governor of Caracas and José Félix Ribas was appointed its military commander.[1] A letter to the Congress of New Granada explained the reasons for these measures.

The new government became a great organizing agency especially in military affairs. The government lasted until January 2, 1814. On that day, the Assembly, meeting again in the temple of San Francisco, vested the Liberator with dictorial powers. In fact, Bolívar already exercised full power, suiting his acts only to the circumstances and to his inclinations, and not inclined to reestablish the institutions of 1811, which in his opinion, were responsible for the fall of the First Republic. That he disliked the federal system, so dear to the Granadians and to the parliamentarians of Venezuela, was shown by the energetic measures which he took immediately. To the governor of Barinas who persisted, declared Eloy G. González, in "discussing forms of government and political systems ninety-six hours after the Liberator's army had triumphantly entered Caracas," Bolívar wrote on August 12[2]:

The division of powers has never established and perpetuated governments; only its concentration has established respect for a nation, and I have

---

[1]Restrepo, *op, cit.*, II, 166; Gil Fortoul, *op. cit.*, I, 221; Mancini, *op. cit., p.*521.
[2]González, *Al margen de la Epopeya*, *Doc.* IV, 759.

not freed Venezuela for any other purpose than that of putting this very system into effect. . . . While the present immediate danger lasts, I shall, despite all opposition, promptly inaugurate the energetic plan which has brought me such success in the past.

A military dictatorship was, in fact, the only means capable of saving the Revolution[1]. Exercised carefully by Bolívar, it manifested prodigious activity even though it was scarcely able to make headway against the reactionary movement which was growing through popular discontent and ignorance, and which was already beginning its formidable offensive. The days of Boves of our anniversaries are of the Terrible Year. It is necessary to remind oneself, in the history of the world, of the barbarian invasions of the Roman Empire, to ponder the savagery of the Asiatic conquerors, Tamerlane or Bayaceto, in order to form an idea of the bestial epoch on the plains of Venezuela. Boves overran them, as Totila did Italy, warring and destroying. The liberating sword in the hands of Bolívar triumphed in war, and brought the newborn independence into being, in an orgy of blood. No other nation in America suffered such frightful slaughters, no other conquered its liberty at such a price as did Venezuela.

Bolívar explained later, in opening the Council of State at Angostura, in November, 1817, the motives which determined his ascension to the dictatorship, in these words:

> When the people of Venezuela broke the oppressive chains that bound them to Spain, it was their first object to establish a constitution on the bases of modern politics, whose major principles are the division of powers and the balance of authorities. Then, condemning the tyrannical institution of the Spanish monarchy, they adopted the republican system as conforming more nearly to justice; and among the various republican forms they chose the most liberal of all, the federal. The vicissitudes of war were so unfortunate for Venezuelan arms that they led to the disappearance of the Republic with all its institutions. There would not have remained a single trace of our regeneration had not a few remaining defenders of the country, returning through New Granada and Guiria, and reestablished the independent government of Venezuela. The circumstances that accompanied this new reaction were such, and the movements of war so extraordinary, rapid, and impetuous, that it was impossible to give the government the constitutional regularity that Congress had decreed in the first period. All the force, and, I may say, all the violence of a military government was hardly sufficient to check the devastating torrent of insurrection, anarchy, and war. And what other government than the dictatorial would have suited such disturbing times? So the Venezuelans thought, and so they hastened to submit to this terrible but necessary administration. The examples of Rome were the counsel and guide of our citizens.

When, in February, 1819, he returned his power to the Congress which he, as the supreme head of the Republic had convoked, a power confirmed by precarious Assembly of Villa del Norte,[2] Bolívar described, in a masterly fashion, the political and military

---

[1]Mancini, *op. cit.*, p. 521.
[2]May 7, 1816.

activity during the busy years since his invasion of the Granadian frontier:[1]

> The epoch of the Republic over which I have presided has not been a mere political tempest, nor a bloody war, nor even popular anarchy. It has been in fact the inundation of an infernal torrent that had submerged the land of Venezuela. What dams could a man—and such a man as I?—interpose to check the sources of these devastations? In the midst of the sea of troubles, I have been nothing more than a mere toy of the revolutionary hurricane, that carried me like a weak straw. I could do nothing, either good or bad. Irristable forces have directed the march of our successes. To attribute them to me would not be just, and it would give me an importance which I do not deserve. Do you wish to know the authors of the deeds of the past and present order? Consult then the annals of Spain, of America, of Venezuela; examine the laws of the Indies, the rule of old mandatory powers, the influence of religion and of foreign dominion; observe the first acts of the republican Government, the ferocity of our enemies, and our national character.

In 1814 the force of the Liberator might have been impotent to stay the infernal torrent, but this force remains in history as a model of human energy.

The Spanish reaction had grown stronger, and barely ten days after Bolívar had arrived at Caracas, he left the city at the head of his reorganized troops, marching to strengthen the line at Puerto Cabello, the refuge of Monteverde. The victories of Bárbula and the Trincheras mark the glorious beginning of the operations. On October 15, the Liberator returned to Caracas, carrying the heart of the Granadian Girardot[3] in a silver urn. On the same day the people of the capital gave him, as Mérida had done, that high title which Congress and posterity have confirmed.

The divisions of patriots were operating against the Spaniards; Urdaneta was sent against Ceballos, the governor of Coro, who had advanced against Barquisimeto; and the Liberator sent Campo Elías against Boves, the master of the plains of Calabozo and Caracas. In Mosquitero, the army was destroyed, even to the last soldier, as one author describes it. Boves and Morales escaped, and Campo Elías, after having punished the people of Calabozo, suspected of royalism, rejoined Bolívar at San Carlos. The Liberator defeated the troops of Yáñez and Ceballos on the field of Arauro, on December 5.

Puerto Cabello, however, was an impregnable bulwark. Boves reorganized his forces. The provinces of Barinas was lost. Bolívar put his hope in the aid from Mariño, but that commander did not seem disposed to lead his army to Centro. Suspicious and distrustful, the hero of New Sparta did not wish to contribute to the success of one whom he considered as a rival, and he persisted in remaining away from the scene of action.

Under such circumstances, the city and the leaders of Caracas named Bolívar dictator, legalizing the authority which he had

---

[1]The source of the excerpt is not given. The address from which it was taken has been translated into English by Francisco Javier Yánes and published in 1919 by Byron S. Adams of Washington, D.C.

exercised. The Assembly of San Francisco possesses a special character, which it is worth while to explain. Mancini described it as follows:[1]

> The meeting of a national Congress was, under the circumstances, impossible. But the tradition of the Open Meeting (*Cabildo Abierto*) permitted the Liberator to consider the municipal assembly as the source of popular sovereignty. It was in virtue of this character that he declared he "wished to place before it the detailed account of his operations."

Political accidents suited the inclinations of Bolívar, who preferred to resort directly to the people to obtain his discretionary powers. The stratagem of the municipal body of Caracas, representative of the Republic, giving authority to a victorious general, was a clever means, useful to the Liberator in confirming his command, and in strengthening his position against popular rivals. Bolívar did not trust much in assemblies, whose permanent control he considered, for our countries, as useless or evil. It may be that his ideas of popular representation were not so different from those which led the insolent Socrates to condemn such assemblies. From another point of view, the Liberator had frequent access to the use of the plebiscite, a device of the Caesars. The idea was firmly impressed upon his mind that these people could not be governed for any length of time except in an autocratic fashion: and he held it to be an absurd illusion to suppose that it was enough to give them a liberal form of government, and to put into operation a strange administrative system, in the hope of changing, at one stroke, social conditions and political ideas. A colonial rule of three centuries had moulded the American character; and extraordinary mixture of races had produced, in America, an inert body of men, without a collective soul, unable to appreciate spiritual postulates of a mixed nature. Superior to the men who surrounded him, in the patriotic exercise of an authoirty which he used for the public good and the public welfare, the Liberator applied a necessary political autocracy, which incited censure of Puritans, and led impressionable writers to believe that imperial ambitions existed where only a genial and vigorous temperament existed. Such a state of affairs was a natural result of his personality, and of the conditions of the elements which he strove to subdue.

On January 2, the Liberator came before the people of Caracas to give an account of his military and administrative operations, and to seek confirmation of the authority which the Granadian Congress had given him. The adversaries of New Granada were numerous in Venezuela. For this reason the conduct of Bolívar removed many of the causes for opposing the Revolution, and convinced the patriots of Venezuela of this nationalist movement. The Liberator, looking carefully to appearances, found the means of loosening the ties which bound him to the federalists of Tunja,

---

[1]*Op. cit.*, p. 522.

whose nebulous idealism he did not approve. In 1814 he incarnated
the Revolution in Venezuela, but after 1820 he was to personify
the American Revolution. Whatever may have been the winds
which propelled his bark, fortune was rapidly pushing the Liberator
into a great movement; and his words, as the Argentinian Carlos
de Alvear later expressed it, became the sword of America and the
ray of liberty.

The Assembly received the vigorous Bolivarian message, and,
in the face of the growing evil that was menacing the Republic,
unanimously confirmed the powers of the General. Bolívar
declared:[1]

> To save you from anarchy and to destroy the enemies who desired to
> continue their oppression, I accepted the soverign power. I have given you laws,
> I have organized an administration of justice and taxation, and, in short, I
> I have given you a government. Citizens! I am not the sovereign. Your repre-
> sentatives should make the laws; the national treasury is yours to administrate.
> All the custodians of public interest should give an account of the use made of
> their powers. Judge impartially whether I have made the sactifice of my life,
> my sentiments, at all times in order to unite you into one nation, to develop
> your resources, or, rather, to create them. I keenly appreciate this moment of
> transmitting this power to the representatives which you are to choose, and I
> hope, Citizens, that you will release me from a position which some of you could
> fill more worthily, leaving to me the honor to which I aspire, that of continuing
> to fight your enemies, so that I may never sheath my sword while the liberty
> of my country is still insecure. . . . Countrymen, I have not come to op-
> press you with my conquering arms; I have come to bring you the power of the
> laws, I have come for the purpose of preserving for you your sacred rights.
> It is not a military despotism that makes a people happy, nor can the command
> which I hold ever be suited, except temporarily, to the Republic. A true soldier
> acquires no right to rule his country; he is not the arbiter of laws or of govern-
> ment: he is the defender of liberty. His glories ought to be combined with those
> of the Republic, and his ambition ought to be satisfied in making his country
> happy. . . . I beg you to relieve me of a burden too heavy for my resources.
> Elect your representatives, your magistrates, establish a just government, and
> count upon the arms which have saved you to continue, always, to protect the
> liberty and glory of Venezuela.

This is the first time that the Liberator had resigned his
command. During the next seventeen years he will often resign
his command, and each time his authority will be restored and
he will emerge stronger, more robust, and more determined than
before.

When elected Liberator he declared:[2]

> My people, no one can possess your sovereignty except through force and
> usurpation. Flee from the country where one man exercises all the powers: it is a
> country of slaves. You have called me the Liberator of the Republic; I shall
> never be its oppressor. My feelings have been in a most terrible struggle with
> my authority. Compatriots, believe me, this sacrifice is harder to bear than the
> loss of life would be.

He directs attention to General Mariño, the very able leader
of the eastern provinces, as a citizen worthy of the supreme power.

---

[1]The source of this quotation is not given.
[2]The source of these passages are not given.

Before the Assembly proceeded to vote, he made these last protests:

> I beg you to believe that my modesty is not meant to deceive you, and to lead you, by this means, to tyranny. I am not like Sulla, who covered his country with mourning and blood; I wish to imitate the dictator of Rome in the disinterestedness with which, having surrendered the supreme power, he returned to private life, submitting himself in everything to the regulations of the laws. I am not a Pisistratus who with eloquent phrases attempts to win your votes while effecting a perfect indifference, unworthy of a republican and more unworhty still in the defender of the country. I am but a plain citizen who always prefers liberty and the happiness of his countrymen to his own advancement.

Bolívar left the capital shortly afterwards for Puerto Cabello. In the meanwhile, Urdaneta triumphed at Ospino. But the events took a turn for the worst when Boves destroyed the battalions of Campo Elías in La Puerta, and went to engage Bolívar in a great contest at San Mateo. At La Victoria, on February 10, the undisciplined soldiers of Ribas retreated when Campo Elías arrived with the remnants of his forces from La Puerta and forced the royalists to flee. Bibas then turned against the bandit Rosetes who was causing havoc and ruin in the valleys of Tuy. This was a Homeric and formidable struggle such as only Venezuela had known. Its warriors were tempered in blood and fire, and were the sowers of liberty throughout the whole continent.

The impetuous attacks of Boves lasted for a month against the republican lines at San Mateo. San Mateo is perhaps the most beautiful page in the story of the heroic life of Bolívar. With a few soldiers the Liberator there defended himself against an enemy three or four times as powerful as his own army, and commanded by one of the greatest generals that America has known. The Liberator never showed himself stronger against death, dominating fortune with his arm. Not for a moment did he yield his inexorable determination to fight to the last. In the midst of the fiercest fighting, he sent this Spartan order to Urdaneta:

> You will defend Valencia, Citizen General, until death. · . .

Boves, retreating with the Spanish troops, was delayed in Bocachica, where he suffered a defeat. Mariño, however, failed to make the proper use of the victory. On May 28, the two liberators triumphed at Carabobo de Cagigal and at Ceballos. A little later Boves destroyed the independent army at La Puerta. This was the great and final battle of the Second Republic of Venezuela. The Liberator left Caracas with the emigration, the unfortunate exodus to the east. With the remnants of the army he fought another battle at Ragua, only to be defeated. The revolt which gave the command to Ribas and Piar proscribed him. In September, Bolívar left the country and went to New Granada.

The Republic fell with him. It did not fall immediately for there remained several units of troops under Cedeño Zaraza and the Monagas in the eastern provinces, even after Urica had left.

In the distant plains, Páez also launched his first attacks against the Spaniards, and developed that strong feeling of discontent which later was to furnish the legions of Apure and the supporters of the Liberator twenty months later with which to conquer Morillo and his great army; and on these plains they were trained. Urdaneta saved the survivors of his division by a masterful retreat, and retired into the interior of the new kingdom.

The Apostleship

WHEN Bolívar was separated from New Granada, where by order of the Congress, he had reduced the rebellious Santa Fé to obedience, by discord, the proscribed took the route to Jamaica.[1] He then devoted his energies to interest the British authorities in the liberty of the Spanish Colonies which had again been forced under the foreign yoke. The Liberator carried on, in this manner, a ceaseless propoganda. His correspondance of that period from his estate in the island has left us a brilliant record. This generous apostleship which caused him, between the two campaigns, to summon the notables of Venezuelan towns to explain and teach them that the fatherland was "a true curse of public rights",[2] with which he began every one of his speeches. This teaching manifested itself in endless exhortations, destined to influence all who, in his opinion, might create a successful movement of sympathy in favor of independence. He carried the vision of the reconquest of Venezuela fixed in his mind's eye, as well as the picture of civil strife in New Granada. He was still planning the Revolution, but his experiences remained to remind him of the need of foreign aid to expel the tyrants of our people. He could not expect outside aid except from England. The neutral apathy of the United States, the economic interests of that nation, and her colonial rivalry with Spain appeared to put her in a position to favor the cause of the patriots. Bolívar continued the relations in Jamaica which he had begun in London as a diplomatic representative to the English authorities, during the period of the First Republic. As a rebel fugitive seeking arms and money to feed the flame of war, he opened the eventual negotiations and prepared the fundamentals of the diplomacy which he was to use as the President of Colombia and Peru. He was an able politician, whose tact and finesse most of Europe admired. His conduct of foreign affairs suggests the same purpose and perseverance with which he pursued and conducted internal affairs, namely, the establishment of a régime of order and stability in the newly created nation states. It is for this one reason that it is important to take careful note of what Bolívar wrote during his residence at Kingston.

In the *Letter to an English Gentlemen* we have a picture of Venezuela of that day.[3] These excerpts from that document are of great interest:[4]

---

[1] The work of Bolívar in New Granada can be studied in Larrazabal, I, 339 *et seq.*

[2] Mancini, *op. cit.*, 481.

[3] *Letters of Bolívar*, 131.

[4] Kingston, September 6, 1815.

"As regards heroic and unfortunate Venezuela, its rise and fall have been so rapid that they have nearly reduced it to absolute poverty, to a frightful desert, notwithstanding the fact that it was the pride of America, one of its most beautiful countries. Its tyrants govern a desert, oppressing the unfortunate survivors who, having escaped death, drag out a precarious existence. Most of the men perish rather than submit to being slaves, while those who live fight with fury in the inland fields and towns until they die, or rush to the coast, there to fall into the hands of those who, insatiable for blood and crime, rival those monsters who first wiped out the primitive race in America. Venezuela had about one million inhabitants. Without exaggeration it can be truly said that a quarter of these have been sacrificed by sword, hunger, disease, travel, throughout the whole country, all, except those of the earthquake, are the results of war."

With profound indignation, he denounced[1]

the execrable atrocities of the archmonster Boves, the devastator of Venezuela. More than eight thousand of her children have fallen victims either through their own acts or by order of this cannibal, and womanhood has been dishonored and destroyed through the most abominable means used by him. Old men and children have perished at the side of the combatants. Nothing has escaped the mad fury of this tiger.

After relating the martydom of the American countries at the hands of the barbarous Peninsula and the fury of its sons, the Liberator implored the aid of the civilized nations, particularly that of England, champion of universal liberty and protector of the weak, adding:[2]

It is now time, sir, and perhaps it is the last time, that England can and should take part in the war of this immense hemisphere that is about to be reduced, if not to perish, unless a powerful nation lends aid to support it. For the condition in which it finds itself by reason of internal disinterestedness in its own salvation, by the vicissitudes of Europe, or by the eternal laws of nature. It may be that just a little help in the present crisis will suffice to save Meridional America from cruel devastations and enormous losses! It may be that when England does finally turn to see this America that there be no land left for it to save.

The Liberator asked for some aid in the shape of guns and money, and promised, even though the aid be small, that he himself will "free half of the world and place the universe in a state of equilibrium."[2]

Bolívar knew the intricacies of British politics, its emphasis upon the practical, the influence of the material on the Cabinet of St. James, and the attitude it takes towards questions of economics, as well as the great influence which commerce has upon the English. He knew the concern with which England guarded its insularity and its profound need of maintaining its supremacy of the sea. He hoped through an appeal to these interests to induce her to see that her continued greatness was closely bound up with her interest in his country. Her interest in Venezuela would not

[1]To the Editor of *The Royal Gazette*, October 15, 1815.
[2]Letter to Mr. Maxwell Hyslop, May 19, 1815.
[3]*Ibid.*

only he helpful to her own country but to the world. He explained:[1]

> The British Government can acquire the provinces of Panama and
> Nicaragua, forming with these countries the center of the world's commerce
> by means of canals which, connecting the two great seas, would shorten the
> greatest distances, and make England's control over commerce permanent.

To the Marquis of Wellesley, Minister of Foreign Affairs of
His Britannic Majesty, with whom he had personally negotiated
for the recognition of the First Republic, Bolívar wrote, on May
27, 1815:[2]

> The balance of the universe and the interest of Great Britain will be united
> with the salvation of America. What an immensely prosperous future does not
> my country offer to its defenders and friends! The sciences, the arts, industry,
> culture, everything which in this day leads to glory and which will incite the
> admiration of the men of Europe and will cause them to fly to America. England,
> will, above all others, see reflected in its country the prosperity of the Western
> Hemisphere. For the prosperity of this hemisphere owes its being almost ex-
> clusively to England. This will be the last period of our existence unless some
> powerful nation does lend us the aid we need. What a pity! We have an enormous
> amount of power by means of which we could build a wall, if only strong and
> able artisans would but construct a wall of liberty about our land. Immense
> regions, traversed by great rivers, sources of agricultural and mercantile riches,
> all will be destroyed by the fury of the Spaniards. Entire provinces have been
> converted into desert, others are the theaters of frightful bloody anarchy. All
> kinds of stimuli have been used to excite the passions; fanaticism has volcanized
> minds; and the result will be the extermination of all organized elements. . . .
> I have seen, my friend and lord, the devouring flame which is rapidly consuming
> my unfortunate country. Not being able to quench it, I have come, after having
> made unheard of and innumerable efforts, to give the alarm to the world, to
> implore for aid, to tell Great Britain and humanity that a great part of the
> human species is going to perish, and that the most beautiful half of the world
> will be desolated. . . . Consider with indulgence, my lord, these transports
> that seem the exaggerations of a madman rather than the account of certain
> facts and exact conditions. It is only the image, faithfully represented, of what
> I have seen, and what will be inevitable if Great Britain, liberator of Europe,
> friend of Asia, protector of Africa, does not become the saviour of America.
> If there remained to me a ray of hope that America could triumph alone, I
> should have no other ambition than that of having the honor of serving my
> country rather than humiliating it by seeking foreign protection for it. This
> was the reason why I left the continent. I come to seek aid; I shall go in search
> of proud capital; if it is necessary I shall go to the pole; and if all are insensible
> to the voice of humanity, I shall have done my duty, even though unsuccessfully;
> I shall return to die fighting for my country.

The country in which the Liberator was now interested had
been enlarged to include the whole of America and not merely
Venezuela, or even the boundries of the vice-regency. "For us,
the country is America," he proclaimed to the soldiers of Urdaneta
in Pamplona.[3] This was a profoundly comprehensive concept for
the men of the Revolution, engaged, as they were, in liberating
their own respective communities.

On May 29, 1815, he proposed to the Duke of Manchester,

----

[1]*Ibid.*
[2]Letter to the Marquis of Wellesley, Kingston, May 27, 1815.
[3]*Proclamation to the Division of Urdaneta*, November 12, 1814.

the Governor of Jamaica, a voyage which he never was able to make. Bolívar proposed "to go to England to employ my forces to procure aid for America which I shall put in a position to pay its gratitude in gains to its well-doers."[1] But finding himself, in September, still on the hospitable island, correcting, with word of mouth and pen, the errors of public opinion regarding the events of the Revolution, he wrote:[2]

> Our discords have their origin in two great fountains of public calamity: ignorance and weakness. Spain fomented one by superstitution, and perpetuated the other by tyranny. In our State before these events of the Revolution, our situation was reduced to nullity: we lived far from all the events that occurred, unused to ponder the events of the world, and separated from everything which develop and enrich our intelligence, or which might give value to our riches and our power. South Americans have for centuries passed as blind men before colors: they found themselves on the theater of action, but their eyes were bandaged: they had seen nothing, they had heard nothing. Why? Because they could not see justice, and could with even less ability hear the truth. No foreign nation has guided us with its wisdom and experience, nor defended us with its arms, nor protected us with its resources.

The Liberator sought "to cover with a veil of shame our differences" and begged the generous excuse of the world for "the turbulent history of Athens, the bloody factions of Rome, the violent civil wars of England, the dangerous dissentions of the United States," which have not prevented these four nations from being "the honor of the human race for their virtues, their liberty, and their glory." And he still insisted on the unfavorable conditions of those countries which made impossible the adaptation of the ultrademocratic institutions to our peoples. "In New Granada," he declared, "the federal institutions and the obstacles with which it was shackled left the executive power so fatally weak, that its power of action has been paralyzed by the very agencies which should have cooperated with it."[3]

It has been said that the letter which Bolívar wrote to an English gentleman, dated, as has already been stated, at Kingston, September 6, 1815, is one of the most interesting documents that we have of this great man. The Liberator really described in a masterly way, in that letter, the state of affairs in America, before and after the first wars for independence; denounced the social and political evils of its countries; indicated the remedies which he believed applicable to those evils; and, with a far-reaching vision, pierced the darkness of the future and prophesied what would be the course of the events of the Continent.

Bolívar presented, at that time, a striking picture of a man, defeated by the Spaniards, expelled from his own country through insubordination and lack of unity among the leaders, a pauper after having been a millionaire, injured even to the point of insult by his "malicious, perverse, and gossipy" servants which he

---

[1]*Letter to the Duke of Manchester*, May 29, 1815.
[2]*Letter to the Editor of the Royal Gazette*, September 28, 1815.
[3]*Letter to Mr. Maxwell Hyslop*, December 4, 1815.

did not pay the usual wages because "I have not a *maravedi*."

It is altogether admirable, I say, the manner in which Bolívar faced misfortune, raised himself by means of an exemplary energy and confidence, and the manner in which he speaks inspiringly of present and future events. A fugitive in one of the Antilles, the Liberator already believed himself inspired with "the national spirit of America," as was said of him ten years later, in Potosí, by an envoy of the Provinces of Rio de la Plata.[1]

The letter is of the greatest value when it discusses the political thought of Bolívar, dealing as much with his abstract conceptions as with its application to the concrete case of the Hispanic-American countries. The Liberator was a sincere Republican, that is to say, he believed in the principle, which he never modified, that theoretically the republic is the form of government most in accord with the dignity of humanity and the purpose of society. The actions and words of Bolívar do not contradict this statement. But Bolívar was, at the same time, judicious and practical. Never did he permit himself to be carried away, in political affairs by illusions, always taking care to stay planted on firm ground, and in realm of safe eclecticism. He did not need, in fact, to explain, at every turn, the elementary principles of constitutional science, or of historical experience, to prove the absurdity of the absolute theory in politics.

Bolívar summarized his ideas of government in this formula: "The system of government is the most perfect which produces the greatest possible measure of happiness, social security, and political stability."[2] Back of that formula lie all the rules which, through the efficacy of proven methods, fulfill the conditions essential to the attainment of the final object of public institutions. We observe that the Liberator, when it came to matters concerning America, remained at safe distances from extremes; and that he idealized a system that offered, according to his views, the greatest gains and benefits without acquiring the vices. His observation was a product of practical experience in the application of general principles and theories in the governing of our peoples. Bolívar sketched, in broad outlines, in the above letter, while dreaming of founding a greater Colombia, the bases of the fundamental laws of 1819 and 1826. He explained:[3]

> New Granada will unite with Venezuela, if they can cooperate in forming a central republic. . The government will be based upon the English system, with the difference that, in place of a king, there will be an elective executive power. And, what is most vital, never hereditary if it desires to be a republic, a hereditary legislative chamber or senate, which in political crises can intervene between popular whims and the functions of government. Also a legislative body, popularly elected, without any other restrictions than those which are imposed upon the English House of Commons.

---

[1] *Vide* Larrazabal, I, 403.
[2] *Message to the Congress of Angostura*, February 15, 1819.
[3] *Letter to an English Gentlemen*, September 6, 1815.

The Liberator seemed to believe that the unity of America is not attainable. Later plans to organize our people into a federation confirm his belief that while it may be "a grandiose idea to plan to form of all the New World a single nation, with a single tie that binds all its parts together," it is not possible because differing climates, different situations, opposite interests, unlike characters, divide America." He desired, however, "more than any other person, to see formed in America the greatest nation in the world, not for its extent and riches, but for its liberty and glory."[1]

Bolívar categorically denied, and never ceased to deny, the theory that the conditions of the New World required the establishment of monarchies in its states. He declared that if "it is not possible to persuade the New World, at this time, to let itself be governed by a great republic," he desired much less the establishment of[2]

> a universal monarchy in America, because this project, in addition to being useless is likewise impossible. . . . A monarchy would be like a great deformity which through its own weight would fall with the first convulsion. . . M. de Pradt has wisely divided America into 15 or 17 independent states, each one governed by its own monarchs. I am in accord as regards the first, that America be composed of 17 nations. As regards the second, even though it is easier to accomplish, it is less useful, and for that reason, I am not of the opinion that American monarchies can be useful. My reasons are these: The best interest of a republic, as generally understood, lies in preserving itself, its prosperity, and its glory. Liberty, since it does desire the establishment of an empire, but rather the establishment of an exact opposite, does not contain the stimulus necessary to incite republicans to extend the boundries of their nation to their own detriment; but in a desire to improve their own interests, and for the sole reason of aiding their neighbors share in constitutional liberty. The republic acquires no right, it gains nothing by conquering, at least by reducing conquered lands to colonies, conquests, or allies according to the example of Rome. Such maxims and examples are in opposition to the principles of justice of the consistent republican, and I should even say more. It is in obvious opposition to the citizens' interest, because a state too extended in itself, or through its dependencies, finally falls into decadence and converts its liberal form into another tyranny, loses the principles that it should preserve, and returns, finally, to despotism. . . . The distinction of small republics is permanence; that of the large ones is uncertain because it always inclines toward an empire.
>
> "Nearly all of the former have lasted a long time. Of the latter, Rome alone lasted several centuries because the capital was a republic, not so the rest of its dominions, governing itself through different laws and institutions.
>
> Very different is the policy of a king. He is constantly inclined to seek to augment his possessions, riches, and powers. And for this good reason that his authority grows with these acquisitions, a condition of great importance not only to his neighbors but also to his own vassals. His neighbors fear him as a formidable power and his empire as one which preserves itself by means of war and conquest. For these reasons, I think that the Americans, anxious for peace, the sciences, the arts, commerce, and agriculture, would prefer republics to kingdoms. It seems to me that these desires are in harmony with those of Europe.

---

[1]*Ibid.*
[2]*Ibid.*

The views of Europe concerning the affairs of the New World were not, precisely what Bolívar then imagined. It lacked certain data and certain information concerning his projects. When he becomes the head of the government of Colombia and Peru he will become better able to judge of conditions and principles, he will modify his opinions, and will pursue his diplomatic negotiations with the vivid comprehension and the extraordinary ability which characterized his activity.

There were two factors, in the opinion of the Liberator, necessary for the triumph of the patriot cause: the union of the Americans, and the aid of a powerful nation. Both of these aims were constantly before him; and it can be truly said of him that he was able to triumph without either of them. Persuasion and the gallows scarcely enabled him to maintain the precarious union of the captains under his Caesarian authority. The heroic British Legion with hardly enough guns to be of any service was all the help the outside world gave to him in his struggle for the noblest cause in history.

The political future of America which Bolívar dealt with in that celebrated letter, contained details that are amazing. The evolution of Buenos Aires, Chile, Peru, Mexico, contained, in his great vision, no secrets for him. He likewise read in his great prophecy, in the words of another commentator of the *Letters*, the picture of the temporary monarchies of San Martín and Rivadavia, the tyranny of Rosas, the oligarchical order of the Araucanian Republic, the fickle politics of Lima, the absolutism of Itúrbide, Maximilian, Porfirio Díaz in Mexico—all passed before the eyes of Bolívar as if he were reading the future.[1] García Calderón declares: "He is a great prophet. Today, after a century, the continent obeys his visions as those of a divine conjurer."

The precipitative war forced the Liberator to leave for the continent. On his departure from Kingston, where he had passed eight months soliciting aid, Petion, President of Haiti, received him with that magnanimous gesture which Torices and Camilo Torres had received him, and gave him "arms, men, munitions, money, and the Moral aid which he needed so much."[2] His sojourn in Jamaica had not been a total loss for the patriotic cause. Apostle of Liberty, Bolívar labored for his ideal, writing in Kingston as much as did the warriors who, on the continent, were struggling against the reconquest. Propaganda absorbed his time. And this time that he thus used brought nearer the hour of his return, the moment in which he would again set foot on the continent, and which he was not to leave until he had realized his marvelous epic.

---

[1] Blanco-Fombona, *Letters of Bolívar*, I, 108. *Vide* also Gil Fortoul, I, 242.
[2] Blanco-Fombona, *op. cit.*, I, 109.

The Provisional Statute

ON May 16, 1816, an Assembly of Notables, meeting at La Asunción, in Margarita, named as Supreme Chief of the Republic, Bolívar, who was, at that time, beginning his drive for independence, as head of an expedition proceeding from Haiti. General Mariño was named the second head of the army. Twenty-five thousand Spaniards occupied Venezuelan territory, under the command of Pablo Morillo and the Canary Islander Morales. In the east, several different chiefs of the patriots were engaged in guerilla warfare, disturbing the royalists. On the plains of the Apure and of the Barinas, stood the Homeric figure of Páez. The Liberator commanded, at the beginning of this crusade, two hundred and fifty men.

An act worthy of mention is the earnest desire which Bolívar always expressed, in offering to surrender his authority, and which carried him to greater power on every occasion, through flattering, we shall not say public sentiment, which did not always exist, but the lack of confidence of the prominent military leaders, and the group of the patricians that represented the ideal and the force of the country. It is better to consider this earnest desire, at times so inopportune, as a definite proof of the Liberator's ability to retain his power even among the crafty schemers who surrounded him. It is a proof of greatness to have been able to win authority in a contest with a revolutionary general, and to have retained that authority discreetly in an atmosphere surcharged with legality and suspicion which the later councils and congresses of Colombia displayed. A profound respect, however, for legal mandates and established formulas characterized the acts of Bolívar as a ruler. It was his spirit, inspired by the literature of the eighteenth century, that retained the respect of the leaders. "I love liberty and I have noble and liberal sentiments," he declared to the citizen Juan Jurado, after the Battle of the Techo.[1] It would, accordingly, be too severe to call the Liberator a hypocrite, judged by his repeated resignations and the continued glamor for great power. He desired to serve, through such conduct, the national cause. He took care always to assure his compatriots of the sincerity and righteousness of his intentions. "I do not need," he wrote to Dr. Gaul, "to exaggerate to you the candor of my character, and the frankness of these feelings which, if my heart does not shelter, would not express, because I am too strong to degrade myself for gain."[2]

What authority did that Assembly of Villa del Norte possess? About the same, probably, as that which, two years before, the

---

[1]The battle was fought on December 8, 1814.
[2]*Letter to Doctor Pedro Gual*, Mompox, February 10, 1815.

Council of San Francisco at Caracas had arrogated to itself in order to invest Bolívar with the dictatorship. Legitimately, or not, he assumed the command, "since independent peoples have done me the honor of investing me with the supreme authority." He hastened to announce, in a proclamation, that the Congress of Venezuela would be reconvened. This promise he repeated, a year later, when, in December of the same year, he arrived in Margarita, with the second expedition from Haiti. He declared to the Venezuelans:[1]

> You were called by me, in the month of May, to constitute the legislative body without my having imposed any restrictions upon you, authorizing you to choose the time and the place. You have not done this: the successes of the war have prevented it. But now you should hasten to do so since the circumstances demand it. . . . The first act of your deliberations will be marked by accepting my resignation.

The Liberator was defeated on July 13th, near Ocumare, which caused a division in the ranks of the patriots, in the form in which it is known. Bolívar reembarked for Guiria, where Mariño and Bermúdez were rising in rebellion, compelling him again to seek refuge in Haiti. MacGregor and Soublette executed a sixty day march across the territory occupied by the enemy, and were reunited with Piar at Barcelona.

These were turbulent months of anarchy, characterized by ignorance and inconstancy. Three or four times Mariño was in open rebellion. Piar, who, as the conqueror in the Juncal, opened the doors of Venezuela to the Liberator, rebelled anew, and ended his life on the scaffold. Páez was the wild horse of the plains. Even the ferocious and heroic Arismendi conspired, greedy for the command. The campaign of Guayana, which gave Bolívar a capital for "his nomad republic", gave him a sufficient number of men for his march through the Orinoco, and definitely established his authority, although this was not accomplished until the year 1817.

In May, Mariño reunited Zea, Urbaneja, the Alcalás, Madariaga, and other chieftains at Caraiaco, made them members of the Congress. He then laid before this body, in his own name as well as in that of Simón Bolívar, the authority which the Assembly of Villa del Norte had conferred on both of them. Those patricians declared the federal system reestablished, and named General Mariño commander of the army, the instigator of the whole nefarious business. Fortunately, the Liberator had troops in Guayana; and Piar, who had just won the Battle of San Félix, remained loyal to the cause. The Congress of Cariaco, an "informal and tumultous council," was no more nor no less legitimate than were the assemblies of Caracas and La Asunción, which gave the command to Bolívar, or the assemblies of Trinidad de Archuna (September, 1816) and of San Fernando de Apure

---

[1]*Vide* Gil Fortoul, I, 244, ff.

(August, 1818), which named Páez the Supreme Chief. But this little Congress was absurd, for it sought to take the military power away from Bolívar, the only man who could use it with success, in order to give it to his lieutenants, who were, without doubt, brave and strong, but incapable of conducting such operations as were needed at the time. The first of these assemblies, it is true, performed the incalculable services of placing the power to wage war in the sword of Páez, while the second, in spite of its failure, only made the authority of Bolívar all the more powerful. The attempt of Mariño had no better results.

The Liberator established himself in Angostura on July 18, and by a series of acts and decrees had, before the end of the year, organized the administrative system. Bolívar had no illusions about the legality of the organism which he had thus created. Some days after he had taken control of affairs, he wrote to Fernando Toro, a refugee in Trinidad: "Some one who calls itself the Government has named you, or better expressed, has called you to serve in the Executive Power. Whether this be legitimate or not, I have approved its action and I call you with even more insistance that this Government."[1] A tribunal of sequestration, a High Court of Justice, civil and commercial tribunals, a Council of State and a Council of Government were instituted. "The purpose of Bolívar," declared Gil Fortoul, "was to organize a kind of Secretariat or Ministry which he could remove at will. Nothing was said about representative government in plan or in that of the following year."[2]

> The government of the Republic was destroyed with the fall of the Republic in 1814, although local insurrections have sustained, precariously, its banners. The Republic again took form at the Assembly of La Asunción, on the island of Margarita. Unfortunately it assumed a military character, a result of a state of war. The third period of Venzuela was not established until the present moment. It is only in this period that we can feel that the roof of our constitution will serve us as a shelter from the tempests. I have been unhappy, and I might say that I have lived despairingly as long as I saw my country without a constitution, without laws, without tribunals, ruled only by the arbitrary power of its commanders, with no other guides than those of these commanders, without any other principles than the destruction of tyrants, and with no other system than that of independence and liberty. I have hastened, removing all difficulties, to give my country the benefit of a moderate, just, and legal government. If the government is not that, Your Excellencies may so decide. My purpose has been to establish it.

Bolívar reaffirmed his intention of creating a central government in these words:

> The Assembly of Margarita of May 16, 1816, declared the Republic of Venezuela one and indivisible. The people and the armies which, up until now, have fought for liberty, have sanctioned, by the most solemn and unanimous confirmation, this act. This act united the states of Venezuela into a single State, and created an executive power, giving it the title of the Supreme Head of

---

[1] San-Miguel, June 27, 1817.
[2] Gil Fortoul, I, 265.

the Republic. So, that there is now lacking only the institution of the legislative body, and the judicial power.

The Liberator defined the powers, and explained the desirability of having these different organisms instituted in this manner:

The creation of the Council of State was the result of a desire to have a body take over the august functions of the legislative power, not with all the freedom which the sovereignty of this body confers, because that would be incompatible with the extension and force which the executive power had received. The Council of State was not only to help free and pacify the country, but also to help create the entire body of the Republic, a task that requires means proportionate to its magnitude and such powers as can reside in the most centralized of governments. The Council of State, as Your Excellencies will see, is destined through its creation to assume in part the functions of the legislative body. To it belongs the initiation of the laws, regulations, and institutions which in its wisdom it judges necessary to the safety of the Republic. It will be consulted by the Executive Power before enforcing the laws, regulations, and institutions which the government decrees. In all difficult cases, the wishes of the Council of State will be consulted, and its advice will have the greatest influence on the deliberations of the Supreme Head. . . . The High Court of Justice, which forms the third power of the sovereign body, has already been established, but its installation not yet effected, since I thought it necessary to consult the Congress concerning such an important institution. I have thought it necessary to consult Congress in regard to its form and the functionaries who are to fill such high positions. The High Court of Justice is the first necessity of the Republic. It will guard and protect the rights of all. The possessions, the innocence, and the just deserts of the citizens will not be trampled upon by the arbitrary power of any military or civil chief, not even by the Supreme Head. The judicial power of the High Court of Justice will enjoy all the independence conceded to it by the Federal Constitution of the Republic of Venezuela. . . . The establishment of a Tribunal of Commerce, or a consular body, has been favored by commercial businesses, and by agriculture, which have so much need of exact and prompt rulings. The erection of the Tribunal of Commerce will acquaint Your Excellencies with the nature of this beneficent body. . . . Ever since the second period of the Republic, there has been a real need of locating the power which should have control of foreign affairs. This power should receive consuls and foreign envoys, conclude commercial treaties, buy and contract for arms, munitions, clothing, and all manner of war supplies. But, above all, the most important matter is that which calls for the creation by the Council of Government of some means by which the functions of the Supreme Head of the State in case of his death. The Republic would suffer considerable trouble if the Council of Government were not established before I begin the next campaign. And so, I rejoice with Your Excellencies now that we have secured this new aid to the Republic.

The Council of State was divided into three parts, namely, State and Treasury (Zea); War and Navy (Admiral Brión); Interior and Justice (Juan Martínez). Each section, moreover, had three votes.[1] The Council of Government was installed on November 21st, and functioned until the beginning of 1819. Its first members were Admiral Brión, Cedeño y Zea, Urdaneta, Tomás Montilla, Roscio y Peñalver, also formed a part of it.[2] The Liberator was busy during the remainder of the year with decrees concerning the sequestration of Spanish property,

---

[1]*Doc.* VI, 154. *Vide* Restrepo, *op. cit.*, II, 427 ff.
[2]*Doc.* VI, 575.

with commerce and taxation, and other matters. He was also
concerned with regulations for the reorganization of the army,
which was to be prepared for the campaign in November.[1] His
influence was such that he was able to establish fair and just legal
proceedings throughout all the branches of the government.[2] To
prevent espionage, he ordered the governor and mayor of Angostura to require emigrants of Venezuela, or foreigners who
return to Venezuela to present themselves to the military commander of the province before communicating with any one;
and to show the public papers, letters, and the correspondance
of which they may be the bearers "under the arbitrary penalty
that may be enacted to cover such cases of disobedience."[3]
As far as the foreigners were concerned, a later decree prohibited
them from enlisting in the militia, or in the army, without their
consent; and exempted all aliens from the payment of forced
loans, and providing that they should only pay the regular
duties on industry and commerce.[4] Still later, by a decree of
October 6, 1817, Bolívar improved the line of division between
the civil and the military powers, in order that the military and
municipal police could function through the military commanding
governors, who in that capacity should preside over the municipality, convoking the assemblies of the heads of families, and
receiving the suffrage of the electors.[5]

The labors of the Liberator were immense, and covered
all the branches of public administration. He was as many-sided
as Preteus. It is only by a knowledge of these facts that the success
of his life in the moral and intellectual desert of America can be
explained. No man in history has shown a greater energy and
wiser intelligence, or achieved greater results with such miserable
tools.[6] The law of 1817 is an excellent example of the character of
his labors, and easily sets his work apart from those who were
laboring for the independence of the Continent. The country
continued to exist through the will of the Liberator. Bolívar was
pleased to create functionaries, and, later, to call congresses.
Venezuela and Colombia were his creations. He was not, like
Washington and San Martín, merely the commander of a revolutionary army; Bolívar was the Father of the Revolution. He
did not win or lose battles merely; he was a great soldier, a great
politician, and a great administrator. He founded nations, made
laws, governed; was an orator and a writer. During the period
which began with the installation of the government of Angostura,
the Liberator revealed his incomparable gifts as a statesman: his

[1]Gil Fortoul, *op. cit.*, I, 264.
[2]*Doc.* VI, 81.
[3]September 25, 1817.
[4]*Doc.* VI, 408.
[5]July 3, 1818.
[6]*Vide* Blanco-Fombona, *The Political and Social Revolution of Hispanic
America,* 99.

great mind worked overtime, not to rest for three years. He always accepted the aid of illustrious spirits, "whose public spirited votes are a great aid in determining questions of high polity," but, always independently, for he desired his country should be free from all foreign intervention in the realms of politics and administration, as well as in the realm of the military.

The authority of Bolívar was of very great value in unifying the country, for the institutions of Angostura were of the utmost importance. The duties of the Executive Power were lightened by the multiplication of its organs, which obeyed the will of the dictator, however, and were, in short, only the members of one single body. While the convenience of Bolívar and the desire of the public wanted to see the government legalized it was also their desire to organize administrative divisions and to modify the powers of the Executive Power decreed by the First Congress. The Liberator always disliked the federal system, and insisted upon the need of having an Executive Power vigorous and robust. He foresaw that an authoritative and personal Executive Power, by virtue of a fatal evolution, would develop in the American countries, in spite of the theory and liberalism of their institutions.[1] He strove to make of this power a beneficial instrument which might later be converted into the scourge of tyrannies. Let us note, on the other hand, the tenacious efforts of Bolívar to strengthen the Executive Power, which his concept of democracy and his temperment led him to assume, as the leader and the educator of the people. Pericles and Augustus, who ruled over two of the most brilliant periods of the human race, would be two witnesses for the acquittal.

One of the most brilliant generals of the Revolution was the victim who supported with his life the edifice of autocracy. A useful, indispensible death was that of the hero of San Félix. "If it were not a just act", wrote Mitre, "it was no doubt necessary, since it destroyed the germ of the civil war which would have led to the dissolution of the army.[2] In reality, Piar, either in conniving with the ungovernable Mariño, or on his own account, made use of his influence among the troops to emulate Bolívar and to undermine his power. It was even declared of him that he organized the nefarious plan of inciting the races to war in order to place "the *mantuanos* of Caracas" in command of the half breeds, whose prototype was the Liberator. A court-martial found the General guilty of "conspiracy against the Government," as the prosecutor Soublette phrased it. That is to say, his action was directed against the authority of Bolívar, and he confirmed the sentence of death, with the reduction in rank,

---

[1]García Calderón has dealt with this phase in his most recent work: *The Creation of a Continent.*

[2]*History of San Martín,* V., 263. (*La Nación* edition).

ordered by the court "against General Manuel Piar, for the enormous crimes of insubordination, desertion, sedition, and conspiracy." The decree by Bolívar of September 6, 1813, was applied in this case, the decree which established the penalty of death for disturbers of the public order. It may be noted that this decree made such a penalty possible when "strong suspicions would suffice for its execution."

Restrepo declared that the Liberator believed that the death of Piar was a necessary sacrifice made in behalf of justice and public safety, in order to prevent greater crimes.[1] It is quite certain that Bolívar did not approve of such a very serious punishment without having given it very serious thought. Proof for this may be found in his letter to General Bermúdez, in which he wrote that "my private desire is now (the trial was in its course) that the court may conciliate the rigor of the law and the dignity of the government with the deserts of the crime . . . I wish that the court, if it applies the major penalty, may open a way, a clear way, for commutation."[2]

When the internal discord had ended, Bolívar was able to begin the new campaign against the Spaniards. The liberated territory was limited, at the end of the year, to the provinces of Guayana, Cumaná, Margarita, and part of Barcelona.

---

[1]Restrepo, II, 242.
[2]*To General Bermúdez, Angostura, October 4, 1817.*

The Congress of Angostura

THE defeat at La Hogaza, of General Zaraza in December, 1817, compelled Bolívar to return to Angostura. He went from that city to join the troops of Páez at Payara, and to begin operations against Morillo who was in Calabozo. The campaign began favorably. But Páez decided that it would be better to retreat towards Apure and attack San Fernando, instead of carrying on war in the mountains of Aragua. The chieftain of the plains was heavily handicapped because he had no cavalry troops; and Bolívar, whose hold upon the soldiery of the plains was a weak one, was compelled to resign himself to the exegencies of the situation, and to agree to a division of the army. The Spaniards defeated him at Semen on March 16, and he had no other remedy but to return to Guayana. The Liberator, defeated, conceived a daring project: he decided to leave a few regiments to engage General Morillo on the plains of Venezuela, while he would cross the Andes in order to carry the war into New Granada. If one considers the very great difficulties in the way of executing this plan: the absolute lack of communications, the slight control which he had over his forces, the possibility of defeat without an opportunity for retreat, and the risk of compromising forever the cause of independence, the plan of Bolívar seems as daring as that executed by Hannibal when he left the legions before the walls of Capua, and marched to attack Rome.

In the middle of 1819, with a handful of soldiers, among which was numbered the British Legion, Bolívar ascended to the top of the American Alps and, after a series of perfect strategic movements, won the decisive battle of Boyacá (August 7), where the Spanish army was taken prisoner. The Liberator entered the capital of the vice-regent, installed the Granadian Santander in the vice-presidency, and made a minor change in the organization of the public administration. The treasury was re-established; a superintendent of the treasury and a court of justice were created; a mint was provided, and, in general, a political and administrative régime, civil and military governors, etc., were established in the provinces. In September, Bolívar returned to Venezuela.

However, before beginning the great campaign, the Liberator decided to convene a Congress that should organize his scheme of government on a firm basis, and to establish the Republic of Colombia. In the Council of State, on October 1, 1818, he made this statement:[1]

> The enemy will be attacked simultaneously on all the points which he occupies, so that, very soon, the happy day will come when we shall see our land free of tyrants, and the government of the Republic reestablished in all

[1] *Vide* Gil Fortoul, I, 271.

BOLÍVAR page 46

its perfection. . . . Even though the moment has not arrived when our afflicted country is to enjoy the tranquility which it should have, to deliberate with intelligence and certainty, we can, however, anticipate all the steps which will hasten the march of the restoration of our republican institutions. . . . I call the attention of the Council particularly to the immediate need of convoking the National Congress: I have not dared to take definite action without hearing an expression of its voice, not feeling myself capable of taking on myself alone the responsibility, or the merit of such important matters. The Council can, if it judges it advisable, name a special commission, charged with the formation of the plan and the method of bringing about a popluar election.

The Council of State named a commission to arrange for the elections, which plan was approved by Bolívar on October 24. Gil Fortoul explained the plan in this wise:[1]

The report declared that the first Venezuelan Congress, having been dissolved by the capitulation of 1812, and since more than four years have elapsed, which was the term of office prescribed for the deputies, the Commission recommended: that since the civil census-roll, ordered in 1810, for the nomination of parochial and provincial electors did not exist, and since there was no time to prepare another such roll, that it was not possible to hold elections in conformity with the systems of the two classes of members, and that, in consequence, a direct election should be held; that the Congress was to be composed of thirty Venezuelan deputies, distributed equally among the six provinces of Margarita, Guayana, Caracas, Barcelona, Cumaná, and Barinas, the provinces of Trujillo and Mérida also to name five deputies when they are able to do so, and an equal number from the province which, though Granadian, considered itself united with the Venezuelans in the war of independence; that the deputies will not only be representatives of their districts, but of all parts of the country; and that, in view of the plan to form a single State of Venezuela and New Granada, the Granadian provinces be invited to name deputies to meet with those from Venezuela, to consider means of recovering their liberty. . . . The elections will be conducted in the imperfect manner which the circumstances demand, and in many sections only through the vote of the military leaders, since the only provinces completely independent were Maragrita and Guayana. In the other parts, the patriots could count only on those sections occupied by their troops.

By making the deputies represent the whole of Venezuela rather than the provinces from which they were chosen, the Council proposed to deprive them of "the provincial spirit," and by that act they hoped to strengthen the ties which bound the provinces to the Republic. In this way, the patricians of Angistura responded to the need of unifying all the peoples of America under the liberating symbol. It has been declared that the causes uniting the peoples of Buenos Aires, Mexico, Chile, and New Granada were identical with those of Venezuela.

The report of the commission declared those Venezuelans voters who, if single, were twenty-one years or over, and if married, younger, of whatever state, so long as they owned landed property, professed a science, or a liberal art, or a trade, and who had, by renting lands for agricultural or grazing purposes, or who had a business with an annual income of at least three hundred pesos. Lunatics, deaf mutes, bankrupts, and public debtors with debts

[1] *Ibid.*, I, 271, 272.

unpaid, unnaturalized foreigners, unless they were enlisted in the armies of the Republic, or had held public employment or office, vagabonds, deserters, criminals, men accused of grave crimes, men who solicited votes, and men separated from their wives without legal cause were not allowed to vote. All civil and military employees, earning an annual income of at least three hundred pesos were also allowed to vote. Officers, sergeants, and chiefs enjoyed the same right. To be a deputy, a man had to be twenty-five years of age or over, a patriot of approved standing, not barred by any provision from voting, a citizen of Venezuela for at least five years previous to election, an owner of property of whatever class, and a resident of the country. Foreigners, although not naturalized, who had served the Republic since the beginning of the Revolution, were also eligible for election as a deputy. Civil, military, and ecclesiastical officials were charged with the duty of supervising the holding of the elections.

The Liberator declared, in a proclamation to the Venezuelans:[1]

> Elect to public office the most virtuous of your citizens, and forget, if you can, in the election, those who have liberated you. For my part, I renounce for ever the authority you have conferred upon me, and I shall never want to be anything more than a simple soldier while the unfortunate war lasts in Venezuela. The first day of peace will be the last of my command.

On February 15, 1819, Bolívar opened the Congress and read his magnificent message. The Liberator sought to constitute a government with which it would be possible to square his acts in politics and diplomacy, and to determine the major activities of the military operations. The Republic, which had not existed up until that moment, except in the "mind and by the sword of Bolívar," acquired shape, in a definite form, and an agreement with the intellects and wills came to lend a real and appreciable aid to the Supreme Head, in the task of creating a nationality, and in preparing, with complete liberty of action from the Colombians, for the liberation of the Continent.

The Republic was not to be dependent upon the caprice of fortune on the field of battle. Under the fiery Bolivarian arm its political and administrative mechanism was to perform its natural functions. The authority of Bolívar acquired legal sanction, and his new title impressed favorably interested foreign nations, and destroyed the suspicious ambitions of his generals. Bolívar was now President of the Republic. The Congress which showed its fickle character, while he triumphed at Boyacá, and after having forced the resignation of Zea, gave the position of vice president to General Arismendi, its munity was stilled by the arrival of the Liberator in September. The revolting deputies convinced themselves that if they wished to continue they must obey implicity the dictatorial will. A little later, in addressing

---

[1] *The Liberator to the Venezuelans. Angostura, October 22, 1818.*

the Spaniards, "the rebel leader" called himself His Excellency
the President of Colombia. Bolívar was placed in a position
which demanded the power of genius. He spoke from the highest
tribunal, in a pompous and solemn manner, to all America, and
was without a rival in all history. Dame Fortune was now tamed,
as one writer expressed it. The stubborn goddess would not then
flee the arms of the man who was tenaciously engaged in pursuing
her for ten years.[1]

In the presence of the deputies from Caracas, Barcelona,
Cumaná, Barinas, Guayana, and Margarita, Bolívar resigned the
supreme command, and declared, "with an extraordinary energy"
that "my sword and those of my illustrious companions in arms
are always ready to maintain the august authority of the Congress."[2] The Assembly named him President, confirmed the
military ranks conferred, and legalized all the acts of his government. By the provisions of the law for the organization of the
army of the Presidency of the Republic, proclamed on February
18, Bolívar became commander-in-chief of the army and the navy,
with the power to appoint all public employees; to impeach
high officials before the Congress for felony, misconduct, em-
bezzelment, maladministration, etc., with the exception of
military crimes, which were to be judged by the regulations then
in force; to negotiate with all foreign governments, submitting
treaties for the approval of the Congress, or its delegates; to
promulgate and order executed all the laws; to order and execute
the decisions of the Congress and the Judiciary, but without a
suspensive veto on them; to mitigate, commute, or even to pardon
capital punishment, first consulting the magistrates; to publish
the tariffs; to give to Congress, or its deputations information, or
accounts which it or they may desire, having the right to with-
hold such information as he felt should be kept in reserve; to
issue letters of marque and reprisal; to raise troops and accept
foreign auxiliaries; and to appoint and remove ministers or
secretaries of the Executive. The Judicial Power was established
eight days later. A Supreme Court of Justice was created for the
capital, composed of five members of whom only three were
chosen immediately, because of a scarcity of lawyers. There was an
Attorney-General of the Republic, duly qualified; and courts of
the first instance distributed throughout the national territory.
In the discharge of their duties, they were to observe all existing
laws which had not been repealed.[3] The Congress passed, in
addition to this, a multitude of laws and decrees for the different
branches of administration; and it should be noted, as one of the
most worthy of its acts, the general pardon for political offenses
which applied to the European Spaniards, "whatever they may

---

[1]*Vide* Larrazabal, I, 510.
[2]*Document VI*, 584.
[3]*Document VI*, 604, 606.

have done against the interests of the Republic and whatever
may be the rank, distinction, or class in which they may be
placed."[1]   The Assembly then began the consideration of the
definite Constitution.

The Constitution which the Liberator submitted to the
legislators of Angostura conformed to the principles that "a
republican government has been and should continue to be the
form of government for Venezuela: its bases should be the sovereignty of the people, the division of powers, civil liberty, the
proscription of slavery, and the abolition of monarchy and of
special privileges."[2]   Bolívar divided power in the classical
manner into the executive, the legislative, and the judicial; and
invented a "moral power, brought from the depth of ancient
obscurity and from those long forgotten laws which had, once
upon a time, virtue among the Greeks and the Romans. . . .
which may be thought to be simple nonsense, but which is not
impossible; and I flatter myself that you will not entirely disdain
a thought which, improved by experience and wisdom, can come
to be the most efficacious."

The English Constitution served as a model for the Executive
Power, since in it "is vested all the sovereign authority pertaining
to, but also limited by a triple line of dams, barriers, and fences. .
The more one examines the nature of the Executive Power in
England, one can find only what leads one to conclude is the
most perfect model, be it for a kingdom, be it for an aristocracy,
be it for a democracy. Let this Executive Power be vested in the
person of a president for life in Venezuela, named by the people
or their representatives, and we shall have taken a great step
towards national happiness."

Bolívar also chose the English Parliament as the model for the
Legislative Power, explaining:

> We have, as Americans, divided national representation into two houses:
> the house of representatives and the senate (the Venezuelan Constitution of
> 1811). The first is composed, very wisely, of the form and power to the require-
> ment of the people to be legislative and wholly representative; and enjoys all
> the powers that belong to it. But it is not susceptible to an essential change
> because it has been established by the Constitution. If the Senate, in place of
> being elective, were hereditary, it would, in my opinion, be the base, the link, and
> the soul of the Republic. This body, during tempestuous political periods,
> would hold the reins of government and check popular whims. A stronghold
> of the government through the proper interest in its own preservation, it would
> always defend it against the invasions which people direct against the juris-
> diction and authority of their officials. We must confess this: most men do not
> know their true interests and constantly try to wrest them from the hands of
> their custodians; the individual fights against the masses and the masses against
> authority. Therefore, it is necessary that there should exist, in all governments,
> a neutral body which always takes the part of the attacked and disarms the
> attacker. This neutral body, to be such, must not have its origin in election by

[1]*Document VI*, 608.
[2]These and the citations given previously are taken from the Message of the
Liberator to the Congress, February 15, 1819.

the government or by the people; but in such a manner that it enjoys full independence and neither fears nor hopes anything from these two fountains of authority. The hereditary senate, as an organ of the people, participates in its interests, feelings, and spirits. For this reason, it should not be assumed that a hereditary senate will lose sight of the popular interests, or forget its legislative duties. The senators of Rome and the lords of London have been the fundamental columns upon which the edifice of political and social liberty has been built.

The Liberator believed that the State should provide special means for educating its future senators; and denies the idea of founding a nobility, declaring:

It is an office for which the candidates should be prepared, and it is an office in which there is need of training and the means necessary to acquire such training. Everything should not be left to chance, and to the outcome of elections. The people deceive themselves more easily than nature perfected by art. Although it is true that these senators would not be born with virtues, it is likewise true that they would be born of well-educated families.

He belived that in founding this institution he had found the means of satisfying the ambitions of the chiefs, and that this institution would preserve with glory the national honor and public interests "until the end of time, a race of virtuous, prudent, and forceful men, which, overcoming all obstacles, have founded the Republic at the cost of the most heroic sacrifices."

The permanency of the judiciary is the basis of the judicial power, that which is closed to outside influences. Bolívar explained his views on the judiciary thus:

In seeking the establishment of judges, in the creation of a new code, I have offered Congress the guarantee of civil liberty, the most precious, the most just, the most necessary. In a word, the only liberty, since without it the rest are nullities. I have sought the correction of the most lamentable abuses which our system suffers, through the vicious origin of the vast amount of Spanish legislation, which, like time, covers all ages and all men, the works of madness as well as of talent, wise productions as well as extravagent ones, monuments of genius as well as of caprice. This judicial encyclopedia, monster of ten thousand heads, which until now has been the lash of the Spanish people, is the most cruel punishment which the anger of heaven has permitted to be grafted upon this unfortunate empire.

As for the moral or Areopagan power, which he considered almost Utopian, the Liberator explained in beautiful eloquence:

"Popular education ought to be the first care of the paternal love of Congress. Morality and education are the props of a Republic; morality and education are our first necessities. Let us take from Athens its Areopagus and the guardians of its customs and laws; let us take from Rome its censors and domestic tribunals, and, making a sacred alliance of these moral institutions, let us introduce into the world the idea of a people which is not content in being free and strong but which also desires to be virtuous. Let us take from Sparta its austere establishments, and, forming with these three pillars a base of virtue, let us give our Republic a fourth power, whose dominion may be the cradle and the heart of men, public spirit, good customs, and republican morality. Let us establish this Areopagus which shall watch over the education of children, over national instruction; so that it may purify that which may be corrupt in the Republic, so that it may root out ingratitude, egoism, the lack of patriotism, leisure, and the negligence of citizens; so that it may detect the principles of corruption, pernicious examples, seeking to correct customs by moral penalties, as laws punish crimes by inflicting penalties, not only which inflicts pain but which mocks them; not only that which attacks them but which weakens them; not only that which violates the Constitution but that which violates public respect. The jurisdiction of this truly sacred tribunal will be effective with respect to education and instruction, and of opinion solely in crimes and punishments. But the annals and registers in which are recorded its acts and deliberations, the moral principles and the acts of the citizens, will be books of virtue and of vice. Books which the public will consult for its elections, magistrates for their resolutions, and judges for their decisions. A similar institution which my seem to be more of chimera than of reality is more easily attainable than those which some ancient and modern legislators have established with less usefulness for the human race.

The moral power conceived by the Liberator, the legislative power composed of two houses, a body charged with the duty of watching over public morality, another to direct the education of children, all have the vague powers, half moral, half judicial of the Athenian Areopagus. Years before, Miranda had advised an institution of censors "who would supervise public instruction and care for the preservation of good customs." The proposal of Rousseau to found a natural and lay religon, with dogmas decreed by the State, may perhaps have served, in a remote way, as an inspiration for the plan of Bolívar, if we consider that the Genevan philosopher, moving slowly toward the ultimate consequences that may be deduced from his idea of the omnipotent State, seeks to justify the intervention of the State in all the phases of social activity. The liberator may say, on more than one occasion, that the constitutional law should not make statutes for matters which pertain only to the internal life of the citizens; his letters may not contain any clause on state religion and his ideas on that point may equal those of the tolerant Locke. But it is undeniable that the teaching of a civil virtue, of the rationalist virtue of Saint-Just and Robespierre, lives perennially in that impregnated soul of the Christian revolutionist of the epoch. A spirit of war and of legislation, Bolívar is likewise an apostle albeit he is late in arriving in an old and sceptical world. In the twilight of the Renaissance, he would have, with Savonarola, organized a militia to care for customs and opinions. . . . .

The person of the Areopagites is sacred. The tribunal is "essentially irresponsible and sacred" and ought to enjoy the filial respect of the citizen and the national powers. The moral house, by means of the press, exercised the censure of public conduct. With an independent and absolute authority, it possessed a vast jurisdiction which went beyond the individual and the family to the moral entity of the State itself. It was the judge of the republicanism of the government and of the observing of treaties. It governed the censorship of the press and of the books after publication, from the angle that its decisions were always theoretical. The house itself, however, could extend its powers to restrain the absolute liberty of the citizens or impede their expressions. It was obligated, on the other hand, with the care of the physical and moral education of children, from birth until the age of twelve. This jurisdiction was exercised in the home and in the school, and had a considerable practical interest because the body was a great council which prepared and executed the systems of education, the establishment of colleges, child hygiene, statistics, etc. One of its duties was the nomination of teachers who, the Liberator declared platonically, deserved to be honored, respected, and loved, as the first and most valuable citizens of the Republic.[1]

If the theory of Bolívar be weaned of all the Utopias in which it abounded and of the pomp with which it was sometimes expressed, originating, as it did, from the philosophical evolution of the previous century and from contemporary romantic literature; if it omitted predetermined premises, illigitimate in the American method, although beyond question in the democracies which inspired the Liberator; if it gave up the idea of a useless examination of details in respect to certain embryo political theories, and in respect to certain unwritten materials, it may be said that Bolívar laid down the constitutional problem of America, and traced the general lines of the system that would have avoided mighty calamities to the new born Republics. Not in vain the genius of the Liberator studied the philosophical and judicial doctrines of all the centuries, and not in vain did his marvelous intelligence permit him to deduce from direct observation sociological postulates of consequence finally proved.

Bolívar had two occasions in which to condense into a code politico-social ideas, and in both he followed the lines which he proclaimed in all his documents. The régime of government of the American countries must be neither a monarchy or an absolute democracy. It was necessary to evolve a system temperate in politics, most nearly free and equal, judged from the point of view of the civil[2], which would improve on the backwardness of those societies, and take into account, at the same time, the conquests of revolutionary thought. This régime must be central, as regards administration, so that the supreme authority might be in a position to exercise its intervention and influence in a direct and effective manner. The federal system was not the proper form, because it was complicated and because of the immensity of the territory, depopulated and without means of communication, and hence it tended to loosen the ties of the provinces to one another, and to provoke divisions and anarchy. A vigorous executive power, creative and paternal, was the axis on which the simple

---

[1] *Vide* Gil Fortoul, *The Moral Power of Bolívar*, I, 545.

[2] The British consul Ricketts, in one of his works, declared that Bolívar believed that the Civil Code "was the only thing which the genius and talent of Napoleon had produced." The Liberators' opinion of Napoleon was quite different when he was not speaking with the English. He declared to General Perú de Lacroix: "In Napoleon we should study the art of war, the art of politics and the art of governing." *Diario de Bucaramanga*, 153.

mechanism turned that preserved the order and liberty of the State. The American Constitution seemed to Bolívar excellent for the Yankees; but "it would be better for America to adopt the Koran than the government of the United States even though it be the best in the world."[1] Bolívar continued:[2]

> The more I admire the excellence of the Federal Constitution of Venezuela, the more I am convinced that its application to our State is impossible. It is a marvel, according to my way of thinking, that its model in North America has continued to exist and prosper, and that it has not been overthrown at the first sign of embarrassment or danger. In spite of the fact that this people is a singular model of political virtue and moral enlightment; in spite of the fact that its liberty has been its cradle, that it has been reared in liberty and that it has fed on pure liberty; I should even say with much respect that this people is unique in human history, yet, I repeat, it is a marvel that a system so weak and complicated as the Federal has been able to rule that country in the difficult and delicate circumstances of the past. But though this form of government be what it has been as applied to the American nation, I must state, that it has never even remotely entered my mind to make a parallel between the position and nature of the two States as distinct as the Anglo-American and the Hispano-American. Would it not be very difficult to apply to Spain the English code of political, civil, and religious liberty? It would be even more difficult to adopt for Venezuela the laws of North America. Does not the *Spirit of Laws* say that these ought to originate with those that use them? That it is a great accident if those of one nation serve another? That the laws ought to be related to the physical characteristics of the country, to its climate, to the nature of the topography, to its location, to its area, to the kind of life of its people? To depend upon the degree of liberty which the Constitution permits, to the religion of the inhabitants, their inclinations, wealth, numbers, commerce, customs, manners? I have here the code that we should consult and not that of Washington! . . . Our weak citizens will have to strengthen their spirit greatly before they can succeed in directing the salutary nourishment of liberty. Their limbs have become numbed by chains, their vision dimmed by the shadows of the dungeons, and their bodies destroyed by abject pestilence, will they be capable of marching with firm step toward the august temple of liberty, will they be capable of admiring its splendid rays and breathing without oppression its pure air? . . . The first Congress, in its Constitution, considered more than the spirit of the provinces than the concrete idea of forming and indivisible and central Republic. Here our legislators surrendered to the inconsiderable obligation, seduced by the dazzling spectacle of the happiness of the American people, thinking that the benefits enjoyed were due exclusively to the form of government and not to the character and customs of its citizens. . . But, though this federal system seemed attractive and might, in effect, be magnificent, it was not given to the Venezuelans to enjoy it suddenly on bursting their chains. We were not prepared for such blessings: a blessing as well as a curse causes death when it is excessive. Our moral nature did not yet have the necessary foundation for the benefit of a government completely representative and so sublime that it could be adapted to a republic of saints.[3]

The poetic soul of Bolívar runs unchecked through the pages of this address, pondering democracy, the only mother of sacred liberty, the virtues of the ultra liberal government which the

---

[1]"Report of Captain Moyer to the Minister of the Navy" in Villanueva, *Ferdinand VII and the New State,* 250.

[2]Larrazabal, I, 567.

[3]The Liberator at the Congress of Angostura. *Vide* also the note of Consul Ricketts to Mr. Canning, February 18, 1826. Villanueva, *The Empire of the Andes,* 104.

constitutionalists of the Year Eleven planned to found popular suffrage, "the only legitimate source of all human power."[1]

These eulogies of the Liberator, sometimes absurdly exaggerated, serve to indicate the difference between the South American method and that of those who nourished and preserved the magnificent plant of democracy. It was a foolish proposition to attempt to rule the gladiators of Sparta with the precepts of the Angora. A people unlearned, fanatical, poor, and a small guiding nucleus taught sufficiently and guided by the generally acredited ideas of the time, were the elements which seemed to suggest the convenience of a régime of government by the higher classes, of an able oligarchy, capable of directing to good advantage the process of our evolution. Captain Malling has put these words in the mouth of Bolívar:[2]

> Of all countries, South America is the least ready for republican government, because its population is composed of Indians and negroes, more ignorant than the vile race of Spaniards from whom we have just emancipated ourselves. A country that finds itself represented and governed by such peoples must go to ruin.

Rear-Admiral Rosamel, also declared:[3]

> Bolívar recognized that purely democratic governments were not suited to these peoples, because they had been accustomed so long to a despotic régime and they were still too near the time when they were Spaniards. Since he found aristocracy established everywhere, he belived that it should be given rights which would give it stability. This manner of determining affairs was, in his way of thinking, the nearest approach to the polity of the European powers. The method of establishing it should present no great difficulties, but he preferred to have such a system proposed by France or some other power, ministers to be sent accredited to propose it.

Finally, Ricketts wrote to Canning, referring to the Liberator:[4]

> "This man summarized his principles thus: that there was not much to hope for from a people that could, unfortunately, be considered as very little superior to a country of slaves; that it ought not to be given more power than it can exercise; that it ought, in view of the conditions existing in them, to establish a mixed government, with authority divided between the executive, the nobility, and the democracy of the country; and that it ought to encourage public education and national industries."

Bolívar desired, without doubt, a republic in conformity with the theory of Aristotle, a government wisely founded on a mixture of the principles of monarchy, aristocracy, and democracy. Caesar conceived of a like régime, and Cicero discussed it in his political works. The predilection of the Liberator for the British Constitution arose as much from a personal examination of those

[1]The Liberator to the President of Haiti, Puerto Principe, October 9, 1816.
[2]March, 1825. Villanueva, *Ferdinand VII and the New States*, 258.
[3]Letter to the French Minister of the Navy, June 4, 1825. Villanueva, *The Empire of the Andes*, 74. It may be assumed that in the words of Bolívar was hidden the artifice to persuade the Parisian government to recognize the independence of Venezuela by sending an official representative.
[4]Lima, February 18, 1826. *Ibid.*, 105.

institutions as from the influence of Montesquieu,[1] who was an Aristotelian. In Bolívar we find the classical error of the author of *The Spirit of the Laws* on the balance of powers. However, he believed that the existence of a nobility in Spanish America was something, historically considered, useful to our political organization, and such a belief proved that he had a definite understanding of the causes that have determined the permanence of the English institutions. In Spanish America, the democratic régime was not an immediate necessity, not a daughter of the social conditions, as in the United States. The creole patrician, who made the Hispanic American Revolution, was called to undertake the direction of those peoples divided by color, by intellectual understanding, and without a collective soul. Samper has denied the existence of this aristocracy;[2] but it is undeniable that there were white nobles who initiated and continued the struggle for independence. "The Revolution, among ourselves, had not a democratic but an oligarchic origin," declared Blanco-Fombona.[3]

The idea of an aristocratic government was associated, in the mind of the Liberator, with the Napoleonic concept of democracy. Because of his abstraction, the Caesarian tendency surprised him, the personal factor, the profound conviction that in every decisive moment of history there was a man who represented the will and the social aspirations, and that, in America, this man was himself. Bolívar loved with affectionate tenderness the great and powerful contintenal country "with the love of those who have been born to exercise it worthily," as it has been beautifully expressed by an historian; and when he followed the unchangeable propositions for public happiness and governmental stability, his great soul as a ruler confounded them with the preservation of his own autocracy. I shall have occasion to return to this interesting factor in the psychology of the Liberator.

Observe how he compared the systems of Athens and of Sparta:[4]

> The wisest legislator of Greece did not see his republic last ten years, and suffered the humiliation of knowing the insufficiency of absolute democracy to rule any particular class of society, even the most cultivated, moderate, and limited, because it shines only through the flashes of liberty. Let us recognize, then, that Solon undeceived the world, and that he has taught us how difficult it is to direct men by mere laws. The republic of Sparta, which seemed a chimerical

---

[1] Gil Fortoul, I, 206.

[2] *Essay on Political Revolutions*, etc. 173. Doctor Arcaya declared that "this *caste* was not an *aristocracy* politically considered," but, becoming remindful of the fact that the democratic ideas did not penetrate "the popular classes except in the 'freed classes' and in 'the whites', the initiators of the separatist movement, it became necessary to speak of them as the *elite* among those who were active in the movement, and that it is necessary to speak of a creole nobility, which prepared for and continued the Revolution. *Vide* Arcaya, *Studies on the Personalities and Deeds of the History of Venezuela. The Social Classes of the Colony.*

[3] Gonzalez, J. V., *Preface to a Biography of José Félix Ribas.* Edition Garnier.

[4] The Liberator to the Congress of Angostura.

creation, produced more real effect than the ingenious work of Solon. Glory, virtue, morality, and subsequently national happiness were the result of the legislation of Lycurgus. Although two kings in a State are monsters to devour it, Sparta had little to fear from a double throne. Athens looked forward to a most splendid position, with an absolute sovereignty, free election for public officials which were frequently changed, and wise and happy laws and politics. Pisistratus, usurper and tyrant, was more valuable to Athens than its laws, and Pericles, though likewise a usurper, was the most useful citizen. The Republic of Thebes lasted no longer then Pelopidas and Epaminondas, because there are times when it is men, not principles, which make governments. Codes, systems, statues, however wise they may be, are inanimate things which have but little influence upon human societies: men, virtuous, patriotic, and illustrious, constitute republics. . . . The Roman Constitution has nveer been surpassed by any people in the world, as far as power and good fortune are concerned. . . Only democracy, in my opinion, is susceptible of absolute liberty, but what democratic government has ever, at one and the same time, united power, prosperity, and permanency? And has it not been true, on the other hand, that aristocracy and the monarchy have held great and powerful empires together for centuries and centuries? What government is older than that of China? What republic has exceeded in duration those of Sparta and Venice? Did not the Roman Empire conquer the world? Has not France had fourteen centuries of monarchy? Who is greater than England? These nations, however, have been or are aristocracies or monarchies.

It may be that the great aristocracies of history impressed themselves too strongly upon the Liberator, who defended with such zeal and decision public liberties against the attacks of personal domination. In Carthage and Sparta, Monarchs often, with the support of the people, encountered, in their path of usurpation, an aristocracy which maintained its rights. The Venetian patrician curtailled, little by little, the autocratic power of the Doges.

In the Middle Ages, the municipal democracy of the Netherlands evolved toward oligarchy, and even when the written constitutions were not modified, the government became concentrated, imperceptably, in the hands of rich merchants, or their descendants who had been enriched by idleness and luxury. This plutocracy which monopolized the course of public affairs, sustained municipal autonomy against the centralizing pretensions of the princes. The British nobility has been, since the time of the Magna Carta, the citadel of popular liberty against the royal power.

The pure democratic institutions should have prevented in America the formation of personal despotisms, usually established soldiers of fortune, whose political and administrative conduct was less productive, than a constituted body could have been, through illustrious elements, and with the necessary preparation for the conduct of that business. In order that a body be enabled to protect its authority unharmed and to resist all attacks, it is necessary that it be protected from bribery and violence, the two means by which acquiescence or inertia are obtained, through its composition and legal powers. This result the Liberator believed he could prevent by the form which he proposed to give to the senate. Bolívar did not wish, however, to delegate absolute power to such a body: his was a system of compensations, a play of balances which would produce, by his concept, equality of proportions, order, and liberty. Add to this an executive power of very great responsibility, of fertile initiative, according to the British model. In spite of his apparent volubility, his brilliant and disordered imagination, the indicision which seem to afflict him at certain moments of his life, and which has caused a foreign diplomat to declare that "The Liberator lacks system", Bolívar had a profound understanding of realities. He was not led astray by "brillaint forms of liberty, but only by their substantial basis," and therefore he recommended to the representatives at Angostura, "the study of the British Constitution, which seemed destined to offer the greatest possible good to the peoples who adopt it." "When I speak of the British Government," he added, "I refer only to what it has of republicanism. . . . although in truth a system which recognizes popular sovereignty, division and balance of powers, civil liberty of conscience and of the press, cannot be called a monarchy, and is even sublime in politics."

A later document compliments and defends the ideas of Angostura. It was in the form of a letter of consequence enveloping the constitutional thought of the Liberator and the bases of his whole system. The hereditary senate was, above all, above criticism. It has been said that Bolívar wished to raise an oligrachy on the ruins of democracy, and to found an instrument of domination by which he could destroy popular control. As a matter of fact, he did not try to "create a nobility" which already existed, nor to preserve for patrician blood the right to hold certain positions. The Senate of the Roman Republic had, in the last days of its existence, opened its doors to the plebeians, who, at the conclusion of the Punic Wars, held the majority in the Assembly. But is was not for that reason that he desired to allow this body to become an agency of aristocratic government. He wished to see it formed not of patricians, but of nobles, of individuals who distinguished themselves in high positions in the service of the Republic. It was to be an oligarchy of the illustrious, renewed constantly and enriched by the capacities of all social classes.

To the criticism of William White the Liberator replied:[1]

It seems to me that you have critized the creation of an hereditary Senate and the education of future senators. The first is in accord with the practice of all democratic republics, and the second is in accord with reason. Education forms a moral man, and to form a legislator it is certainly necessary to educate him in a school of morality, justice, and law. You cite me England as an example contrary to my system, but would not my system do much good in England? As regards my Senate, I will say that it is not constituted as an aristocracy nor as a nobility, the first with the right to govern the republic, the second to have offensive privileges. The purpose of my Senate will be to temper absolute de-

---

[1]Doc. VI, 698.

mocracy. It is to unite the absolute government with a moderating institution, because it is an accepted principle of political science that the absolutely democratic government is as tyrannical as a despot. Can only a temperate government be free? How do you wish me to temper a democracy except by an aristocratic institution? Though we do not wish to unite the monarchical form with the popular one which we have adopted, we ought at least to make certain that there will be in the Republic an unalterable body which will assure it stability, since without stability every political principle will be corrupted and will end in destruction. Be good enough to read my address as a whole and not merely its parts. Its unity proves that I have very little confidence in the morality of our citizens, and without republican morality there can be no free government. To maintain this morality I have invented a fourth power which develops virtues in men and maintains it in them. This power likewise seems defective to you; but, my friend, if you wish a republic in Colombia, you must also desire that there shall be political virtue. The establishments of the ancients prove to us that men can be ruled by the most severe precepts. All the experience of history proves that men submit to the laws which a capable legislator requires of them, and only so far as a strong magistrate applies them. Draco gave Athens laws of blood, and Athens endured them, and even observed them until Solon sought to reform them. Lycurgus established in Sparta what Plato dared not dream of in his *Republic*, if he had not had for a model the legislator of Sparta. To what have men not submitted? To what would they not still submit! If there be a just violence it is that which is used in favor of good and consequently happy men; and there is no legislative liberty but that which is directed to honor humanity and perfect its lot. All the rest is pure illusion and perhaps a pernicious illusion.

Bolívar professed belief in the theory of Montesquieu concerning the nature of laws and believed that they ought to be adapted to the special conditions of every country. Political virtue which the illustrious jurist considers with Aristole indispensible for the stability of a republic did not exist in America, and therefore the Liberator tried to found institutions which were in accord with the disposition of those people, and not a false democracy. He who pretends that such ideas belittle Bolívar will fall into the same absurdity as those who censure Socrates, Plato, and Aristotle, who were in their own time the three greatest citizens of Athens, and the greatest adversaries of the democratic principle. Nor was the Liberator the only one who believed that a pure democracy should not be established in the new States. Peñalver declared in the embryo Congress[1]:

> An Executive Power for life, a powerful senate, and a house of representatives elected for seven years are, in my opinion, institutions suited to the state of the civilization and the customs of the Venezuelans, because it is these that most nearly approach a monarchical government to which they have been accustomed without having been separated from the republican which they desire to adopt. The term of office of these magistrates will give the continued vigor and force which a new government needs to establish itself.

Bishop Mendez, while opposed to an executive for life, advocated the hereditary senate which he believed to be "conducive to stability and social permanence." "There are in republican societies offices whose permanence of tenure is dangerous and unfortunate," he declared, "to the peoples who are governed

---

[1] *The Liberator to William White, San Cristóbal, May 26, 1820.*

by their extremes. Of this type is the executive power. . . .
A factious, unstable, and changing senate is an imbecilic body,
incapable of suppressing the madness of a people or its government."[1]

The Congress of Venezuela refused the project of Bolívar for
an hereditary senate, the life term of the presidency, and the
fourth power which it characterized as inquisitorial. The president
of the republic was to be changed every four years, while the
senators were to hold office for life. The federal system was, however, not adopted, and the Republic of Venezuela was proclaimed one and indivisible.[2]

The fertile year of 1819 came to an end with the Liberator
believing that he had the chance to put into practice his favorite
scheme, which he had been nursing for a long time, and which
had been intensified through observation and by the events of
the last months of that year: namely, the founding of Colombia.
On December 14th, Bolívar reported to Congress the fortunate
result of his campaign and asked for the creation of the new
Republic:[4]

> this generous people (The Granadian) has offered all its properties and all
> its lives for the country. Gifts all the more meritorious when they are spontane-
> ous! The unanimous determination to die free and not to live as slaves has given
> to New Granada the right to our admiration and respect. Its desire for a union
> of its provinces and of these with the provinces of Venezuela is likewise unanim-
> ous. The Granadians are fully convinced of the immense gain that will result
> to both peoples by the creation of a new republic composed of both of these two
> nations. The reunion of New Granada and Venezuela is the only scheme that
> I have proposed since my first battles: it is the vote of the citizens of both
> countries, and it is the guarantee of the America of the South. Legislators! The
> time for giving a firm and lasting base for our Republic has arrived. It is for you
> in your great wisdom to declare this great social act and to establish the prin-
> ciples of the pact upon which this vast Republic is to be founded. Proclaim it in
> the face of the world, and my services will have been amply rewarded.

The Fundamental Law of Colombia, decreed on the 17th of
the same month, established a Republic out of the military
Captaincy of Venezuela, the Kingdom of Santa Fé, and the
Presidency of Quito, this last country being still occupied by the
troops of the King. The city of Rosario de Cúcuta, on the Gran-
adian-Venezuelan frontier, was chosen for the meeting of the
First Congress of Colombia for the following year. In the meanwhile, the Liberator was named the Provisional President of the
Republic, General Santander, Vice President of Cundinamarca,
and Juan German Roscio, Vice President of Venezuela.

Bolívar promptly returned to the army to aid in the preparation for a new campaign. The Assembly of Angostura, in spite
of its admirable labors, left no pleasing memories with him, due

---

[1] *Doc. VI*, 698.
[2] *Vide* Gil Fortoul, I, 280.
[3] Note to the Secretary of Foreign Affairs, Dec. 31, 1813. Larrazabal, I, 250.
[4] *The Liberator to the Congress of Angostura.*

nodoubt to the affair of Arrismendi and the tenacious opposition to the constitutional projects submitted by him. In a letter to Peñalver, the displeasure of Bolívar is noted in the first words:[1]

> From Roscio and Soublette you will learn what I said to them concerning war, peace, and the usurpation of this late Congress, and from you, as president of this enemy body, Señor Roscio, who knows very well that the laws of the Indies authorize the opening of the proposals of Morillo, and who knows from memory the Book of the Maccabees, so that no one may interfere. Do you know that I am going to say nothing about this negotiation? God is on high, the Deputation very distant, and the Congress of Colombia very near, in order that it may give its vote to Cato and the Senate, while Caesar sleeps, and our Cicero returns to his legation.

----

[1] *The Liberator to Peñalver, San Cristóbal, September 24*, 1820.

Colombia

GENERAL MORILLO, acting on the instructions given him by the new constitutional Government of Spain, began, in the middle of June, 1820, negotiations with the Liberator for the purpose of putting an end to the armed conflict. The Spanish delegates proposed the adoption, at San Cristóbal, of the Constitution of Cadiz, and the recognition by Colombia of the sovereignty of the Peninsula. On such a basis the negotiation was useless, and it was only after the loss of much time that a treaty was signed at Trujillo, of armistice and for the regularization of the war, and which meant the recognition of the independence of the Republic.[1] A monument in Santa Ana commemorates the embrace of Bolívar and Morillo. Colombia sent two plenipotentiaries to Spain to negotiate a final peace.

At the end of the six months' armistice, the city of Maracaibo, which had, until that time been faithful to the King, proclaimed its incorporation with the Republic of Colombia in January, 1821. Urdaneta hastened to send a garrison to Maracaibo. This was considered by General Latorre, commander-in-chief of the royal troops, replacing Morillo who had been recalled to Europe, as a violation of the treaty. A decisive battle took place on June 24th on the famous field of Carabobo. The second Carabobo was a triumph for Páez and the British Legion. The general of the plains who had had several successes to his credit during the last few years, such as the capture of the fleet, the attack upon the Quesaras del Medio, and the advances on Mucuritas, threw the full weight of his division in the battle of that day, a battle which was decided by the unbreakable firmness of Colonel Farriar and the English contingent. Latorre took refuge in Puerto Cabello, the last bulwark of the peninsulars, and where they kept up a resistance until November 10, 1823. Bolívar, after having organized his conquests, set out for New Granada.

Gil Fortoul cites, in describing the condition of affairs in Venezuela which, during the period, had not been improved, a very interesting document. It is in the form of a letter in which Vice President Soublette gives an account to the Liberator of the troubled conditions existing in that country, scarcely emancipated, of the ambitions of the military element, and of the character of the great leaders. Páez and Mariño, above all, alarmed this

---

[1]Señor Jules Basdevant, professor of the University of Grenoble, has recently published, in the *Revue de Droit International Public*, in Paris, an extensive commentary on this convention, which possesses notable characteristics of originality, and which put an end, legally, to the war to the death. The treaty of Trujillo was frequently broken, particularly by the Spanish commanders, especially by Brigadier Morales.

correspondent. He pointed out that where these leaders operated "nothing moved regularly or smoothly" and neither were "the taxes organized." And more than that "there was no one to give strength to our forces since His Excellency the Commander-in-Chief (Páez) was amusing himself in Achaguas. If I were sure that he would not return, I should go to Valencia, and, unmindful of the whole world, confine my attention to the territory this side of the Apure, and I should leave Páez to his own little territory; because I can count on no taxes and no organization in that province. This they do the more easily since they know that you are in Peru, and hence they are losing time."[1]

The Liberator appreciated fully the magnitude of the dangers of this situation, and did not conceal his concern over these anarchical elements which were numerous in Venezuela, and with which, nevertheless, it was necessary to build the national edifice. Titanic was the effort of Bolívar and prodigious his constancy, as he prosecuted the task alone, against all, convinced in the depth of his soul that his edifice would fall to pieces, even before his death, and every effort to bring order out of this chaos was useless. Bolívar succeeded, in fifteen years of struggle, with the heorism of his soldiers, in ejecting the Spaniards from America. But the rights which heroism confer were the major obstacles in substituting a regular administration for the arbitrary despotism of the battlefield, the qualities of justice in place of the sword, and scrupulousness in handling public funds in lieu of the customary rapine of war. The Liberator met, on the very first day of peace, the covetousness and turbulent ignorance of the generals; and, later, the suspicious scrutiny of a group of ideologists who, enmeshed in their own interests, caused Colombia and America countless damages. Gaul received the confidential prophecy:[2]

> You cannot form an exact idea of the spirit which animates many of our military men. They are not those which you know there. Men who have fought a long time believe themselves very meritorious, and consider themselves humiliated and miserable and without any hope of plucking the fruit conquered by the sword. They are determined plainsmen, and never believe themselves the equal of other men, who know more, or seem better. I myself who have always been at their head do not yet know their capacity. I treat them with the greatest consideration, but not even this consideration is sufficient to inspire in them confidence, and the frankness which should exist between comrades and fellow-citizens. Be persuaded, Gaul, that we sit on an abyss, or rather on a volcano, ready to erupt. *I fear peace more than war*, and with this I give you an idea of all that I do not write and which cannot be written.

The poverty of the men made Bolívar desperate. "All is a chaos: nothing good can be done, because the good men have disappeared, and the bad have multiplied," he wrote to Peñalver.[3]

The attacks of which he was becoming the victim filled his heart with the venom of disconsolation. The first accusations of

---

[1]Gil Fortoul, I, 305.
[2]*The Liberator to Doctor Pedro Gaul, Guamare, May 20, 1821.*
[3]*The Liberator to Fernando Peñalver, Valencia, July 1, 1821.*

tyranny begin the rude campaign of improprieties, of systematic opposition, of criminal assaults which his enemies make in order to destroy him. There was born, in this epoch in the Liberator, a superb disdain for the mob of demagogues and for the greedy politicians who prepared to ruin the country. This disdain became the infinite sadness which Eloy G. González has described for us. His love of Colombia, his high integrity, and the irresistible and happy spirit of leadership prevented Bolívar from realizing his desire to retire from the command, which he announced on so many different occasions. The documents, nevertheless, reveal, a significant state of mind which must be noted. The presidency was for this man a torture, not in itself, but because of the embarrassments which he encountered in the exercise of its power, for power proved to him the inadequacy of his creative genius against the destructive forces which assailed him. The impressionability of the Liberator was great, and the scratches which continually rub against his skin provoked those brusque movements, those momentary falls followed by sudden reaction, which result in an angry blow, or in a bitter upbraiding.

Bolívar had hoped for much from the First Colombian Congress, installed in Rosario on May 6, and which was to prepare the statute for the Republic. The movement of the ideas born in this assembly quickly brought disillusionment to him. When all the preparatory measures had been taken for its installation, Bolívar wrote from Trujillo to General Azuola, that it was necessary for Congress to assemble soon in order to elect the high officials, that he was tired of ruling, and of hearing himself called ambitious, and that he was useful only as a soldier. "If they force me, I shall desert," he added.[1] And to Peñalver: "I am tired of ruling this republic of ingrates; I am tired of being called a usurper, tyrant, despot, and more tired even of them."[2] Mariño, Urdaneta, and Santander seem to him well suited for the supreme power. From Guanara he complained also of the calumnies and accusations of which he was the object, of his fatigue, of his ruined health, and declared again his resolution of serving "while Colombia lasts, or his life lasts, but only in war."[3] Doctor Gaul urged him to go to Rosario in order to inspire Congress to greater activity in its deliberations. Bolívar replied:[4]

> To what purpose, when I have important expeditions under way, at precious and unique moments? I know what I can do, my friend, and I know where I am useful: be assured that I am useful only for fighting, or at least to go with the soldiers, preventing others less able than I am from leading. All the rest is an illusion of my friends. Because they have seen me guide a ship in a tempest, they believe I could be admiral of a fleet. . . . You say that history will say wonderful things of me. I believe that it will say nothing so

[1] Trujillo, March 9, 1821.
[2] Barinas, April 21, 1821.
[3] Guamara, May 24, 1821.
[4] Maracaibo, September 16, 1821.

great as my resignation from the command, and my absolute devotion to arms
to save the government and the country. . . . History will say: Bolívar
took the command to liberate his fellow-citizens, and when they were free he
left them to govern themselves by their laws and not by his will. That is my
answer, Gaul; the other reasons you will see in my letter to the vice-president. .
You have wished to intimidate me with vain fears; I see danger only in the
frontiers. The Goths only are our enemies; the others are enemies of General
Bolívar, and he does not fight them; it is necessary to flee from them to conquer them.

On the eve of his departure for the southern campaign, where
he went first "to relieve Colombia", then to liberate Peru and
create Bolivia, Bolívar declared to General Montilla: "I hope to
return from Quito within six months, to establish myself in San
Mateo, because I am tired of ruling and shouldering responsibilities; but the country can always count on my arm."[1] The Liberator
soon recognized the grave and growing divisions, the latent
anarchy, the weakness of his projects, due to the activities of the
Congress; and was oppressed by worries. But he was still in
possession of the strength of his genius, pressed the termination
of the war, and marched anew to gain battles and build up cities,
leaving to his adversaries the time to prepare in obscurity the
ruin of Colombia.

The Fundamental Law of Angostura was ratified July 12
by the Congress of Rosario, which adopted, on the following 30th
of August, the Constitution of the Republic, with a central form
of government and with popular representation, the country
being divided into provinces governed by representatives chosen
freely by the Executive. The Executive Power was exercised by
a president, and in his absence by the vice-president, elected
for four years. A house of representatives, elected for the same
length of time, and a senate, half of whose membership was renewable every four years, formed the legislature. A high court
of justice and subordinate tribunals made up the judicial power.[2]

The Liberator took the oath before the Congress as President
of the Republic, and delivered one of his magnificent discourses.
No assembly, since the days when Athens heard the glorious
voice of Pericles, has listened to ideas nobler or more elevated

---

[1] Rosario, October 5, 1821.

[2] General Antonio Nariño, vice president, whom Bolívar charged with the
installation of the Congress, presented a project for a constitution with federalists
tendency to it, obscure in form, with a single house, a senate which was "simply a
tribunal of justice for the violation of political laws, like the high court of justice
is for the violation of governmental laws, which was also subordinated to it: a
tribunal which under this form is found in all constitutions, and which is of supreme
importance to cut off in time the abuses which are likely to be introduced in the
constitution." Without doubt, Nariño imitated the project for the federal constitution of the state of Cartagena of 1811, which instituted a conserving senate to
judge the violations of the Constitution. (*Vide* his *Message to Congress, Doc.
VII*, 604). The General left the Hall of Sessions when his project was rejected.
Years before, he proposed for New Granada in *La Bagatea* a central government
with an elective aristocracy. Restrepo, I, 120.

from the mouth of a soldier or governor. "They were the most eloquent words of his life", wrote Bartolomé Mitre. Bolívar swore that the Constitution "will be, together with independence, the holy alter on which I shall make all my sacrifices." He asked Congress for authorization to wage war in the South, to liberate Ecuador, still Spanish, and

> when I ask ardently that you will not be deaf to the clamor of my con-
> science and of my honor which call on me with great cries that I be no more than
> a mere citizen. I feel the necessity of leaving the first post to which the people
> have nominated me as the chief of its heart. I am son of the war, the man whom
> battles have elevated to the magistracy. Fortune has sustained me in this rank
> and victory has confirmed it. But these are not the titles necessary for justice,
> happiness, and national will. The sword which has governed Colombia is not the
> balance of Astrea, but a lash of genius that sometimes the heavens let fall to
> earth for the punishment of tyrants, and a warning to the people. This sword
> is useless the day peace begins, and that should be the end of my power, because
> so I have sworn to myself, because I have promised it to Colombia, and because
> there can be no republic where the people are not certain of their power. A man
> such as I am is a dangerous citizen in a popular government; he is an imminent
> threat to a national sovereignty. I wish to be a citizen in order to be free, and in
> order that all others may be free. I prefer the title of citizen to that of Liberator,
> because the latter emanates from war, and the former from the laws. Change
> for me, Sir, all my privileges for that of the good citizen.[1]

The constitutional principles enunciated by Bolívar at Angostura, and amplified by the code of 1826, were not adopted by the Colombian Constitutional Convention, as may be observed, without fundamental alterations. The life presidency, the hereditary senate, and other bases of the system were rejected. The Liberator received the Charter of Cucuta with coldness, and no favorable comment came from his lips for those institutions which he had sworn to defend with his goods, his blood, and even his honor. It is of course true that, when he announced, on his departure for the campaign, in a proclamation to the people, he expressed himself as follows;[2]

> The General Congress has given the nation that which it needed: a law
> of union, of equality, of liberty; it has formed a family of many peoples. . . .
> Your representatives, imbued with the sacred origin of their authority, preserve
> the greater part of the power for the sovereign, which is the people: to the
> depository of public power they have committed the pleasant task of doing you
> good without being able to harm you.

General Santander tells us that Bolívar informed him of his desire to resign the presidency and go to the southern campaign because "he was convinced that he could not govern under the Constitution promulgated by the Congress."[3] Fortunately, as always, the Liberator kept the authority.[4]

----

[1]October 3, 1821.

[2]*To the Colombians, Rosario, October 8, 1821.*

[3]*Archivo Santander*, I, 57.

[4]Bolívar, declared Mitre, "showed on this occasion as he did in the remainder of his grandiose and brief expression that if he harbored great ambitions he was not a despot, nor wished to be a tyrant. He had the moderation which was a part of his natural authority, adhering to his personal power." *History of San Martín*, V, 333.

As a matter of fact, the fundamental features of the new institutions diverged more and more from the conception which Bolívar had of them, for he hoped "that all parts of the government and administration should have the vigor which can be maintained only by a balance of powers, and not only between those members which form the government, but between the various sections of the country", that Colombia should be content" with moderate pretentions, forming itself in a way suitable to its conditions, its spirit, and its circumstances"; "that we should not aim at the impossible, that we should not in our efforts to elevate ourselves to the region of liberty descend into the region of tyranny" because "abstract theories are those which produce the pernicious idea of unlimited liberty." Very little is to be found in the Constitution corresponding to the wish of "a government eminently popular, just, moral, repressing tyranny, anarchy, and crime, a government which establishes innocence, humanity, and peace. A government which causes equality and liberty to triumph through inexorable laws."[1]

The Liberator divined the evils which this Constitution conserved for the country for it opened the doors to demagogy. Congress, in its independence of action, had worked for an incoercible rebellion, ignoring the Liberator's charges that it attacked this principle, in order that it might eliminate his imperious and dominating personality, in order to wrest the Republic from his control. Before the birth of the factions which were to destroy Colombia, Bolívar judged it necessary to quiet the suspicious, suppress his ambitions, and promise to separate himself from the command of the army as soon as the war had been won.

On October 9, a Congressional decree conferred on the Liberator dictatorial powers for the duration of the campaign, and authorized him to organize the territories which he might emancipate by his arms. General Santander, Vice President, was charged with the Executive Power in Bogotá, capital of the Republic. On the same day, Bolívar left Cúcuta for the South.

---

[1] *The Liberator to the Congress of Angostura, February 15,* 1819.

The Campaign in Peru

THE first clash between Colombia and Perú came about over the possession of the province of Guayaquil, which had proclaimed its independence from Spain. It was in this epoch that the zenith of the influence of the Liberator in the destines of America was reached. Bolívar arrived at Guayaquil on July 11, 1822, and received, fourteen days later, the visit from José de San Martín, formerly general of the troops of the Government of Buenos Aires, the liberator of Chile, and, at that time, commander of Chilean expedition at Lima.

An important personage in the southern wars, General San Martín had conducted a brilliant campaign of the Andes to liberate Chile, and had won the battles of Chacabuco and Maipú, which gave him first place among the chiefs of Argentina. His operations formed, in connection with the manœuvers which preceded the battle of Boyacá and the strategy of Ayacucho, the brightest pages in the military history of America. The illustrious soldier, with the title of Protector of Perú, had organized a government in Lima, which had been abandoned by the Spaniards —who were preparing in the Sierra for the offensive—and came to Guayaquil as advocate of the claims of Perú to this territory, and with the proposition to agree with the Liberator as to what help Colombia might give Perú, and for the form of the political organization which might seem the most suitable for the new States.

The nature and the result of the conferences of Guayaquil are recorded in a private note from the secretary of the Liberator addressed to the Department of Foreign Relations at Bogotá.[1] The tendencies of General San Martín were monarchical. For this reason and also because he did not believe in the efficacy of republican institutions for America, he suggested to the Liberator the necessity of establishing in these countries constitutional monarchies ruled by European princes. This insinuation was made with particular reference to Perú, where the general from Rio de la Plata beleived he could impose his views. Secretary Perez gives, in a note referred to above, the following exchange of views:[2]

His Excellency (the Liberator) replied that it was unwise to bring European princes to America or to Colombia because they were factors foreign to our race; that His Excellency would oppose, if he could, that form of government, but declared that he would not oppose the form of government which a State might adopt of its own free will; adding to this what he thought of the nature of

---

[1] *Vide The Letters of Bolívar*, I, 422.
[2] *To the Secretary of Foreign Relations of Colombia, Headquarters of the General of Guayaquil, July 29*, 1822.

government, referring to his address before the Congress of Angostura. The Protector replied that it would be better to have the prince arrive later, but His Excellency declared that he would never favor the coming of such princes; that His Excellency would prefer to invite General Itúrbide to crown himself rather than that Bourbons, Austrians, or other European dynasties should come. The Protector of Perú said that there was a large number of lawyers in Perú who favored a republic, and he complained bitterly of the character of these intellectuals. It is to be presumed that his plan now is to set up a monarchy on the principle that the throne is to be offered to a European prince; and that if it should prove unwise to have him come over at once, to have him come later when he is more popular and stronger. If the words of the Protector are sincere, no one can be farther from desiring a throne. He appears to be thoroughly convinced of the burdens of ruling.

General Tomás Cipriano de Mosquera, who was afterwards President of New Colombia, was secretary to Bolívar and was also present at the conferencies. In a work published forty years later, Mosquera ascribed the following words to the Liberator:[1]

My dear General, we have no elements of monarchy in this God's earth. Let the republic be formed; it will produce dignity in man. Necessities and habits of work will be developed for the social welfare; this will produce material riches which will bring commercial industry. With it immigration from Europe, where land is lacking for the proletariat, and which is available among us, will be induced to come. It is not possible to stop human progress; and if you should succeed in planting monarchies in the New World their duration will be ephemeral, the kings will fall by rebellion of their guards of honor, in order to establish a republic, because once the idea has spread, as among us, it cannot be extinguished. I agree with you that there might occur a new revolution after independence has been conquered if good sense be wanting in the election of public officials. Grave and of transcendental importance is the question which we have discussed, but it is difficult to change the principle which was adopted after twelve years of a glorious struggle filled with examples of abnegation and patriotism. . . . Neither we nor the generation which is to follow us will see the brilliance of the Republic which we have founded; I consider America to be in a chrysalis; there will be a metamorphosis in the physical existence of our inhabitants; finally, a new blend of all the races will produce a homogenous people. We may not stop the march of mankind with institutions exotic, as I have told you, to the virgin territory of America.

And General San Martín responded: "I only hope that before I close my eyes I may celebrate the triumph of the principles which you defend." Mosquera returned in 1829 to find the Liberator in Quayaquil, and declared: "I found him possessed with the same ideas of a monarchy being incompatible with the needs of Colombia and Perú."

The Argentine general considered the project of Bolívar to federate the American republics very fine and useful, at least those of Colombia and Perú; but insisted, above all, which was natural to his soldier's temperment, on the advantages which these institutions gave from a military point of view. In addition, he promised the Liberator that he would try in the Congress

---

[1]Doc. XII, 754. General Rufino Guido, of the staff of San Martín wrote in a letter to Bartolomé Mitre that Mosquera did not attend the conferencies. And that Mosquera's testimony could not be taken as historically accurate.

of Lima, to bring about a satisfactory solution of the question of the frontiers between the two countries.

Bolívar had, as we have seen, a special system which he believed best suited to America, and it is not strange that he objected to the proposition of his interlocutor. Consul Ricketts declared to Canning, some years later: "He (Bolívar) sees no objection to the presence in Brazil of an emperor, nor of a federal government in the sister Republic of Buenos Aires, but he has his special plan for governing Colombia, Perú, and Bolivia.[1]" The Liberator had no confidence in democracy for our countries, and a monarchy inspired him with the same uneasiness. It has also been declared that his character prevented him from submitting to a power greater than his own, or to the playing of a role like that of a satellite.

The point of real interest debated at Guayaquil who should assume the liberation of Perú, which territory was still occupied by the Spaniards, with the exception of Lima and a few points on the coast? General San Martín sought aid from the Colombian army which the Liberator desired to lead in person. The former came to the point where he offered to serve under orders from Bolívar: but as there was no agreement, the Argentinian, disgusted, returned to Lima on July 28, where he resigned his command and retired from public life.

The two men left different impressions. "General San Martín came to see me at Guayaquil," wrote the Liberator, "and seemed to me to be the same as to those who have most favorably judged him, such as Francisco Rivas, Juancho Castillo, and the others."[2] Larrazabal informs us that Bolívar "judged General San Martín as he should: a man without duplicity and good." The captain of La Plata, on his part, expressed his impression in an enigmatic phrase to O'Higgins, Director of Chile: "The Liberator is not the man I imagined." Nevertheless, in announcing to the Peruvians the aid from Colombia, he exclaimed: "The 26th of July last, when I had the satisfaction of embracing the hero of the South, was one of the happiest days of my life. Let us all express our eternal gratitude to the immortal Bolívar." And later he had formulated the judgment which Mitre has recorded: "It may be said that his military achievements have, with reason, entitled him to be considered as the most extraordinary man that South America has produced. What characterizes him, above all, is the

_____

[1]February 18, 1826. Villanueva, *The Empire of the Andes*, 103. In this same note it is claimed that the Liberator said, with regard to South America, "I do not claim that republican is superior to any other system, but it is better suited to the imperfections of the elements of our countries. Its establishment will lead to despotism and tyranny". I believe that he speaks of the "republican" he means the "democratic," because the latter would be in keeping with the ideas of Bolívar.
[2]*The Liberator to Peñalver, Cuenca, September 26*, 1822.

constancy which difficulties do not impair. He never allows himself to be weakened, no matter how grave the dangers."[1]

The separation of the Protector from the negotiations of
Perú was imposed by force of circumstances. A stranger and
isolated in a country which he could not impress and whose
sympathies he could not capture; object of the suspicions of the
Peruvian leaders; knowing no other profession than that of arms;
without prestige in Chile; "without support of his own country,[2]
General San Martín lacked the authority to impose his personality,
to dominate anarchy, and to finish the war. He was not "properly
speaking a politician. He did not possess administrative talents
nor wide vision of political matters."[3] Matters in Perú grew
more complicated daily, and San Martín felt himself incapable of
guiding them. Thus, as his minister Montegudo tells us, "he
was firmly of the opinion that he should not continue as governor:
he is a man of war and averse to the tasks of the cabinet."[4]

On the departure of San Martín, the Peruvians returned to
the man of genius who incarnated liberty and bore in his brain
and his arm the support and force to evict discord and conquer
the Spaniards.[5] A plenipotentiary of President Riva Agüera
declared to the Liberator, in Guayaquil, the desires felt in Perú
that he should enter their territory at the head of the Colombian
army. The congress of Bogotá authorized this, and Bolívar,
on his arrival in Lima, September 1, 1823, found the Marquis de
Torre Tagle in the Presidency. On the 10th of the same month, the
Peruvian Congress conferred full military powers on the Liberator
throughout the whole extent of the country.

If the action of Bolívar in Perú had a decisive influence on the
destiny of America and of the revolution, Lima, in turn, exercised
a more important one on the Liberator and on the march of events.
The political atmosphere, from that time on, was different from
that in which the personality of Bolívar had emerged, and in
which his power had developed. A worldly and brilliant society,
perhaps the richest in America, faithful to the ideas and the
traditions of the court of the viceroy, governed by great lords,
jealous of their hereditary importance, as much so as were the
Colombian soldiers of their recent prerogatives; a dignified
Catholicism, tempered by the scepticism which is natural to
centers of culture, and constituting a characteristic of that
genuinely Spanish culture; a people lazy, capable neither of
practicing nor of enduring Venezuelan adventures, content with
the wealth of the great and their own poverty; an administration

---

[1]Mitre, *History of San Martín*, VI, 179.
[2]Mitre, IV, 197.
[3]Mitre, IV, 313.
[4]*Memorial*, Quito, March 7, 1823.
[5]Later, the Liberator declared as "an act of ingratitude" the conduct of the
Peruvians toward General San Martín. *A View of Spanish America*. Quito,
April, 1829.

which encouraged forgetfulness of political aspirations by reason
of its benignity and effeciency; the double atavism, Ibero-Incaic,
working on the ideas of a people half breed, imaginative and
voluble; with a profound inclination toward peace and tranquility; such are some of the conditions which give to the Peruvian
evolution a peculiar character.

From the political point of view, when the revolution arrived
in Perú, after devastating the rest of the Continent, the question
of the form of government assumed a most important form. The
tendency toward monarchy, which also became manifest in Buenos
Aires, became pronounced from the first moment of emancipation,
even when the Spaniards still occupied the major part of the
territory. And this tendency coincided with the personal ideas
of General San Martín, who entered into a treaty with the enemy
in order to establish a monarchy, and, as has already been explained, he spoke of the same matter to the Liberator. The
influence of Lima extended to Colombia, where during the fifteen
years of war, no one had spoken of any system other than the
republican. The proposition to crown Bolívar, conceived by some
soldiers in Caracas and Bogotá, was coincident with the apogee
of Bolívar, and of the interchange of ideas between Colombia
and Perú. In this latter country, as in the rest of America, the
traditional was monarchical.[1] The nobles of Lima tried to direct
the revolution toward a monarchy in the same way as the Mexican
clericals, by reason, pressed toward Itúrbide. High revolutionaries
did not exist, and the extensive war in Colombia had not developed
meritorious and ambitious generals. The liberating movement
found the old Incaic empire encircled by a considerable number of
barricades, which were, in the long run, demolished by the torrent,
but which in an appreciable degree influenced its course. The
Peruvian tradition suggested an expedient to Miranda, when he
sought in London to interest the British Government in his
dream of redeeming America. This Generalismo imagined that
the restoration of the throne of the Incas would incite the native
element to support his attempt, and to overcome the scruples
of the English rulers. It soon became evident, however, that the
revolution in Peru, as in the rest of America, was to be carried on
without outside help, and against the half breeds and the Indians,
by the force of the white creoles alone.[2]

---

[1]The monarchy offered to America stability and independence; it would have
prevented civil wars and half a century of anarchy. It was the only real American
tradition. The revolutionary battles gave a hegemony to ambitious generals:
against these, a central government, above the quarrels of the factions, would have
defended liberal institutions. A constitutional prince would have brought unity to
these divided nations, continuity, under the force of which parties and classes,
themselves ambitious, would have finally arranged themselves. The social elevation
of the half breeds and mulatoes would have been less violent. Garcia Calderón,
The Latin Democracies of America.

[2]Quite the contrary happened in the French Revolution, which, as Tocqueville

As soon as he approached the Peruvian frontier, the Liberator became aware of the monarchical tendency of that country, which were given disturbing support by the plans of General San Martín, who offered to go to Spain in search of a Bourbon prince to crown him in Perú[1]. Bolívar dispatched, as early as September, 1821, to his envoy near to this General, Colonel Ibarra, instructions that he should inquire into the truth of these matters, for he feared that the projects attributed to the famous Argentinian would lead to a "scandal" for our republics, and encourage Spain to continue the war. Bolívar ordered his envoy to protest in the name of Colombia against a proposition contrary to republican institutions, contrary to the objects of the conflict, and to the most earnest desires and votes of the peoples for liberty.[2] In addition to this, referring to the pact in the Plan of Iguala between Itúrbide and Viceroy O'Donojú, the Liberator wrote to General San Martín: "Transplanted to the New World, these European princes, supported by the kings of the Old, may cause serious changes in the systems and governments of America."[3] On this point, Bolívar was adamant: "Never, General, shall I help to move to the New World the sprouts from the old dynasties of Europe. If we should attempt such a thing, Colombia as one man would say to me that I had made myself unworthy of the name of Liberator."[4] According to San Martín, Bolívar added that, as a last resort, the kings could only be Americans.[5]

The Liberator foresaw the development of affairs in Mexico and the coronation of Itúrbide: "The turn which the revolution has taken in Mexico these last days shows clearly what will be its result: a monarchy, to which European princes will be called and which will be established there, and, when contrary to all probability, none comes, the crown will go necessarily to the

---

observes, was prepared by the cultured classes and carried out by the common people.

For an account of the state of morals and politics in Perú at this time consult the *Memorial* published in Quito, in 1823, by Don Bernardo Monteagudo, minister of General San Martín.

[1]The plan of making Perú a kingdom "was a set idea" in San Martín, declared Mitre (IV, 260). Consult the proposals made in Punchauca to the Viceroy Laserna by General San Martín, on June 2, 1821. Consult the instructions given to del Rio and Paroissen, on the 25th of December following, by the Consul of Lima. These men had been chosen to go to Europe to look for a sovereign for Perú. The instructions were signed by Don Joséde San Martín, Torre Tagle, Monteagudo, and others. The Liberator wrote to General Santander, July 29, 1822, a day after the departure of San Martín that the latter "says that he does not wish to be king, but neither does he want a democracy and that he does want a European prince to come to reign in Perú."

[2]Vide Villanueva, *Bolívar and General San Martín*, 205.

[3]*The Liberator to General San Martín, November 15,* 1821.

[4]Mosquera. Publication cited.

[5]*General San Martín to Don José J. Pérez, Agent of Chile in Paris.*

most audacious and resolute pretender in Mexico."[1] Months
later he wrote to Peñalver;

"You must know that Itúrbide has made himself Emperor, by the grace of
Pio, the first sargeant: without doubt he will be a good emperor. His empire will
be great and happy, for his claims are legitimate according to Voltaire who
declares: the first king was a fortunate soldier, alluding without a doubt to
Nimrod. I fear much that the four purple covered planks called the throne will
cause more blood than tears, and give more uneasiness than repose. Many
believe that it is easy to wear a crown, and that all adore it, but I believe that
the time of monarchies, is past; and that until the decadence of man no longer
permits a love of liberty, thrones will be out of fashion."[2] Bolívar held these
sentiments unchanged when, a year later, he declared in a toast at a banquet
"that the American people should never consent to raise up a throne."

In addition to these differences of principle which divided
public opinion, there existed a well developed anarchy in Perú at
the time the Colombian divisions entered the country. Twenty
thousand Spaniards prepared to descend from the Sierra to give
battle to a patriotic army, which one may say never existed.
Riva Agüera and Torre Tagle disputed over the Presidency,
preventing common action and wasting the last resources of the
Republic. The Argentine troops of the Callao garrison supported
the Spanish, and surrendered the fortress to the royalists (February, 1824); and some time later, Torre Tagle himself deserted.
A decree of the Congress then conferred the dictatorship upon the
Liberator. A little before, General Sucre had been named commander of the army.

The Peruvian war was painful to Bolívar, because he had to
struggle both against the enemy and against the national element
either aggressive or inert. He had assumed the command because he was convinced that he alone could destroy the Spaniards.
"Yielding to the universal vote, I have decided to make a new
sacrifice for the independence of America, undertaking this
heavy duty," he declared to Revenga.[3] And before the discord
and the attempts of Congress to deprive him of the authority
which had barely been conferred upon him, he wrote to Torre
Tagle, who was still president and a patriot: "You must know
that the country cannot save itself thus. My own has achieved
liberty because it was united and obedient, not always voluntarily,
but always constant. De Pradt declares, with much reason, that
the weapon of the masters of war is despotism: that is to say,
command without limit and obedience without investigation."[4]

During all the months that his command lasted, until Ayacucho, he protested against the difficulties of the campaign,
and the lack of money. The war became difficult. "I have
complained to the Government, threatening to leave Perú,"
he declared to General Sucre, "within a month if they do not

---

[1]*The Liberator to General Soublette. Bogotá, November 22, 1821.*
[2]*Cuenca, September 26, 1822.*
[3]*Lima, October 30, 1823.*
[4]*Pativilca, January 7, 1824.*

give me money for the army."[1]   And he gave these momentous orders: "We must, dear General, be deaf to the clamor of the whole world, because war thrives on despotism and is not made from love of God. Stop at nothing, show yourself to be a terrible, inexorable character.[2]" Money was found, the churches being forced to contribute their treasures for the public good; an army was created; anarchy was suppressed. And in this cyclopean task of organizing Perú, the Liberator was greater than ever and the Continent was liberated.[3]

Bolívar conquered the royal army, on the 7th of August, on the field of Junín. Junín was the battle of the nations of the New World. There the cavalry of the Argentine Necoechea and the Peruvian division under Lamar fought gloriously by the side of the troops from Colombia. On this symbolic ground America fought united, and the spirit presiding over its liberty was incarnated in the man representing the genius of the race. On December 9th, Sucre won the victory of Ayacucho and finished the epic cycle of the revolution.[4]

While successes of this type were achieved in the South, grave difficulties developed in Colombia. The first symptoms of discontent manifested themselves in Venezuela, at the time of the promulgation of the Code of Cúcuta, long before there was formed around General Páez the party which, in 1830, was to begin the movement for dismembering the Republic. The authority of the cacique of the plains was not yet established, nor did there exist the monarchical influence of its allies, when the Municipality of Caracas passed, in public session, the reservations to this new constitutional canon, and expressed itself in favor of a modification of many of its provisions.[5] The initiative taken by certain

---

[1]*Pativilca, January 16*, 1824.

[2]*Pativilca, February 8*, 1824.

[3]See how O'Leary described the magnificent activity of Bolívar. *Narrative*, II, 255.

[4]Historians find that nearly five hundred warlike engagements took place during the fifteen years, and over an area of 7,500,000 square kilometers. A French officer, Colonel Baron d'André, who has traveled in America, declared, referring to the formidable author of the Epopeya: "He was a superhuman genius, who, conquering truly inconceivable difficulties, shines with unequalled brilliance in the military history of the world."

[5]*The Act of the 29th of December*, 1821. The Government of Bogotá declared this Act and that of the 3rd of January following were "miserable and extemporaneous protests," and saw in them "a disagreeable example which may prove to be very serious, in places where the whole people have received loyally the Constitution and in which our enemies see with our view, expecting to see the Republic go forward in unison through the new system. . . . The Municipality of Caracas, taking counsel from the department of Quito and from the province of Caracas, has arrogated to itself a power which no one recognizes." The Intendent of Venezuela expressed himself in a like manner to the Secretary of the Interior, February 26, 1822. The City Council explained and excused its conduct on the 15th of the following July. *Vide* José Joaquin Guerba, *The Convention of Ocaña*, 42.

municipalities, during the period of the war, was fertile in results for the national cause in the veneer of legality which it gave to the authority wielded by the generals, in the absence of congresses or legitimate assemblies; and when the Municipal Council of Caracas passed these serious reservations it followed, to a certain extent, the tradition of debating in these embryonic bodies questions of public interest. But the usurpation, which in abnormal times rendered signal services and were justified, violated at the time and would violate in the future the sovereign law, weakened the prerogatives of the Congress and set an example deplorable for the destinies of the country. Municipalities were converted into instruments of disorder and, in the hands of intriguers, contributed powerfully to the triumph of a bad cause.

New Granada enjoyed a preponderant position in the Colombian Union, and the military men of Venezuela, who had won the common independence, were humiliated by the ascendancy of the cultured Granadians which became more pronounced each day. Neither Urdaneta, nor Soublette, nor Mantilla, called to high positions, men of exalted patriotism, permitted themselves to be actuated by petty ideas. But, behind them surged the warlike and covetous mob, which wished to keep *what they had conquered by the sword*, and for whom government and order were a nuisance, above all, in the hands of others. There existed, besides, in Venezuela a group of chieftains who would have preferred the establishment of a federal system in place of a central government at Bogotá with full power. And finally it was said that, if Colombia had numerous supporters in New Granada, it was because the Union served to govern the Venezuelans badly and from afar. With such elements, and because of certain unfavorable geographical and social conditions, the future could not be peaceful.

As far as it concerned Bolívar, Venezuela respected him, Bogotá feared him. Absence reduced the respect and changed the fear into hatred. The Liberator tried in vain to calm the impatient ones, to disarm the angry, and multiplied the promises that when the war was ended he would surrender the command. In a letter to Briceño-Méndez, he insisted on his intentions: "The first day of peace will be the last of my public life," he declared.[1] A little later he wrote: "I have reached the end of my career and now it is necessary that it decline, and, because of this fact, it is necessary that I arrange for myself an honorable and gentle fall, because if I do not do so in a manner to please myself, I may do it with violence and the loss of all my acquisitions."[2] Knowing the scruples of those who did not cease to oppose him and accuse him of being a despot, Bolívar affected an absolute respect for law and government. While preparing for a march to Perú, he wrote to the Marquis del Toro: "I will tell you, however, something

[1]*Guayaquil, August 11*, 1822.
[2]*Guayaquil¹ August 29*, 1822.

about the state of affairs: we have sent six thousand men to Perú; we have not raised them ourselves in order not to violate the law; I hope for the permission of Congress to do so. . . . If the Congress will not let me go into Perú, I shall go to undertake an immense task to permit Colombia to avoid making new sacrifices which are about to ruin her."[1] And to Peñalver he recalled that the installation of the Congress of Angostura had given him a greater reputation than his past services, "because men desire that they be served to suit everybody, and the way to please them is to invite them to participate in the power and the glory of command."[2]

Bolívar sent to Santander, on January 9, 1824, from Pativilcar, his fifth resignation of the presidency of Colombia, and, some days later, confided to General Sucre the hopes he placed in that manœuver: "I have sent my resignation to the Congress, expressing much disgust because of the ingratitude of the people. This step must produce, as it did in Lima, some result. If not, I shall separate myself wholly from the service, for I am determined not to let Colombia be ruined in my hands, and much less to liberate her a second time: such a work is not to be done twice."[3] Disillusion had filtered into this soul of granite. The spiritual illness of Bolívar, like the misfortunes of Colombia, is incurable. From this time forward we hear him, in his flowing and prophetic language, mingle his woe with the woe of his country. He wrote to Santander:[4]

> The age of ambition is the age I am in. Rousseau declared that at forty years of age ambition leads men. Mine, on the contrary, is finished. You, who are young, and Sucre, who is young, should follow for ten years more the career which I abandon. Happy are you who are now in the age of hope! In the meantime, I hope for nothing and I fear everything. I have been loaded with such encomiums and blamed for such vices that I hope for nothing from one or the other: both are sufficient for any mortal.

And to Peñalver he wrote:[5]

> Every day I pity more and more the fate of my country, and every day it appears to me more hopeless. In this unlucky revolution, defeat and victory are equally unhappy: I must ever shed tears over our fate. The Spaniards will be finished soon, but we—when? Like the wounded deer we carry in our bssom the arrow, and it will bring us death ultimately, because our blood is our poison. Happy those who die before seeing the fatal sequel of this bloody drama! At least to them will remain the consolation of a ray of hope giving them an illusion of what will never take place. That is all I expect after the end of the war.

Moreover, neither fatigue nor resignation which seem to have overcome him prevent this prodigiously energetic being from continuing the fight for liberty and from multiplying his efforts to consolidate the countries of America. Bolívar possessed the

---

[1] *Guayaquil, May 30*, 1823.
[2] *Idem. id., id.*
[3] *Pativilca, January 16*, 1824.
[4] *Ibid., January 23*, 1824.
[5] *To Don Fernando Peñalver, Chancey, November 10*, 1824.

blind confidence in the future which never abandon great imaginative minds, and which, in exceptional cases, permits the
sustaining of the will and the robust mind. The independence
of America was the realization of the Casacoima. It is surprising
to see this man in such an epoch, and many times during the same
day, deliberating over high politics, scrutinizing the future,
with seeing eyes, and losing himself in lyric dreams, inexplicable
to those who do not study the depths of his extraordinary mind.
When he seized control of the war and politics in Perú, when every
action is necessary to carry out his formidable task, and his
attention is divided between Lima threatening and Bogotá
intriguing, when the engagements at Pativilcar seemed to have
exhausted all his energy and the recent events destroyed his
illusions, Bolívar realized that his master Don Simón Rodríguez
had returned to America, and proud of his work and of his fame,
forgot the failures and the difficulties, forgot the enemy and the
woes of the country, wrote a beautiful letter to the itinerent
scholar in declamatory style which reminds one of the *Delirio*.

In Bogotá the opposition did not concern itself with admiration for Colombia, but in attacking her. The Liberator still
enjoyed sufficient prestige to prevent the darts of the adversary
from being turned against his path of glory, but events came to
link themselves together and the end was approaching. The
Colombian Congress, jealous of the power of Bolívar, revoked, on
July 28, 1824, the extraordinary powers which it had conferred on
him in the decree of October of the Year 21; and took from him the
command of the expeditionary army, which the Liberator had
entrusted to General Sucre.[1] In December, he resigned for the sixth
time the Presidency of Colombia, a resignation not accepted by
the Congress.

After Ayacucho, Bolívar convoked the Peruvian Congress,
surrendered the dictatorship, and communicated his intention
of moving against Upper Perú in order to organize it. On this
occasion he declared:[2]

> Legislators! In restoring to the Congress the supreme power which it
> placed in my hands, may I be permitted to congratulate the people because
> they have become free of what is the most terrible thing in the world, from war
> by the victory of Ayacucho and from despotism by my resignation? I ask you,
> let there be proscribed forever such a tremendous authority! This authority
> which was the sepulchre of Rome! It was laudable, no doubt, in Congress to fix

---

[1]The historian broke a confidence of the minister of Chile in Bogotá concerning the end of the power of Bolívar. According to that diplomat, the arrival
of Valdez at Laserna, after Junín, which doubled the forces of the royal army, put
the patriots in such a grave danger that a council of the superior officers, composed
of Sucre, Santa Cruz, Lara, Lamar, Miller, Córdoba, Gamarra, and at which the
Chilean general O'Higgins were present, judged that "the Liberator ought to retire
from the campaign to serve the general cause of America." Sucre should assume
command of the army in the event of the retirement of Bolívar.

[2]*The Liberator to the Congress of Peru, February 10, 1825.*

its laws on the bayonets of the liberating army in order to leap over horrible abysses and to survive furious tempests; but now that the nation has secured domestic peace and political liberty, laws alone should be permitted to rule.

The high Assembly was known to prefer the dictatorial power in the hands of Bolívar and that it decreed him great honors.

The deputies of Upper Perú reconvened in Chuquisaca, July 10, 1825, voted the creation of a sovereign state with the name of the Republic of Bolívar, and elected the Liberator as Supreme Chief, who delegated the power to Marshall Sucre. In the following year Bolívar sent to the Congress of the new Republic his plan of the Constitution.[1]

---

[1]*Vide* Gil Fortoul, I, 346.

The Hispanic American Ideal

AN ample American nationalism, which exalted on occasions the tremendous struggle against the Spaniard, the only foreigner which we really know, formed in Bolívar the political program which considers, long before Monroe, that America is for the Americans.[1] Ten years before, to be exact, the Liberator expressed the idea of freeing the Continent from all European rule, when the President of the United States, acting on the suggestion of Great Britain[2] expressed the idea in a formula which has been successful, and which has been converted, by the Anglo-Saxons into a base of American public law.

The Liberator proclaimed, at the restoration of the Granadian Union in 1815: "This half of the globe belongs to those whom God has placed on its soil, and not to those refugees from the other side of the ocean who, to escape the blows of tyranny, come to establish it on our ruins.[3]" We have already seen what was the conduct of Bolívar when the circumstances and the motive led

---

[1] All the world knows", declared Morton Fullerton, "the idea of Bolívar contained in the phrase 'America for the Americans' and which is frequently confounded with the Doctrine of Monroe. If the famous message of President Monroe of the 2nd of December, 1823, without prejudice, it will be seen that the motives of these two American statesmen were separated by the whole of the height of the Cordillera of the Andes, but that Bolívar and Monroe both agreed in prohibiting the Western Hemisphere to the monarchical systems of Europe founded on the theory of divine right. Their declarations implied an incompatibility between certain traditional conceptions of government in Europe and that of the American idea of government. In origin, the doctrine of Monroe, like that of Bolívar, was directed against a certain form of government and one way inquire whether Monroe had the intention, also, of protectiug his neighbors of the South against the ambitions of a government, albeit European, which was truly representive and in extent to that which Monroe saw in the plan of the Holy Alliance." *The United States and the War*, 42, 1916.

[2] The Monroe Doctrine was, in reality, an alliance with Great Britain for the defense and the common security of both States." Morton Fullerton, 41. "The Monroe Doctrine, in the sense in which it was formulated conjointly with Madison and Jefferson, called for a political alliance which England and the United States should follow on the American Continent against the powers, a policy which originated with England, but which came from Washington in order to have it appear that it was a matter wholly separated from the Mother Country. Sir Thomas Andrea Cook, *The Original Intention of the Monroe. The Fortnightly Review. September*, 1898.
Address of Bolívar, January 23, 1815.

[3] In an article published in the *Figaro*, February 21, 1927, Morton Fullerton insisted: "Is it not the existence of the great fleet of England which alone gave to the Monroe Doctrine its secular reality?" History asks and conserves the same identical question. England alone possessed, during the nineteenth century, the desire and the power to defend our countries from a European attack. At the present time, Europe neither desires nor dares to attack us and the larger number of the Latin Republics are, on the other hand, in a position to defend themselves without aid from the outside. Note of 1927.

the North American Government to enunciate Monroeism. The decree of war to the death was a nationalist explosion to effect a heroic medium in order to impregnate with iron and blood the soul and ideals the vast organism of the Continent. However, Americanism for Bolívar does not mean Xenophobia. A universal spirit, an electric and elevated intelligence, the Liberator was not the man best suited to separate himself from the world and to escape its contact. At no time in his life, even when America kept him most occupied, did Bolívar forget Europe. Sufficiently lustrious to hold for fifteen years the attention of the world, the care he took not to lose the favor of liberal Europe is a proof of the greatness of his thought and of his mission. He cultivated important relations in foreign lands; he was proud of the admiration which he inspired on the other side of the ocean; his associates, Wilson, Ferguson, O'Leary, Peru de la Croix, were foreigners. Above all, the Liberator realized that America must receive for a long period of time a gush of foreign blood into its immense arterial system, and which must refine the race of the future. "We must encourage the immigration of people from Europe and North America so that they may establish themselves here, bringing their arts and sciences. These advantages: an independent government, free schools, and intermarriage with Europeans and Anglo-Americans, would change the character of our people, and make them illustrious and prosperous. . . . We need mechanics and farmers, and the country must have them to progress." Neither as politician nor as sociologist could Bolívar be an exclusionist. As for his sentiments, we could hardly find a better formula to express them than that from the lips of the statesman of the Plata to the Anglo-Saxon postulate: "America for Humanity."

Bolívar is, *par excellence*, the apostle of American solidarity. "Let us make," he explained, completing the idea previously expressed, "let us make it so that love, with its universal tie, will unite the sons of the hemisphere of Columbus, and so that hate, vengeance, and war will be evicted from our bosoms, permitting them to be employed on the frontiers only, and against those only whom they may be justly used: against the tyrants."[1] Later he wrote from Jamaica:[2]

> It is a grandiose idea to try to form the whole of the New World into a single nation with one soul which leagues its parts with itself and with the whole. As it has a single origin, a single tongue, the same customs and the same religion, it should have a single government, which would confederate the different states which are to be formed. More is not possible because remote climates, diverse situations, opposing interest, and dissimilar characteristics divide America. How beautiful it would be if the Isthmus of Panama were for us what the Isthmus

---

[1]Bolívar's resolution against the Spaniards was immovable. Recall the decision of the *junta* of November 20, 1818, and the reply of the Liberator to the governor of Cartagena, when he proposed to send them to Spain.

[2]*Letter to an English Gentleman, Kingston, September 6, 1815.*

of Corinth was to the Greeks! Would that some day we might have the good fortune to install an august Congress of the representatives of the republics, kingdoms, or empires to discuss the high interests of peace and war with the nations of the rest of the world. This kind of cooperation might take place in any happy period of our regeneration; other hope is groundless. Such was the plan of the Abbot St. Pierre who conceived the laudable dream of reuniting a European Congress to decide the fate and interests of those nations.

In 1826 Bolívar convened a Panamerican Congress at Panama.

In the middle of 1818, when Colombia was born, the Supreme Chief of Venezuela, meditated on his project for a federation of our people, and from the fortress of Guayana, when Páez had not become submissive and when the cliques of the East were barely held in check by Piar, declared to the Americans of the Extreme South: "Inhabitants of Rio de la Plata! The Republic of Venezuela, although covered with mourning ,offers you its brotherhood; and when covered with laurel it shall have expelled the last tyrants which profane its soil, then it will invite you to a single society so that our standard may be the unity of South America."[1] The proclamation was accompanied by a letter to Don Juan Martin Pueyrredon, Supreme Director of the United Provinces, in which he wrote:[2]

Your Excellency may assure your noble countrymen that they will be treated and received here only as members of a friendly republic and as members of our Venezuelan society. There should be only one country in America, now that we have a perfect unity among them. When the triumph of Venezuelan arms have completed the work on independence, or when more favorable circumstances permit more frequent communications and closer relations, we shall hasten to seal, on our part, with the greatest interest, the American pact which shall form of our republics a single political body, and present to the world America with an appearance of majesty and greatness without precedent among older nations. Thus, Most Excellent Sir, may America, if the heavens yield us this desired goal, be the queen of the nations and the mother of republics.

After the armistice of Trujillo, the Liberator wrote anew to Pueyrredon:[3]

I had the honor, last year, to advise Your Excellency of the first successes of the revolution of the Peninsula and the firm resolution of Colombia not to desist from its noble undertaking, nor to enter into any transaction with Spain until there should be accepted, as the only base, the recognition of the absolute independence of the American republics. . . . Mutually bound among themselves by the definite pact and the identity of reason, as are all the republics who fight Spain, our conduct should be uniform and similar. No one may attack one without equally injuring the others, and likewise supporting one means supporting the other. . . . My object is confined to assuring Your Excellency of the conduct of Colombia on this occasion, presenting it to the consideration of Your Excellency, and of the heroic people whom you worthily rule, in testimony of the purity of its sentiment of unity and friendship with which I wish to see our relations bound, not as between two distinct peoples, but as between two brothers, who mutually support each other, and protect and defend each other.

It is plain that besides the interest which he displayed in the

---

[1] *The Liberator to the Argentines, Angostura, July 12*, 1818.
[2] *The Liberator to the Director Pueyrredon. Id., id.*
[3] *The Liberator to the Director Pueyrredon, Tunja, February 4*, 1821.

material union of our peoples against the common enemy, Bolívar conceived of America as a moral unity, destined to develop uniformly in the future. "His American patriotism seems to me sincere," wrote Captain Moyer to the French minister of the navy.[1]

In 1825 the Liberator spoke, in definite terms, of a project for the confederation of the South American republics, revised later, in view of the special conditions in Chile and Argentina, of the five nations which he founded. "In Chile," he wrote to General Heres, "the people, called together by Freire, have established a new reform in the government, in which the mountebanks have held the preponderance of power. It would be well to enter into communication with gentlemen, and learn what they think of Chiloé, the federation, and harmony with us. See Blanco on this business and write to General O'Higgins what you know, so that he may learn about this revolution or this reform."[2] He gave expression to his hopes to Marshall Santa Cruz: "South America will, without a doubt, form a genuine confederation during the first years of their existence, and this I see more clearly every day. If I stay in the south of Colombia a few years, taking for granted that Congress will allow me to do so, I flatter myself with the belief that our republics will be so closely united that they will appear, not as nations, but as sisters."[3]

The Government of Buenos Aires sent, by October, a mission, headed by General Carlos de Alvear, to offer the Liberator the congratulations of the Provinces of la Plata, and to solicit his alliance against Brazil. Bolívar welcomed the Argentine envoys in Potosí with benevolence and cordiality, but he avoided compromising in a struggle which seemed to him, as an American, to be a civil war. He wished, nevertheless, to flatter Buenos Aires by criticizing the conduct of the Emperor in the Question of Banda Oriental, the more inexplicable in the case of a prince "who is involved in our noble insurrection, and who has risen to his throne, not on weak supports, but on the indistructible basis of the sovereignty of the people and the sovereignty of the laws. . . . A prince who seemed destined to be the friend of his republican neighbors."[4] On the question of an alliance, renewed later, Bolívar declared to General Alvear: "Your first demand appeals greatly to my own personal desires," adding that he would like to have the tie of "this Republic (Bolivia) with Argentina" be made" to extend to all Spanish America on the proposed general plan of federation."[5]

[1]Villanueva, *Ferdinand VII and the New States*, 251.

[2]*The Liberator to the General Heres. Tinta, July 29*, 1825.

[3]*The Liberator to Marshal Santa Cruz, Plata, November 25*, 1825.

[4]*Address of the Liberator at the Reception to the Envoys from Buenos, Potosí, October 16*, 1825.

[5]*The Liberator to the General Alvear, Plata, December 5*, 1825.

At this time the attempts to establish a monarchy began in Colombia and Perú. The anti-republican sentiment was great in this latter country. Antonio Leocadio Guzman was sent to Lima from Caracas to advance his "Napoleonic ideas" to Bolívar. There were some who pleaded for the Bolivarian federation, and the Liberator said of these to Santander:

> There are also others who wish me to be the absolute master of the South, figuring that Chile and Buenos Aires will this year need my protection because war and anarchy are devouring them. The emperor and Chiloé will destroy these countries. I reject this promptly, of course, because it does not enter into my idea of things. As to the proposition of this Government with reference to the federation, I declare to you that, because of delicacy, I have abstained from intervening in its resolutions. I foresee that here in Perú they do not wish to put themselves, helplessly, in a close federation: the ideas they present to me are honorable, but there are always mental reservations. Besides, they are afraid of the expenses, for they are very poor and much in debt; here they owe much to the whole world."[1]

In the following year Bolívar explained, finally, his project for a confederation of his republics, and in that spirit wrote to certain persons.[2] The organization made necessary by his successes consumed his time, and he resolved to fight with energy the menace of a crown which was opposed to his ideas and politics for America. The Liberator tried to unify the nations which he has emancipated through his legal and effective direction; and to prevent the petty ambitions and criticisms from aggravating the diversity of interests among them, dividing them for a long time, sterlizing great efforts, and precipitating them into despotism, or anarchy. The political analogy which a writer finds in it with the Confederation of the Rhine, established by Napoleon, is ingenious but inexact. It would mean, moreover, imagining, as the analogy pretends to find, as regards hidden tendencies, a relation between the Code of Bolivia and the consular Constitution of the Year VIII. In a letter to General Antonio Gutierrez de la Fuente, the Liberator expounded his project;[3]

> After having considered with infinite pains, persons of the best judgment and I, we have agreed that the only remedy we can apply to such a serious evil is a general federation between Bolivia, Perú, and Colombia, closer than that of the United States, governed by a president and a vice-president, and controlled by the Bolivian Constitution, which may serve for the particular States and for the general Federation, with such modifications as may be necessary. The purpose of this pact is perfect unity under a federal form. The government of the federal States, or particular States, will be under the control of the vice-president, with their chambers for everything dealing with religion, civil administration, economics, and, briefly, everything except foreign relations and war. Each department will send a deputy to the federal Congress, and these will be divided into sections, each section containing one-third of the deputies of each Republic. These three chambers, with the vice-president and the secretaries of State, who will be elected at large in the Republic, will govern the Federation. The Liberator, as Chief Executive, will visit the departments of

---

[1]*The Liberator to General Santander, Magdalena, February 21*, 1826.
[2]*Vide* O'Leary, *Memoirs*, II, 582 ff. Edition of Madrid, 1915.
[3]*The Liberator to General Gutierrez de la Fuente, Lima, June 17*, 1826.

each State every year; while the capital will be at a central point. Colombia should be divided into three States; Cundinamarca, Venezuela, and Quito.

The Federation will take the name it may desire; there shall be a flag, an army, and a single nation. It may, however, prove absolutely necessary to have Boliva and Perú adopt this plan, because of their relations and because of the need they have for each other due to the local situation. After that it would not be difficult for me to get Colombia to adopt the only path to salvation.

Bolívar, expecting the dissolution of Colombia, considered it desirable to precipitate it in the form best adapted to conserve the ties which, in his mind, were indispensible for the future. A confederation would compel a reform in the statutes of Colombia, and permit, in a certain fashion, the satisfaction of the desires for autonomy manifested by the various departments of the Republic. He maintained that the union of Bolivia and Perú was necessary, and the Liberator expected that he would be the head of this immense dominion for life. He was pleased with the idea of consolidating his work and of strengthening the union of the peoples while saving liberty. He wrote to General Gamara:

The prospect of a great people, governed by authorities united together, circumscribed in their power, eminently lovers of the national glory, is enchanting. Thus a people makes itself as firm and immovable as a rock. Perú may attain this situation without new sacrifices. It only needs new functionaries who will be able to ignore minor resentment and have their vision fixed on the great object: the conservation of the Republic.[1]

The events in Venezuela, the insubordination of General Páez, and the unruly politics of Vice-President Santander, compelled Bolívar to return to Colombia. In the midst of the preparations for this march, he promised General La Fuente: "I shall soon return from my trip to Colombia, I shall be in Lima, at least by September of next year, to install the new Congress, elected under the new Constitution, or to see the Congress of the Federation of the sister States. This will be the end of all my work, and if not I shall give up the race."[2] In the meantime, the Panamerican Assembly, convoked by the Liberator, had assembled at Panama. There were present at this gathering representatives from Colombia, Mexico, Perú, and Central America.

The thought of a federation of the Bolivarian republics had not reconciled its author to the federalist tendencies, which he had opposed since 1811. He so explained his views to the above correspondent: "Many have confused the idea of a federation of the States with that of the provinces, believing that was under consideration in the public papers. But do you believe, General, that I should be capable of imagining that you would be false to your principles, to order, and to your friends? . . . As for the Government, I can assure you that the information which was given to me on the Araquipa has always been honorable to you. General Santa Cruz and Señor Larrea have written to me in

[1]*The Liberator to General Gamara, Magdalena, June 30,* 1826.
[2]*To General Gutiérrez de La Fuente, Magdalena, July 3,* 1826.

the same sense, believing that you were very far from favoring a project which would certainly produce sinister results."[1]   A great confederation between nations, such as was conceived by the Liberator, was logical in theory, if one considered the existence of a certain number of States, constituted in this or that manner, with individual characteristics, which could have, as in North America, grouped themselves and undertaken a common existence under better conditions.   But a provincial federation like that recently adopted by some of our countries, was to Bolívar absurd, because it would have been necessary to breathe life into nothing, create organisms, and by a simple decree, set them to carrying out unnecessary measures, without origin and without a basis.

As to the political organization of the new entity, the Liberator, in the hope of accomodating his Code "to small states, encased in a vast confederation, applying the part which belongs to the executive to the general government, and the electoral power to the individual States. There could not possibly be any advantages secured from this arrangement, or even any appreciable degree of duration, judged by the spirit which guides us in this labyrinth."[2] In the following chapter, we shall study the Constitution which Bolívar introduced to the Bolivians as the most liberal in the world,[3] and which Marshal Sucre presented to the Constituent Convention of Bolivia in 1826.

Don Bartolomé Mitre has discovered in the meeting of the Liberator and General San Martín the contact of two tendencies toward the hegemony of the Continent, that of Colombia and that of Argentina. I confess that I do not see this discovery clearly. At least I find the words inexact.   The two things which clashed there have been called the great American politics of Bolívar and the politics of the estuary of the Rio de la Plata, personified, a little later, in Rivadavia and defined some years ago by Zeballos.[4]

---

[1]*Idem., id., Caracas, April 11,* 1827.

[2]*The Liberator to General Páez, Lima, August 8,* 1826. The thought of Bolívar did not find acceptance at the hands of his contemporaries. Many years afterwards, such great spirits and loyal supporters as Larrazábal and Baralt, were not able to defend it. The latter of these two writers declared that the project of a federation was "indigenous in the political genius of the Liberator." There will be found in the *Bulletin de la Bibiotheque Américaine,* in Paris, correspondance in the month of October of 1915, and with the signature of Jean Péres, ideas more exact: "His ideas on international law, which concerned all attempts to establish, in one great federation, the republics of the western Continent, constitute the parts of his international law which are the most definitely established. The brilliant light of the 18th century, enamored of reason and justice, refined everything. An ideal for international relations was formed which, when desired, is easily realizable between peoples of the same blood and the same language. It has been unable on many occasions to prevent civil war, but it has given to America a model for Europe, which, when the admiration of Bolívar will have been more fully realized, can translate into reality his great principles."

[3]*The Liberator to the Bolivians, Chuquisaca, January 1,* 1826

[4]Vide Blanco-Fombona, *The Political and Social Revolution of Hispanic America* 93.

The problem of the Liberator was not how to establish a hegemony in these countries, nor was it an effort to bring about a "unification of South America," which Bolívar always believed impracticable. When the newspapers of Buenos Aires, in 1825, attributed to him the idea of forming "a single government for all America", a note from the Secretary General denied the accusations.[1] The confederation of the Spanish Republics, which the Liberator desired, was neither the unification of America nor the Colombian hegemony. The project is based, on the contrary, on that equilibrium between nations which may be called the moral and material weight, which excludes the idea of individual domination and guarantees the independence of the people. The bonds between these States: race, religion, language, and history, enabled Bolívar to believe in the possibility of a foundation of a vast organism which would avoid the contentions of the nations. The union of the Iberian-American peoples will be a reality in the future, because of the material necessities, and of the imponderable agents which direct the course of history. At that distant hour of realization, we will not forget that Bolívar tried to make us gain one hundred and fifty years of history.[2]

---

[1] *The Secretary General of the Liberator, Cuzco, July 4,* 1825.

[2] The Bolivian Congress ratified, on December 27, 1826, the treaty of federation concluded between the plenipotentaries of Bolivia and Perú on the 15th of that same month, with certain modifications. The Bolivian Federation had at its head the vitalizing influence of the Liberator. It had a federal congress composed of nine deputies from each State. The Supreme Chief commanded the army and the navy, conducted the foreign relations, appointed diplomatic and consular agents, etc. The federal States were autonomous in such matters as concerned their economic organization and their internal affairs. Colombia was invited to adhere to the pact, the formalities of the beginning of the activities of the federation until this matter had been settled. The presidency of the Liberator was the main cause of the pact of this personal union, which gave to Bolívar the power to name his successor. At his death the right to modify the pact rested with the Committee of Foreign Affairs of the Congress of Bolivia, the legislative bodies of the federal States being at liberty to continue in the federation or to dissolve it. *Vide Doc. X,* 706.

The remainder of this chapter is deleted, as an unnecessary polemic.

The Constitutional System

THE government, in the Bolivarian Republic, was popular and representative. The people exercised the sovereignty through four divisions of the supreme power: the electoral, legislative, executive, and the judicial. In each province there was a body chosen by universal suffrage, composed of electors, one elector for every ten citizens, and renewed every four years; and which had for its principal duties: To train the citizens for the exercise of their rights; to elect and prescribe the term of the members of the respective houses; to propose to the executive power, the candidates for the prefecture of the department, governor of the province, the mayor of the cantons and municipalities, as well as for the curacies and the vicarages; to propose to the prefect of the department, candidates for mayors and justices of the peace; to propose to the senate, the members of the courts of the judicial districts and the judges of the courts of first instance. Bolívar explained, in his message to the Constituent Congress of Chuquisaca, the reasons which induced him to constitute this power: "The electorate," he declared,

> Has received powers not permitted in other governments which consider themselves most liberal. These attributes approach the federal system. It has appeared to me not only convenient but useful, and also easy to concede to the immediate representatives of the people, the privilege most desired by the citizens of each department, province, and canton. No other object is as important to a citizen as the election of his legislators, magistrates, judges, and clergy. The electoral colleges of each province represent the necesssities and interests of those they serve, to complain of the violations of the law, and of the abuses of the magistrates. I venture to say with some exactness that this representation divides the rights enjoyed by the individual governments of the federated States. In this fashion a new weight has been added to the balance against the executive, and the government has acquired more guarantees, more popularity, and new rights, so that it surpasses the most democratic of governments.

The Liberator attempted to assign to the people the largest number of rights compatible with a strong government, equally removed from tyranny and the dangers of anarchy. He conceived for these countries only a central administration capable by extension of its powers of watching the operation of the powers and embracing all the manifestations of national activity. To obtain this, Bolívar did not hesitate, to concede to liberal public opinion the real speculative items which did not disturb his system. It is necessary to consider the great cleverness needed for legislation in America at a time when the legislator was accused of aspiring to tyranny or to a throne, in order to explain the weaknesses found in the Bolivarian institutions. The Liberator knew that, in reality, a representative government could not be established there, that democracy in any form was Utopian; that the constitutional false-

87

hood would bring new elements of decomposition like all inapplicable theories, and would precipitate our peoples into civil war behind the illusive flags and under the dictatorship of factions.   But
in order not to give way before the contemporary world, or to condemn his efforts to sterility, Bolívar found it necessary to confine
his political thoughts within what was possible in the general lines
of the plan of government emanating from the revolutionary furn-
ace.   The electoral body, in the Bolivian Constitution, was one of
the weaknesses which brought upon the Liberator the charge of
contradiction.   The democratic concept for its creation did not
exist in America.

Bolívar explained the conditions necessary in an elector in the
following words;

> Nothing is required in the elector except ability.   Nor is wealth necessary
> in representing the august function of the sovereign.   But it is very necessary to
> know how to write one's vote, to sign one's name, and to read the laws.   It is
> also necessary to know a science or an art in order to assure the individual an
> honest living.   No one but the vicious, the lazy, and the absolutely ignorant
> should be excluded.   Wisdom and honesty, not wealth, are required for the
> exercises of public power.[1]

There were three chambers exercising the legislative power:
that of the tribunes, that of the senators, and that of the censors,
each composed of thirty members for the first twenty years.
The legislative body, formed by these, names the president of the
Republic for the first time, and confirms his successors; approves
the election of the vice-president, and the secretaries of State;
decides whether its members are, or are not, to be placed on
trial, also whether the vice-president or the secretaries of States
shall be placed on trial; elects, from the lists presented by the
electoral body, who are to fill the vacancies in each of the chambers,
etc.   The members of the legislative body enjoy immunity for their
opinions expressed in the exercise of their functions.   The Bolivarian commentary indicated the idea back of this innovation of the
legislative power.   It was a question of establishing a healthy
equilibrium, and of preventing frequent conflicts between the
two classes of chambers from disturbing business and reducing
the value of the initiative peculiar to each one.   "In all business
transactions between two adversaries, a third is named to arbi-
trate the differences," he declared, "and should it not be absurd
that in the gravest interests of society this providence dictated
by an imperious necessity be disdained? . . . .   Modern
congresses, they tell me, have been composed of only two sections.
This is because in England, which has served as a model, nobility
and the commons were represented in two houses; and, if in
North America, the same was done without nobility, it may be
supposed that the custom of being under the English government
inspired this imitation.   The truth is that two deliberating bodies

---

[1] *The Liberator to the Constituent Congress of Bolivia, May, 1826.*

fight perpetually, and for this reason Siéyes wanted only one. A classic absurdity!"

The origin of the three chambers being the same, the election by the same electoral body, its members possessed the same source of authority, and preserved equality even to the form of their election. Tribunes, senators, censors were mandatory of the second grade who differed from each other in age and in their functions. To be a tribune, it was necessary to be twenty-five years of age; and its chamber initiated measures relating to peace, war, and the treasury. "It has the immediate control of the branches which the executive administers with less interference of the legislative." The members served four years in the exercise of their duties, and were renewable every two years. It was the duty of the senators, who must be thirty-five years old, to take the initiative in the formation of civil and criminal law, judicial and ecclesiastical law; to show vigilance and knowledge in the trials of the judges and magistrates; to make nomination of the members of the supreme court of justice, of the prelates and other ecclesiastical functionaries, and submitting their names to the house of censors; to elect from the lists submitted by the executive of the electoral bodies, the prefects, governors, and mayors; and to regulate the right of patronage; etc. "The work of the senate relates primarily to religion and law." The senators were elected for eight years, with one-half of that body renewable every four. The chamber of censors watched over the observance elected for eight years, with one-half of that body renewable every of the Constitution, laws and public treaties, and imposed punishments for the violations of them before the senate; it could request the senate to suspend the vice-president and the secretaries of State; and, in such a case, if the two chambers were in accord over the matter, could constitute itself the national judge and the supreme tribunal without appeal. The censors proposed the laws of economy, of the press, and of education. They had to be forty years of age, and served for life. "They exercise," declared Bolívar,

> A political and moral power similar to that of the Areopagus of Athens and the censors of Rome. They will be the critics of the government and will see that the Constitution and the treaties are religiously observed. I have put under their aegis national justice, which must decide the good or bad in the administration of the executive. The censors protect morality, science, art, education, and the press. The most terrible as well as the most august function belongs to the censors; they condemn to eternal opprobrium usurpers of sovereign authority, they confer public honors for the services and virtues of illustrious citizens. The balance of glory is placed in their hands and for this reason the censors should lead an innocent and stainless life. If they fail in their duty they could be accused for minor faults. To these priests of the laws I have entrusted the conservation of our sacred tables because it is they who must cry out against the profane.

The center of public authority and the guarantee of the stability which the creator aimed for in this system was the president of the republic, incumbent for life, responsible to no one, and with the power to designate his successor, whom the legislative body must confirm. The president appointed and suspended the secretaries of State, who with the vice-president, chief of the cabinet, carry on the business of each administrative department; he published and enforced the laws and the sentences of the tribunal; he commanded in person the national army and navy, and appointed the officers of that service; declared war, previously decreed by the legislative body; he directed diplomatic negotiations and made treaties, subject to the subsequent ratification of the same by the chambers; he appointed diplomatic and consular officers and those of the treasury, and approved the nomination of national functionaries; he received foreign ministers; he exercised the powers given him by the law of ecclesiastical patronage; he could commute capital punishment. It was not permitted him to deprive citizens of liberty or property. His age could not be less then thirty years. He formed, with the vice-president and the secretaries of State, the executive power. "On him rests all our order without being responsible for it." Bolívar believed that his executive had all the powers of the North American. He gave to the executive a term for life, imitating the government of Haiti. "This island," he wrote, "found itself in permanent insurrection; after having tried the empire, kingdom, republic, all the known forms of government and some new ones, it was forced to turn to the illustrious Petion to save it. They confided in him, and the destinies of Haiti no longer vacillated. They elected Petion for life, with the power to choose his successor. Neither the death of this great man, nor the succession of a new president, have caused the least danger to the State: everything has carried on under the worthy Boyer, in the calm of a legitimate rule. It proves triumphantly that a president for life with the right to select a successor, is the most sublime inspiration of the republican order." The Liberator, also, pointed out that since the president of Bolivia did not appoint the judges, magistrates, or ecclesiastical officers, he lacked influence; and since these officials owed him neither power nor fortune, would not make themselves accomplices of tyranny, but against which they would form a power of vigilence and opposition. "If to this consideration are added those which are naturally born of the general oposition which a democratic government has to meet in all the phases of its administration, it would appear proper to feel sure that the usurpation of public power is less likely in this government than in the others. The constitutional limitations on the president of Bolivia are the lightest known; he merely appoints the officials of the treasury department; in peace and war he commands the army. I have here his duties. . . . The customs officers and the soldiers are the only agents of this minister," added the Liberator, as Bentham would have said, "they are not in truth the most likely to capture the public favor; therefore his influence will be almost nil."

The vice-president of the republic, appointed by the president, was responsible, with the secretaries of State, for the active administration which devolved upon the executive. He was the successor to the president. Bolívar explained that the custom then followed in the United States of naming the first minister to succeed to the chief magistracy inspired in him the idea of establishing such a law. "Nothing is so convenient in a republic as this practice: it unites the advantage of placing at the head of an administration a person experienced in the management of the State. . . . Through this provision the elections are avoided which produce a great commotion in a republic, anarchy, which is the luxury of tyranny, and the most immediate and terrible danger of popular government. Witness how this practice succeeds, as in the legitimate kingdoms, the mighty crisis of the republics." The Liberator legislated, let us remember, for Latin America, and attempted to prevent the farces, the usurpations, daughters of human nature, exaggerated in those countries by a combination of circumstances, which made impossible the normal exercise of the new institutions. Bolívar stated that the liberal constitution was in the civil legislation, and, in accordance with this opinion, he did not believe it necessary to compensate liberalism of the civil régime with certain restrictions which, in the political order, he considered indispensible in establishing public stability.   He showed himself inexorable when there was under consideration the question of establishing social and civil equality of the citizens, which he desired to be complete.   But the thesis of absolute liberty carried with it, in his mind, certain reservations.[1] The philosophic materialism of the Liberator is shown in his constitutional ideas, especially in his conception of the State and of the individual, of authority and of liberty. He found that the last is inevitable in a properly constituted State, as a logical consequence of an ideal order. His inclinations, however, took him away from social spirituality, and he did not believe that liberty was essential to society. His ideal would be a republic, equalitorial and virtuous, working for the common progress, under a paternal and respected government. The proposition of Bolívar may, either in general theory or in the application to the concrete American case, be open to the censure of technicians and of historians, but it bears the earmarks of a legislator as original as the most celebrated of the ancient world. "All his works," declared a writer, who is not a devotee of the Bolivarian glory, "of the political order, as well as of the military, are so character-

---

[1] As a matter of fact, his constitutional propositions deal more with civil than with political liberty.   Jean Pérez, *Bulletin de la Bibliotheque Americané,*. No. 1, *October,* 1915, *Paris.*

istic that it has been found necessary to invent words to distinguish them."[1]

The Liberator also justified the institution of succession of the vice-president in the following words:

> The monarchy which governed the country had obtained its title through the system of inheritance which made it stable, and through unity which made it strong. Thus, while a sovereign prince may be a spoiled child, cloistered in his palace, educated by adulation and led through all the passions, this prince, which I might dare to call the irony of many, commands the human race, because he preserves the order of things and secures obedience by a firm power and a constant action. Observe, legislators, that these advantages are to be found in the presidency for life and in the hereditary vice-president.

It is difficult to say to what extent Bolívar was right in giving to executives the virtues of force and stability, at the same time that he guaranteed liberty. Marshal Sucre, who tried the Constitution for two years as president of Bolivia, and who was one of the most clear-thinking and enlightened spirits of the New World, declared that the powers of the Bolivarian executive were insufficient and his stability illusory. The Marshal, whose government was an illustrious page in political history, would have preferred to grant the president a greater degree of power and initiative, and freed him from much of the limitations which embarrassed his control and his regulation of public negotiations. We may consider the criticism well founded since Sucre, an energetic administrator, could not save the Code from complete failure. The difficulty consisted, perhaps, in the contradiction in the fundamental principles of the system, some ultrademocratic and inapplicable to our countries, others sufficiently reactionary to alarm the liberal element and to serve as a banner for ambitious demagogues. The defect in this régime was in this combination, which made it a curious trial of political electicism. In point of fact, it was a summary of classical institutions for which there were wanting only a people capable of realizing them. The social evolution of America, which has meant a century of governments, fruitful in producing a dread of liberal principles, strangled this Bolivian Constitution, as well as the later ones; but it has proved that the Liberator was right, in his general beliefs, by the degree in which it demonstrated that the fatal type of the American government would be, for some length of time, that of personal authority, sometimes brutal and pretorian, sometimes civilized and benign, according to the character of the powers and the vague influence of the written laws. Bolívar had declared in Angostura that when he gave to the executive powers more far-reaching then those usually given to it by contemporary institutions, that he did not attempt to create a tyrant, but "to prevent that belligerent despotism from being the immediate

---

[1]Mitre, VI, 227.

cause of a circle of vicissitudes in which anarchy would, in turn, be replaced by oligarchy and monarchy."

In the Bolivian Constitution, the judicial power was exercised by a national court of justice, composed of seven members and a prosecutor, by a court established in each judicial district, a judge of the first instance in each court, and a justice of the peace in the cities and towns. The magistrates served during good behaviour: The magistrates could not be removed except for cause and under the conditions provided by the laws. The supreme court took cognizance of the criminal charges against the vice-president, the secretaries of State, and the members of the chambers. It took cognizance also of cases ordered by a previous decree of the legislative body, and of cases relating to the exercise of ecclesiastical patronage by the civil authority, etc. The Liberator declared to the Constituent Congress;

"The judicial power I propose will enjoy absolute independence: nowhere in the world does it have so much power. The people nominate the candidates and the legislature selects the individuals which are to compose the tribunals. If power does not arise from this source, then it is impossible to conserve, in all its purity, the safeguard of individual rights. These rights, legislators, are those which are constituted by liberty, equality, security—all are the guarantees of the social order. The true liberal Constitution is in the civil and criminal codes. The tribunals exercise the most terrible tyranny by means of the powerful instruments of the laws. The executive is, ordinarily, merely the depository of public affairs, while the tribunals are the arbitrators of private matters, of individual matters. The judicial power determines the good or the evil fortune of the citizens. If there be liberty, if there be justice in the republic, they are distributed by this power."

And Bolívar concluded with this phrase which reveals the depth of his thoughts on the Constitution:

It matters little sometimes what the political organization may be, if only the civil organization be perfect. For then the laws are obeyed religiously and are considered as inexorable as destiny.

In the project of the Constitution of Venezuela in 1819, the Liberator provided for a president for life, an hereditary senate, irremovable judges, and a fourth power, called the moral. For Bolivia, seven years later, he retained his idea of the presidency and the magistrates. He modified the legislative power, introducing in the plan for life censors the idea of the moral power, which is so dear to him. The political speculation of Bolívar always follow identical lines with perfect equanimity. Even the contradictions which his life offers and the unexpected atagonism of his ideas affirm the greatness of his genius and the superiority of his spirit, if the teachings of Boutmy be true that "the contradictions are natural to men who have thought much, created much, and destroyed much."

As for the internal government of the republic, there was a prefect for each department, a governor for each province, mayors in the cantons, and alcaldes and justices of the peace in the municipalities. The term of office of these officials was placed at four years for the first three, and at two for the others. The Liberator recommended, to the Constitutional Convention, that the regulations for the internal government be good. "Remember legislators," he declared, "that nations are composed of cities and villages and that the wellbeing of these comprises the happiness of the State. You can never give too much attention to the good government of these departments. This fact is of the first importance in the science of legislation, but which is, nevertheless, insufficiently appreciated."

The national military force was composed of the regular army and navy, of the national guard, and of bodies of the militia to prevent smuggling. "The purpose of the army," declared Bolívar, "is to guarantee the frontiers. God help us from the army ever turning its arms against the citizens. The national militia is sufficient to preserve internal order."

The formation and promulgation of laws, the administration of justice, the position and responsibility of public officials were regulated in special provisions of the Constitution.

The republic was and always should be independent of all foreign domination and never could become the patrimony of any person or family.

The conditions required to become a citizen were also enumerated, the means by which their prerogatives might be lost or suspended, and the duty of the nationals toward their country.

The Constitution guaranteed civil liberty, personal security, property, equality before the law, freedom of speech, press, and work, freedom of movement, inviolability of the home, and a fair proportion in the payment of taxes. Slavery and torture for forcing confession from criminals were abolished; justice through oath was established; no citizen could be imprisoned without a warrant, which warrant must set forth the cause of arrest, and without a written order from a competent judge, except in the event of being caught in the act, or in other cases expressly defined by law; confiscations and punishments of cruelty and great infamy were prohibited, punishment being limited to imposition of capital punishment. The authorities might not suspend the Constitution or individual rights, except in specific cases and for a definite period of time. Bolívar made these wise observations on the rights;

> The most perfect guarantee has been established: civil liberty is the true liberty; the rest are nominal, or of little influence upon the citizen. Personal security has been secured, which is the aim of society and from which the others emanate. As regards property, that depends upon the nature of the civil code which you, in your wisdom, will soon establish for the happiness of your citizens. I have preserved intact the law of laws: equality, without which all liberties, and all rights perish. For it we must make all sacrifices; at its feet I have placed, covered with humiliation, the infamy of slavery.

The Liberator refrained from legislating concerning religion, obeying the reasons which we shall mention in another part of this book. But as the cult practiced in the republic was Catholic, he sought to provide, in the fundamental Code, for the nomination of ecclesiastical officials, and the right of the exercise of the patronage, which, in imitation of the Colombian Statute two years previously, the State assumed over the Catholic Church. The Colombian law of patronage, which was in accord with reality and the conditions of the time, was likewise adopted in Venezuela, and is one of the few laws among us which has resisted the combat of parties.

Bolívar repeated on occasions that this Constitution was the true expression of his philosophical thought and the creed of his politics. There existed no other act, no other document which contradicts that fact. The Liberator believed that his institutions, at an equal distance from turbulent democracy, which he considered dangerous for America, and from monarchical principles, which were those which he did not prefer in general theory, could be applied with relatively good results, and which might correct our social vices and our lack of political knowledge. In his address to the Constituent Congress, Bolívar condemned every effort to alter the republican form of government which the new States had adopted, at the very moment when his greatness subjected him to the flattering offers of a crown. He exclaimed:

"And more, liberty today in America is indestructible. Observe the wild nature of this Continent how it protects us, and which expels the monarchical order. The deserts call for independence. Here there are no great nobles, great ecclesiastics; our riches are nearly nothing, and at this time they are hardly that. The church, while it enjoys an influence, is far from aspiring to rule, being satisfied with its preservation. Without these supports tyrants are not permanent, and if some ambitious ones attempt to raise up empires, Dessalines, Cristóbal, Itúrbide will tell them what they may expect. There is no power more difficult to maintain than that of a new prince. Bonaparte, conqueror of all armies, could not triumph over this law, stronger than all the empires; and if the great Napoleon did not succeed in maintaining himself against the league of republicans and aristocrats, who can succeed in America in founding monarchies on a soil illuminated with the brilliant flames of liberty, which devour the thrones that are built, to elevate scaffolds in their places. No, legislators, you need not fear pretenders to the crown; they will have the sword of Damocles over their heads. The resplendent princes who obscure themselves until they construct thrones built on the fragments of liberty will erect tombs on their ashes, which they may display to future centuries as the result which their fatal ambition preferred to liberty and glory."

After having concluded this magnificent piece of politics and literature in the address to the Assembly of Chuquisaca, Bolívar concluded with an expression of gratitude in his heart to the country which had taken his name:

Since your rapture did not find a demonstration, befitting the warmth of your sentiments, you obliterated your name and gave that of mine to all your generations. This, which is unheard of in the history of the centuries, is yet one of the most sublime of generosities. This deed will show to posterity that there will be in the thought of eternity that which may strengthen the possession of your rights, which is the right of exercising political virtues, of acquiring brilliant talents, and of the joy of being a man. This deed will prove, I repeat, that you were destined to receive the benediction of heaven in preserving the sovereignty of the people, the only legitimate authority of the nations.

The new Code was maintained for two years in Bolivia, under the government of Marshal Sucre, who never accepted the presidency for life. The Council of Government of Perú, in virtue of the vote of the people, exercised in the acts of fifty-nine electoral colleges, decreed that the Republic should also adopt the Constitution, and named the Liberator president for life; but the insurrection of Bustamente and the departure of the Colombian troops from Peruvian territory provoked a reaction against the Statute of Bolívar, whose adoption was declared illegal and contrary to law. "The destiny of this Constitution," wrote Gil Fortoul, "was the same as that of nearly all of the Spanish American Constitutions: it ended in tumults, and was replaced by another which proved inferior, since it was of insufficient merit."[1] This author affirmed, however, that the constitutional projects of the Liberator are the most notable politico-philosophical speculations of our history. For my part I have declared that the principles of the Bolivarian system, as generally happens with the systems adopted in Latin America did not correspond with the need demanded in giving life and stability to the institutions. The revolutionary ideal, impelled by the inflexibility of newly discovered theories, consulted, in imposing them on a new society, neither the interest not the local contingencies. The Code of the Liberator contained the prime vice which Croiset assigns to all these systems; it was beautiful, but without life. "The codes, systems, statutes, however wise they may be," wrote Bolívar himself, "are dead letters as far as they influence society." No constitutional mechanism, thinks Boutmy, possess efficacy and virtue of itself: its vitrue results from the social and moral forces which promote it and maintain it. A proof of this truth is found in the fact that the North American Constitution, so much praised even by Bolívar, is, in the final analysis, conflicting, and offers imperfections which does not prevent it from being an example of singular longevity. The spirit of the English institutions, the Tory tendency, much more in fashion than the revolutionary doctrines, truly inspired the Liberator when, in order to put his powers under protection from the oscillations of political life, gave them life of themselves, capable of resisting all attacks. The secular balance of the factors that exercise public power in England had so much influence on his mind that he forgot that it is impossible to create by decree the elements which exist naturally in Great Britain. It is unquestionable, nevertheless, that the Bolivarian régime was worth much more and better adapted to certain conditions of American society than the ultraliberal Constitution which supplanted it. "In the writings

---

[1]Gil Fortoul, I, 349.

of Bolívar are to be found the best program of political and social reforms for America," declared García Calderón.

When General Santander did not abandon his conservative ideas to convert himself into a demagogue, when he did not also find the "absurd" Bolivian Constitution a "dangerous novelty," he believed that this Code was liberal, popular, and strong. Marshal Santa Cruz, who had solid gifts as a statesman, re-established the system in Bolivia. Antonio Leocraddio Guzman, the ardent apostle of Venezuelan liberalism, wrote, concerning the Code:

> Bolívar, in conceiving and publishing this project, has placed himself between two worlds, has drawn from one the most sublime features of liberty, and from the other the most solid basis of government; has given the first more extension and more beauty, has reduced the second to reasonable limits. It may be said that he has rebuilt human institutions, and presented to the world the product of all of them polished by the anvil of his sublime reason.

The Constitution of Bolivia is the type of those liberal statutes which the peoples of Europe gradually adopted after the re-action of 1815. The Sardinian Code of Charles Albert, for example, which may serve as a model in this case, was conceived and formulated on the same basic principles. In general, Bolívar imitated the basis, and quite often the form, of the Constitution of France from 91 to 93, as well as that of the Fructidor of the Year III. His electoral power was inspired by the electoral power established by these Constitutions. His liberties and guarantees he derived from the Declaration of the Rights of Man and the Bills of Rights of those of the North Americans.[1] Guerra declared: "As may be seen in certain general points, the Bolivian Constitution differed little from those of the other republics and particularly that of Colombia. If a parallel study be made of these several Constitutions it will be found that many articles have been copied textually and others only slightly modified. In the internal structure of the Bolivian Code there was nothing un-

---

[1] Don Bartolomé Mitre declared that Bolívar was inspired by the institutions of Siéyes. VI, 229. The Tribunal of Siéyes, of the year III, was a body which proposed the laws, which were voted on by the legislature and executed by the government. The *Constitutional Jury* (*jurie constitutionnaire*) took cognizance of the violations of the Constitution. In the Year VIII this system suffered modifications: The Council of State interpreted the laws, or better, the laws that were presented to it by the tribunals. One tribunal, directly representative of the people, proposed or interpreted them before the legislative tribunal: this body chose from among those submitted and proclaimed them laws. A prosecutor or protector of the senate took note of the controversies over the violation of the Constitution, taking the matter before the legislative body and before the tribunal. Bonaparte reformed the project of Siéyes: depriving the tribunal of the right to propose laws, reduced the number of the members of the legislature and the senate, substituting by proclamation three consuls. It was the Constitution of Frimario of the Year VIII, in which a conservative senate, elective for life, from the lists sent to the consuls, to the tribunals, to the legislatures, to the justices and financial commissions. The government proposed the laws, the tribunals discussed them and defended them rom attack before the legislative bodies, by the means of three orators; and the First Consul promulgated them.

usual in the method followed nor in the division of its parts." The
essential difference lay in the life and irresponsible president, with
the right to designate his successor in the person of the vice-president; in the division of the legislative into three houses, of which
one, that of the censors, was for life; in the creation of the electoral
power; in the irremovability of the judiciary.[1] It was the first
American Code which did not establish a State religion. If the
immediate example of Bolívar of creating the life president was,
as he himself declared, following the example of Haiti, it is well not
to forget that in this country they copied, with faithfulness, the
various French institutions. Before Petion and Boyer, a senate
of the 18th of Thermidor of the Year X, had given to the First
Consul, then enjoying a life term, the right of designating his
successor. The Statutes of the Revolution, of the Consulate, and
of the Empire, the Charter of 1814, the Supplemental Act, the
Project of Manuel, of June, 1815, had a decisive influence upon
the formation of the Bolivian Code. From there came the principles of the irremovable judiciary, applied also in England and
in the United States. From this last country the Liberator took
the greater part of the executive powers, the cabinet without
parliamentary control, and the participation of the houses in
international affairs.

It may be pertinent, perhaps, to cite, in the examination of the
Bolivarian institutions, as antecedents, the constitutional projects of Miranda, for it is well known that the ideas of this man
had great influence on the Liberator. The Generalissomo submitted to Pitt, in 1790, a program of Roman quality in which we
find: an upper house, or life senate, appointed by the inca, or
emperor; two censors elected by the people every five years to
watch over the behavior of the members of the senate and to
punish them by expulsion; the vigilence of the censors was
exercised, likewise, on the behavior of the youth and on public
instruction; the ediles cared for the roads and monuments; the
questors had control over the revenue. Later Miranda conceived
the project of a federal establishment for America with an executive of two citizens, elected for ten years with the name incas,
and, as a legislative power, a council or parliament, selected by the
provincial assemblies. The electoral power of Bolívar approxi-
mated the conceptions of Miranda. The latter created the court
and the judges for life, and suggested the adaptation of the
English and North American principles to the judicial mechanism.
The religion of the State, Catholic, did not exclude liberty of
sects.[2] It is proper at this juncture to indicate the criterion which
Bolívar followed in the matter of popular sovereignty, at least the
criterion which he proclaimed in his letters and public documents.
The Liberator abandoned the ideas of Montesquieu to adopt the

---

[1] José Joaquin Guerra, The Convention of Ocaño, 64.
[2] *Vide* Gil Fortoul, I, 512.

broader theory of Rousseau, if we take into account, for example, his concept of the nature of representative government. The people are the only sovereign, he declared, and members of the legislative power are its agents. Here, however, are found one of those contradictions, which are not rare with Bolívar, in the hereditary senate, and the perpetual censor repudiated by Jean Jacques, who affirmed that the legislative power should be composed of members who were removable and with limited power. The same was true of the life presidency. Nor did the Liberator institute universal suffrage, which is the essence of real democracy, the application of the principle of popular sovereignty. It is true that the electoral power represented a considerable democratic organism, although it was composed entirely on a ten percent basis of the voting citizens. The basis of public power for Bolívar, as for Miranda, was privileged suffrage.

No one in America was as well prepared as was Bolívar to be the legislator of these tumultuous democracies. The Thinker of the Revolution, as he has been called the brilliant writer, whom I have quoted several times, united in his person military power and the extraordinary ability of a popular leader. Two men who knew him intimately and who have been called the evangelists of the Liberator have left us some lines which may be given as an appropriate conclusion for a chapter that has explained the political system of Bolívar. General Perú de Lacroix wrote:[1]

> Besides the vivacity of his spirit, he has the quick and right judgment, knows how to compare and properly appreciate things, and he possesses the uncommon talent of knowing how to apply his comparisions according to places, circumstances, and time. He knows that such and such a thing is good in itself, that it is excellent, but that it is not proper at the moment, or that it is good here, but not there.

General O'Leary, on his part, has written:[2]

> Profoundly versed in the history of the human race, and well instructed in the theories of public science, he recognized the institutions, which in ancient and modern times, have elevated nations to prosperity and glory, or influenced their decay and ruin. He possessed another quality even more essential: he had a perfect knowledge of the world, and given, as he was, to the study of the human heart, few individuals have had more or better occasions than he to acquire this knowledge, and, there are few, who have had a more lively perception and a more delicate tact. . . . From the northern extremity of Colombia to Potosí he was familiar with each place and its productions, and even with its individuals, customs, habits, and inclinations. In his constant travels through all those lands, he tried with insatiable curiosity to constantly inform himself concerning objects that might seem important, investigating all the inhabitants, situations, or professions, placing them in such a way as to give him satisfactory information. He fatigued lawyers and doctors with questions on professional matters, and inquired of the clergy the nature of the most frequent secret crimes in their parishioners acording to the revelations in the confessional.

---

[1] *The Diary of Bucaramanga*, 90.
[2] *The Diary*, II, 453.

The Bolivian Constitution is the work of a man who tried to temper the absolution of theories, and adjust the result of a direct observation to written postulates.

The Diplomacy of Bolívar

THe first efforts of South American diplomacy were directed toward obtaining the moral and material support of the two powers interested in aiding the Revolution: England and the United States. Both countries assumed a favorable attitude toward the proposals for the independence of the Hispano-Americans, and the first missions appointed by the Junta of Caracas to solicit foreign aid were sent to London and to Washington in 1810. The Government of the United States, the year previously "had suggested to prominent men of the Spanish Colonies that, if they proclaimed their independence, the North American Congress would recognize the mission that might be sent and would consider a confederation of all America."[1]   As regards English politics, Mancini declared that, in spite of egoism, variations, and fluctuating leaders, this policy was necessary, as one of the original factors of the South American Revolution.[2]   It is known that, in addition to the aid asked from abroad, the Junta of Caracas solicited from New Granada the coordination of the forces of the two countries in order to attain autonomy.[3]

It would not fall within the limits of this work to treat of the fluctuating history of our diplomacy, and I shall limit myself to consider the personal activities of Bolívar, and to point out, in a hurried way, the tendencies of his foreign politics in the general exposition of his ideas. I shall pass over in silence, as far as possible, all that does not particularly concern the Liberator, or which was not derived from his immediate inspiration or construction, or through the importance of the result and indispensible line of his diplomatic work. I shall only have time to mention the missions of Farjado, Clemente, Peñalver, Vergara, Zea, and Revenga-Echeverría.

The object of the mission of Bolívar and López Méndez to London, in 1810, can be summarized thus: Venezuela, as an integral part of the Spanish Empire, sought maritime protection to defend it from a French attack; the people of the Captaincy wished to have His Britannic Majesty lend his good offices to aid them and to preserve peace with all the nations; Venezuela did not object to His Majesty interposing his friendly mediation to continue his cordial relations of commerce and mutual aid with the Mother Country.   The English Government listened to the

---

[1]Gil Fortoul, I, 128. *Vide* also Mancini, 309.

[2]Mancini, 97.

[3]Madariaga concluded in Bogotá, on May 28, 1811, a treaty of friendship, alliance and confederation. This tentative (plan) to unite Venezuela and New Granada aroused the sympathies of the Granadian provinces. *Vide* Restrepo, I, 272. The first Venezuelan Constitution expressed the desire to have the benefits of this plan extend to all the peoples of "Colombia," that is to say, of America, by means of a Continental Congress.

solicitations of the mission and insisted on the necessity of an arrangement which would permit Venezuela to send auxiliary troops to Spain in its struggle against Napoleon. British politics pursued two primary objects: the development of commercial prosperity, and the war against the Emperor. When England had weakened Napoleon and turned its attention toward the Holy Alliance, we see her separate completely her cause from that of Spain, and placing herself on the economic basis, aid the rebellion of the colonists and allow them provisions. From necessity, the Government of London had impeded every foreign aid designed to help the Spanish reconquest. From a knowledge of such deeds comes the force of the efforts of the independents to convert the sympathetic tolerance of the Cabinet of St. James into definite recognition and the necessary protection. The Revolution was disposed to repay the cooperation of Great Britain, and it is significant that Miranda, when he was planning to found a vast empire of all the Spanish colonies, really thought to leave in the free hands of England, Brazil and the Guianas, as the price of eventual aid.[1]

There were moments when it was feared that Spain would obtain from Europe a fleet and an army to subdue the Americans, but the English Government made effective opposition to such tentative plans. The Czar Alexander, head of the Holy Alliance, recommended, in 1817, a meeting of plenipotentaries, like that of Vienna, in which Spain would be represented, doubtless with the proposal for a discussion of the question of the insurrectionary colonies. London declined the proposition, and the Conference of Aquisgrán brought together only the members of the European Directory. The matter thus lay between the Czar and Great Britain. Alexander had, at that time, two policies: one which he played in Germany to oppose the preponderance of Austria, which included the Germanic Confederation and frightened Prussia with the spectre of the Revolution; and the other which induced him to support Ferdinand VII in his desire to subdue the colinists. Thus, while he favored the liberalism of the German princes, the Czar incited Europe to lend its aid to the despotism of Madrid, and with it opposed, at the same time, the commercial ambitions of England in the New World and the propositions of Austria in Germany, attacking in the latter country the formidable plan of the counterrevolution which Metternich approved at the Conferences of Carlsbad and Vienna. England, on her part, remained inexorable, as far as permitting an armed force for reconquest was concerned. Some years ago I took the opportunity to explain that the view of Metternich on the real purpose of the Directory was that it had helped to moderate the desires of the Czar and that it had also dissuaded the Powers from undertaking a distant and absurd adventure.

In France, with Napoleon fallen, the Cabinet found itself

[1]Gil Fortoul, I, 97.

bound to the general politics of the Holy Alliance, and naturally sympathized with Ferdinand VII. Chateaubriand had, for an instant, the idea of transforming the rebellious colonies into autonomous kingdoms, governed by princes of the house of Bourbon. Such a project never was accepted by the King of Spain, and, besides, in order to realize the plan it would have been necessary for France to supply an armed force which it was not disposed to do at the time. Chateaubriand recognized the impossibility of a reconquest, and believed that Spain ought to decide to treat with its subjects in the colonies.[1] The Marquis of Clermont-Tonnerre quieted the Americans by declaring, in a note to the governor of Martinique, that his Government had no aggressive intentions.[2] The Governor of this island informed General Páez of the sentiments of friendship of the Cabinet of Paris,[3] and Rear Admiral Rosamel carried instructions to[4]

> deny the rumors that enemies of France, or persons jealous of its prosperity, seek to diffuse, attributing to its Government intentions hostile to the new States of South America with whom it maintains only the most amicable dispositions.

Finally, the French Government formally abjured "all intention to work against the colonies by force of arms."[5]

Canning, who was not disposed to form with the new States "any political tie that goes beyond the relations of friendship and Commerce"[6] solicited from the Government of Washington an energetic declaration respecting whatever plan of foreign intervention in the Hispanic American conflict might exist, and warned the European courts that Great Britain would recognize the independence of the colonies, in case any nation should aid Spain, or in case it should propose to establish new restrictions on commerce. At the same time various British confidential agents and consuls were accredited in certain cities of South America.[7] The interference of the French in the affairs of Spain provoked the Cabinet of St. James, by a series of pretexts, to advance each day and to reveal its intentions. In January, 1824, Canning expressed the desire that the Spanish Government should be the first to recognize the independence, and in the following May declared that England would do what she thought best, without being influenced by hostile sentiments, but without considering what the Spanish Court might think of the matter. In the month of July, negotiations were concluded for a commercial treaty with the Argentine Confederation. Finally, a note of January 1, 1825, informed the foreign ambassadors, residing in

---

[1]Villaneuva, *The Holly Alliance*, 81.
[2]*Ibidem*, 77.
[3]*Doc. IX*, 299.
[4]*Rear Admiral Rosamel to the Liberator.*
[5]*Declaration of the Prince de Polignac to Canning. Conference of October 9, 1823, Doc. IX*, 104.
[6]*Canning to Polignac, Conference citada.*
[7]1823.

London, that Great Britain would recognize the independence of the new countries, accredit representatives in their capitals, and conclude with them treaties of commerce and friendship.

From this year there ceased to be any apprehension or danger for the republics of the New World from foreign sources, and while the recognition was not effected before, it was, as Debidour explained, because England feared that the Czar sought, as a pretext, the English intervention in America, to intervene, in his turn in Greece, and to create there an undesirable situation.[1]

The United States appeared as a moral factor of great influence in the process of our emancipation, and the American politics guided itself in particular accord with the suggestions of London. After the victory of Carabobo, the meeting of the Frist Colombian Congress, and the beginning of the southern campaign proved, in the opinion of that country, our triumph, the House of Representatives pronounced itself in favor of the abandonment of the policy of neutrality, and voted recognition.[2] In the following year, Monroe made his famous declaration, and minister Anderson presented his credentials to Vice President Santander.[3]

The foreign politics of the newly created republics should consider, besides the particular activity of each one of the great powers, what has seemed to me, indispensible in explaining great events, the situation that the making of the independence created on the great peoples of the Continent with respect to their mutual relations, and from that, the attempts to obtain, through one means or another, general cooperation, which guaranteed common independence and defence against the foreigners. We have seen that the Liberator was an ardent and noble champion of the idea, which gave the impulse to the establishment of Colombia. The diplomatic action of Bolívar was inspired by the proposition to form a confederation which would embrace all the peoples from Mexico to Rio de la Plata, and to acquire for this immense but weak defensive organism the guarantee of Great Britain. His efforts are known to have obtained from 1815 the help of the English, and his efforts later developed to bring about the His-

---

[1]On May 12, 1826, the Liberator wrote to the Marshall of Ayacucho: "Do not fear the Emperor of Brazil, since England is with us in this matter and will preserve harmony from neccessity and from politics. The United States, with Russia, and France, are working with Spain to have her recognize us. For the same reason, it will not be necessary to raise the number of battalions to six hundred, instead of to one thousand, as I have written before. The Emperor of Russia is not Constantine, as is reported, but his brother Nicholas. The latter has the principles of Alexander, while the former is a Cossak." Years afterwards, Bolívar pointed out to Sir Robert Wilson the convenience which would have come to England from the negotiations of Greece to bring about the solution of the Holy Alliance and to attack Russia," a colossal threatener which deserves to be cut in marble by the whole of Europe, to prevent her suppression." *Bucaramanga*, April 16, 1828.

[2]March 28, 1822.

[3]*Doc. VIII*, 335.

panic-American Union. The Congress of Panama was the zenith of this useless and grandiose diplomacy.

Shortly after the founding of Colombia, the Liberator had sent by the Government, Don Joaquin Mosquera, as plenipotentaries to the republics of the South, with the intention of inviting them to ally themselves against Spain, and to send representatives to a Panamerican Assembly, which "should serve as a council in great conflicts, as a point of contact in common dangers, as an interpreter of public treaties, in case of any doubt, and as a conciliator in differences that may arise." Santamaría went to Mexico, provided with the same instructions. Mosquera concluded treaties of alliance and friendship with Chile and Perú, whose Governments welcomed with enthusiasm Bolívar's project, but collided in Buenos Aires with the narrow policy of Rivadavia, who found that the proposition for a congress of arbitration in American questions was "a dangerous and useless imitation of the Amphyctionic Council of ancient Greece."[1] From that time forward, "the Argentine Government, strong in its principles, opposed the plan of the Congress of Panama, composed of the republics subject to Bolívar's influence, and the project failed."[2] Mexico received gratefully the offers of Colombia, and negotiated a treaty. The Bogotá Cabinet adopted the following bases for a federal system: the American States united themselves perpetually for peace and war with mutual guarantees for the integrity of their territories, in accordance with the *uti possidetis* of 1810; as regards personal rights, commerce, and navigation, the Latin Americans were to enjoy the same rights as the citizens of the country in which they should reside as citizens or transients. To perfect this compact, and with the plan as suggested above, there should be convoked in Panama an assembly composed of delegates from each nation; the pact was not intended to impair the exercise of sovereignty by the contracting parties.[3]

The negotiations were carried on very slowly, and as the Peruvian campaign absorbed the Liberator entirely, the execution of the plan was delayed five years. It was only in 1823 that there was concluded a treaty of alliance and defence with Buenos Aires, and another of friendship and perpetual confederation with Mexico, and in 1825 a treaty with Central America. The Government of Perú divided the honor of the project with Colombia from the very beginning.[4]

Two days before Ayacucho, the Liberator sent to the South American nations his famous circular, inviting them to appoint representatives to the Panama Congress. Bolívar declared:

---

[1]Mitre, VI, 166.

[2]*Ibidem*, VI, 226.

[3]*Exposition of Minister Restrepo to the Congress of Colombia*, March 21, 1827.

[4]On July 6, 1822, a treaty of perpetual union, league, and confederation was signed between Colombia and Perú, and likewise a convention relative to the meeting of the Congress of Panama. Doc. VIII, 453 and 455.

After five years of sacrifices for the liberty of America, to obtain the system of guarantees which in peace and in war are to be the seal of our destiny, it is now time that the interests and the relations which unite the American republics, formerly Spanish Colonies, should have a base which last, if possible, during the life of these governments. To establish this system and to consolidate the power of this great political body belongs to the exercise of the sublime authority which should direct the politics of our governments, whose influence should maintain the uniformity and their principles, and whose name alone should calm our storms. An authority so respected can exist only in an assembly of plenipotentiaries, appointed by each of our republics, and under the auspices of victory obtained by our arms against the Spanish power.

Colombia urged, in the meanwhile, the Government of Buenos Aires, then under Las Heras, to ask Brazil and Guatemala to agree to the assembly, and to order its minister in Washington to learn how the Government of the United States would view the realization of the project, and, at the opportune moment to invite it "to send its plenipotentiaries to Panama, in order that, in union with those of Colombia and its allies, they may concert together to effectively resist all foreign colonization on the American Continent, and the application of the principles of legitimacy to the American States in general."[1] The Government of Colombia also invited Canning to send representatives, and suggested the conclusion, eventually, of an offensive and defensive alliance between Great Britain and the Confederation.

The Liberator attached great importance to the internal stability of the new States because of the effect it would have on his foreign policy, and worked constantly to consolidate those governments, even offending foreign nations, especially France and England, for the betterment of our institutions by being a conserver and a source of strength, in order to inspire confidence. He wrote to General Santander:[2]

I believe that France must be made to understand that I am not very far from lending myself to the ideas of the Holy Alliance, and by means of my influence the reform of our government can be made without the sacrifice of a war which may decide the fate of the universe. I believe that America can be saved by these four means: First: a large army to preserve and defend us. Second: a European policy to save us from the first blows. Third: England. Fourth: the United States. But all of this must be well managed and by a very good combination, for without good control there can be no good results. I insist, besides, on the Congress of the Isthmus of all the American States, which is the fifth means. I must add that the greatest energy ought to characterize our deliberations, to prevent us from being isolated between the people and the enemy. Belive me, my dear General, we shall save the New World by putting

---

[1]*Vide* O'Leary, *Narrative*, II, 536. The Mexican Government believed it would be wise to invite the United States. Consult the reply of Guadalupe Victoria to the circular of the Liberator, O'Leary, XXIV, 256.

[2]*The Liberator to General Santander, Lima, March 17*, 1825. The italics are in the original. *Vide* also the letter from Bolívar to Pueyrrendon, Tunja, February 4, 1821, and what was written by the chargé d'affaires of Colombia in London about his interview with Mr. Cockburn, Caracas, April 24, 1827. Today, as never before, the Latinamerican Governments need to have the program of Bolívar as the basis of their foreign policy.

ourselves in accord with England in *political and military matters*. This simple statement ought to tell you more than two volumes.

It should be noted that Bolívar, at this time, never proposed the adoption of the monarchical system as a form of government, but merely to found an aristocratic republic, the eternal ideal of the Liberator. A letter by Bolívar to Hutardo, written in this period, is the best proof that he was less disposed than ever to abandon "his political ideas." In this document we find the following concepts:[1]

The fact is, it seems, that France takes, as a pretext to make war on us, the democratic system we have adopted in our government. The French ambassador, in one of his conferences with Mr. Canning, told him that England, united with the rest of Europe, ought to interpose its mediation, in order to have us adopt, at least, aristocratic systems. You know, as the whole world should, from my address to the Congress of Venezuela, that my opinion then was that we should plan our legislative power on the British Parliament. You are, accordingly, authorized expressly by me to explain to the British Ministry, my views on government. They are quite clearly stated in that address. These views, expressed with vigor, should enable the British Ministry to declare that the hopes of France for a reform in our Constitution are well founded. But all this cannot take place until it is definitely known, by means of very definite proofs, that France and the Holy Alliance are determined to fight us because of our democracy. If the British Government should find it convenient, to avoid war, *to offer my political views to the allies* as a means of preventing open hostilities and for beginning negotiations, which should have for its object, the liberty and independence of America, modified through *governments of mixed aristocracy and democracy*, you are authorized by me to inform the Biritish Government of my determination to interpose all my influence in America to obtain the reform which will bring us recognition from Europe and the peace of the world.

This unchangeable thought of Bolívar is confirmed by what he wrote, years later, to Doctor Vergera, minister of Foreign Relations:"Only the structure and solidity of the government and its warlike attitude brought about the recognition of our sovereignty by the powers of the first and second order."[2]

The Liberator observed, in his interviews with the various foreign agents, a primary rule of diplomatic education, which consists in flattering the interlocutor, accepting, when the contrary does not seem necessary, his ideas and tendencies. Bolívar declared himself a fervent democrat in the presence of a North American official, who might publish such sentiments in the land of Washington,[3] while his phrases to the English Captain Malling, badly interpreted, according to a later statement of the Liberator, were intended to suggest to the British Cabinet the possibility of a conservative reaction. It may be that the vehemence of his temperment caused Bolívar to give expression to words of much

[1]*The Liberator to Señor Hurtado, Lima, March 12,* 1825. This letter, taken from a paper in Caracas of recent date should not be considered as an isolated one. From 1825, Bolívar sought to establish in America the principles of his Code.
[2]*The Liberator to Doctor Vergara, Popayán, February 6,* 1829. *Vide* also the letter of Bolívar to the same, *Guayaquil, September 20,* 1829.
[3]*Visit of Commodore Hull to Bolívar, May,* 1824. *Doc. IX,* 308.

gravity, such as those which Captain Malling attributed to him: "If the British Government should come to propose the establishment of a regular government, that is, a monarchy or monarchies in the New World, it would find in me a firm and constant supporter of those ideas, and disposed to support in everything the sovereign which England might want to establish and maintain on the throne."[1] These words must not be taken too literally. Bolívar declared to Consul Ricketts that "Captain Malling did not fully interpret his thoughts in his notes."[2] And it is necessary to note, with Gil Fortoul, that the Liberator was at the height of his power and glory in 1825, that he enjoyed the admiration of Europe, and that he was the arbiter and lord of America. Whoever studies this great spirit will never believe that Bolívar would, at least in this epoch, make himself into an instrument of a foreign prince. "The most likely thing is that Bolívar, clever diplomat as he always was, made use of this sailor to sound out the Cabinet of London, with the intention of gaining its sympathy and support in the questions to be considered at Panama, and in favor of his projected expedition to Cuba and Porto Rico, which offended the United States."[3] It should not be forgotten either that the Liberator was in the habit of launching certain disconcerting insinuations. He wrote to Sucre once that "he saw the crown on the forehead of the Marshall of Ayacucho," and at another time he offered to General Páez his support in case the vote of the nation should call the plainsman to the throne.

It is important, moreover, to verify the absolute purity of historical sources before forming a definite judgment. One of the books of Carlos A. Villanueva, rich in facts and interesting documents, supplies, in a communication of Consul Sutherland to the English Government, a notable case on inaccuracy. Villaneuva took care to mark the errors of the English official in giving an account of his political conversations with General Urdaneta.[4] It

---

[1] Villanueva, *Ferdinand VII and the New States*, 259.

[2] Villanueva, *The Empire of the Andes*, 104.

[3] Gil Fortoul, I, 456. Bolívar was a master in politics. He did not hesitate to use what one might call small means when he judged that necessary. His instrutions to General Heres, dated at Ica, April 20, 1825, are very significant: "In diplomatic matters," he declared, "I will give you a good maxim: *calmness, calmness, calmness; procrastination, procrastination, procrastination.* Compliments; vague words; consultations; investigations; contortions of arguments and requests; references to the new Congress; disputations over the nature of the question and of the documents. . . . and always much inactivity and much silence in order to give in to the contrary view. Excuse yourself on the ground of being a military man; that you do not know the nature of the negotiations now pending (verbally); that you are an official *ad interim* and that the affairs of Perú are very delicate. Above all, act in conformity with good principles and universal justice . . . . We need rectitude in our conduct and an appreciation of the greatness of our age."

[4] Villanueva, *The Empire of the Andes*, 193, *passim*.

is quite evident that there has been no criticism of these new documents which, in point of fact, do not alter in any essentials the actual historical criterion.

Rather than impose upon his compatriots a foreign prince, the Liberaotr held to the Constitution as the bond for all the peoples of the Continent, to the idea of the greatness of the country, capable of resisting morally and materially the attacks from without and from anarchy from within. To guarantee the stability of this organism, Bolívar hoped to obtain the benevolent cooperation of the great powers and as England was the only one of these, which by reason of political and economic interests, could lend itself to the proposition,[1] he directed his efforts toward her. Great Britain, however, did not wish to have our peoples form an alliance in which the United States should be a member and "looked at it with great dread."[2] at the same time that the Cabinet of Washington followed with uneasiness the unifying projects of the Liberator, according to the declaration of Secretary Clay to the commissioner of Charles X in Spanish America.[3] In addition to the cunning and similtaneous hostility of these Governments, the troubles of the plan multiplied in direct proportion as the general conditions of our countries became anarchical and without a guide in a sea of antagonistic aspirations. The Liberator had conceived the idea of yielding *the needle of the balance* to England, that is to say, to put under the protection of a great power the enormous and precarious machine of his Amphyctionic League,[4] not only to defend it against Spain but also from the aggressions feared on the part of the Holy Alliance,[5] and to balance the inevitable influence of the United States. Great Britain then appeared as the champion of liberty and the protector of the weak peoples. In its manifesto of August 2, 1825, the Greek Government announced its determination to solicit an English protectorate. O'Leary declared, however, that Bolívar "did not overlook the danger of admitting so powerful an ally into the League."[6] A letter to the Colombian minister of Foreign Relations

---

[1] *The Liberator to General Sucre, Guayaquil, May 24*, 1823. "We need goad the English to an intervention in the peace of Spain or to force them to come to our aid," declared Bolívar to General Santander, *Pativilca, January 23*, 1824.

The interest of Great Britain has always been intimately leagued with the safety of our countries, while the false English General Homer Lea has written that "England and not the United States gives guaranties for the independence of the American peoples, and the basis of their secutity rests on the maintenance of the British Empire much more than on the Monroe Doctrine."

[2] Mr. Canning's Instructions to Mr. Dawkins, March 18, 1826. Villanueva, *The Empire of the Andes*, 152.

[3] Villanueva, *The Empire of the Andes*, 147.

[4] Consult the piece of paper sent by Bolívar to Consul Ricketts, as published by Villanueva, in *The Empire of the Andes*, 144.

[5] *The Liberator to General Sucre, Trujillo, April 9*, 1824.

[6] *Narrative*, II, 542, *pessim*.

contained the following explanation of the fears of the Liberator in this matter:

> For the present, it appears to me that an alliance with Great Britain will give us great importance and much respectibility, because under its shadow we may grow, become men, become educated and strong, so as to appear before the nations with a degree of civilization and of power which are necessary in a great people. But these advantages do not dissipate the fears that this powerful nation may be in the future sovereign over the councils and the dicisions of the Assembly; that its voice may be the most penetrating, and that its will and its interests be the soul of the Confederation, which no one will dare to irritate for fear of arousing an irrisistible enemy. This is, in my mind, the greatest danger of mixing so great a nation with the others that are so weak.[1]

When various countries of America adhered in principle to the project of convoking a Congress in Panama, the Colombian Government communicated to Perú the matters it felt should be considered in this Assembly, to wit: the confirmation of the treaties of offensive and defensive alliance between those countries confederated against Spain, or any other country trying to subjugate them; the proclamation of neutrality and friendship of the American States for the foreign countries; the measures which should be taken in regard to Cuba, Puerto Rico, the Canary Islands, and the Philippines; and the celebration of treaties of commerce and navigation between the allies. Other questions should be studied by the confederates and the neutral powers represented in the conference. Such were: First: the adoption of means to make effectual the Pronouncement of President Monroe, in order to frustrate in the future all attempts to colonize the American Continent. Second: the establishment of accepted principles of international law, in order to avold conflicts over controversial points and particularly those which could be settled among themselves, one of which might be a belligerent and the other a neutral. Third: to determine the political and commercial relations among the contracting parties and the States which, like Haiti, had declared their independence from the metropolis without being recognized. Fourth: to abolish the slave trade. Fifth: to determine the subsidy and the respective contingents of the conferedates in case of foreign atack. Sixth: to adopt a plan of hostilities against Spain, in order to oblige her to recognize the independence, on the following bases: prohibition of all commerce, direct or indirect, with the Peninsula, permitting the confiscation of the cargo and the ship transporting it; prohibiting the return to America of those Spaniards who had emigrated during the revolution and the sequestration of their property; to encourage a system of corsairs against Spanish commerce; and an agreement among the confederates not to ac-

---

[1] *The Liberator to Minister Revenga, Magdalena, February 17, 1826.* Bolívar always maintained that it was necessary to insist upon the greatest degree of autonomy as far as England was concerned. "Great Britain," he declared, "is worthy of the considerations which it demands but without degradation." *Instructions to the Council of Government of Perú*, O'Leary, *Correspondance*, XIII, 88.

cept a separate peace. Seventh: fixing the territorial limits among the States in conformity with the *uti possidetis* of 1810. Eighth: in view of the fact that America needed a long period of rest and peace in order to recover from its evils and certain recently considered tendencies, there should be established what part of the new republics should be considered as representative of the national sovereignty and will, seeking the manner in which this declaration might have the desired legal effect. Ninth: the former point having been determined, a statement should be made to the effect that the American States, far from fomenting and aiding the dreams of those ambitious ones who intended to disturb the public order, would cooperate for the purpose of protecting the legitimate governments with all possible means.[1] Tenth: on ratifying the treaties approved by the Congress of the Federation, a decreee should be proclaimed declaring that the said convention formed the code of American public law, binding upon the States which took part in the Congress. These bases were approved by the Government of Perú, according to the definite instructions which its delegates received.[2]

Later, the Government of Bogotá, suggested to its allies the addition of other points for study, which were: First: the establishment of a penalty of exclusion for the State which did not conform to the decisions of the Confederation, using this as a means of arbitrating the disputes of its members. Second: prohibition of confederates from contracting alliances with foreign powers, or among themselves to the exclusion of other American States. Third: the institution of compulsory arbitration by the Confederation in disagreements which might occur between one of its members and a foreign power. Fourth: the authorization of the Assembly of the Isthmus to conclude by itself, or through the means of delegates, in the name of the Confederation, treaties of defensive alliance with other nations. Fifth: periodical meetings of the Congress of Panama.[3] These additions altered some of the original bases, as, for example, the one dealing with the sovereignty of the contracting parties in their relations with foreign countries. As regards the rights given to the plenipotentiaries to sign treaties of alliance, Bolívar found that excessive. "Of the others," he declared, "the additions seem to me as just and as beneficial as the remainder of the plan, and I believe, as you do, when adopted by the American Continent and Great Britain it will present an immense mass of power which must necessarily produce stability in the new States."[4]

---

[1]In this epoch the tendency toward autonomy became pronounced in Venezuela, and may be the circumstance which influenced the Government of Bogotá in suggesting the eighth and ninth provisions.

[2]O'Leary, *Correspondance*, XXIV, 259.

[3]O'Leary, *Narrative*, II, 542 *passim*.

[4]*The Liberator to the Minister of Foreign Relations. Ibidem.*

As the suspicions which the Congress incited in England disappeared, Canning applauded the general program and decided to send an agent.[1] Holland, did the same. The British Government, on naming a commissioner, sought, however, particularly to prevent the Congress from adopting plans which might disturb its politics. "Whatever project for placing the United States of North America at the head of an American confederation, in opposition to Europe, might be proposed would be highly disagreeable to your Government," declared Minister Canning in his instructions to Mr. Dawkins. England had an effective and indisputable interest in the independence of the Spanish colonies, but she did not desire to see America rise united and formidable, in any manner whatever, with the ideal of Panama as a standard in the hands of Bolívar, attempting a gigantic conflict of ideas and tendencies between the two worlds. The English influence in Rio and in Buenos Aires contributed powerfully to prevent Brazil and the Provinces of la Plata from taking part in the Congress. Great Britain, on the other hand, did not deny Colombia or any other country at war against Spain the right of operating against the Iberian Antilles; but, knowing the attitude of the United States, the Cabinet of London sought to avoid complications which might arise out the act of an occupation of the island by the Americans of the North. As regards arbitration, Canning held that the principle was not objectionable, provided always that its application be limited to the relations of the American States among themselves, and not to any possible difficulties with a foreign nation.[2] It is to be noted that the Liberator did not wish to have the United States create a prepondering position for itself in America. On the contrary, he was disturbed by their future ambitions, and their "arithmetical conduct of business,"[3] did inspire in him great sympathy. Mitre pointed out that Bolívar declared to the Argentine envoys in Potosí that "he had been of the opinion of not inviting the United States to the Panama Congress, which invitation had been given by Vice President Santander exclusively through his own initiative."[4]

The United States were alarmed over the eventuality of an invasion of Cuba and Porto Rico, on the part of Colombia or of Mexico, and this apprehension seemed to have been influential in the decision of the Government of Washington to send a mission to the Congress. It was hoped, in this way, to prevent the extension of hostile operations and to aid in bringing about an end of the war. The wish for a concilation led the North American

---

[1]O'Leary, *Narrative*, II, 575. Villanueva, *The Empire of the Andes*, 142.

[2]*Instructions of Canning to Mr. Dawkins. The Empire of the Andes*, 149.

[3]*The Liberator to Don Guillermo White, San Cristóbal, May 1,* 1820. *Vide* also, among others, Villanueva, *op. cit.*, 143.

[4]Mitre, VI, 221

Cabinet to suggest the idea of mediation of the Czar of Russia between Spain and the rebelling colonies. On April 27, 1825, Secretary Clay informed the United States Minister at Madrid that his Government was satisfied with the present condition of the Spanish Antilles and did not desire any change. Clay insinuated a possibility of a North American occupation if the *status quo* of the islands were interferred with. Under pressure from Washington, the Colombian Government gave to the representative of the United States in Bogotá the assurance "that Colombia would not undertake without the gravest of motives any operation of great magnitude against Spanish Antilles," and offered to present the matter for consideration in the Congress of Panama.[1]

By virtue of the invitation to assist at the Assembly, mentioned above, the Committee of Foreign Affairs decided that the House of Representatives of the United States should vote the funds necessary to send a mission. The Committee gave this favorable opinion in view of the fact that, according to the treaties of Colombia with the other nations of the Continent, the meetings at Panama "would not affect in any manner the autonmous exercise of the national sovereignty of the contracting parties in respect to its laws and the organization and the form of the respective governments."[2] In May, 1826, the Government gave instructions to its delegates to the Congress "purely diplomatic" of Panama: the mission was to oppose any project for the establishment of an Amphyctionic Council to settle controversies of our States among themselves; it might treat with all or each one of the nations represented on commerce, navigation, maritime code, the rights of neutrals and beligerents; it was to abstain from taking part in the deliberations concerning the state of war bewteen Spain and its former colonies, but not those which consider the eventualities of an attack by the Holy Alliance, in which case the delegates "could form an offensive and defensive alliance," an inacceptible proposition, since according to the principles of American politics and for other reasons, such an alliance would be useless.[3] On the whole, the Government of the United States refused to follow the grandiose path which Bolívar had tried to lay out for the meeting of the Congress. The adoption

---

[1]*March 17*, 1826. Consult the notes of Revenga, Secretary of Foreign Reations of Colombia, to the minister to this Republic of Perú in Lima and to the minister of the United States at Bogotá. O'Leary, *Correspondence*, 483-506. The Liberator insisted, in 1827, on his project for an attack on the Antilles and sought to bring about a war between Spain and England in order to send General Páez with six thousand men to Puerto Rico. The United States would certainly have hesitated to go to war against an ally of Great Britain. *Letters of Bolívar to the Marshal of Ayacucho, Caracas, February 5 and 28*, 1827. Consult the *Autobiography of Páez*, I, 377, *passim*.

[2]*Doc. X*, 459. The question of the abolition of slavery caused concern in the Southern States, where it was opposed.

[3]*Doc. X*, 311.

of obligatory arbitration, which today forms the base of the
treaties of peace and friendship concluded later by the Cabinet of
Washington;[1] the perfection and definition of the Doctrine of
Monroe as a principle of public continental law, guaranteeing to
all our countries integrity and sovereignty not only against
Europe, but likewise against the imperialistic ambitions of any
nation in America; the creation of a vast and powerful agency of
universal equilibrium, founded on diplomatic necessities and
politics, supported by a true and just conception of a genuine Pan-
americanism: I have here a program to which the representatives
of the great democracy of the North were not authorized to sub-
scribe. The Bolivarian Doctrine was the defense of all the American peoples, through a confraternity and mutual guarantees,
opposed to the declarations of Monroe, which Saenz Peña critized
as uncertain and egotistical.[2] Of the deputies from Washington,
one died on the road, and the other arrived too late.

The Argentine Government, in considering the proposal to
assist at the Congress, which "left to consider the idea of establishing a definite authority which could preside over the confederation of the American States, which make uniform their
foreign policies and arbitrates the differences that may arise
among the confederates. . . . considered as the most
effective means of assuring the internal order of each State, the
harmony between them, and the security of all against foreign
enemies" and even when "the National Executive may not be of
that opinion" the Aregntine Government, I say, submitted to its
Constituent Congress a project for a law which would authorize
it to conclude a treaty of defensive alliance with the other nations
of America against Spain and other foreign powers and to send
its plenipotentaries to Panama.[3] The plan was not realized.

The minister of Brazil in London informed that of Colombia,
Señor Hurtado, that his Government would send representatives
to the Congress, to take part in its deliberation of general interest,
"compatible with the strict neutrality that the Emperor maintains

---

[1]A journalist versed in universal politics, in a recent book, full of thought and
good sense, even though at times obscure and pedantic, describes the proba-
bilities and uses which the treaties on arbitration proposed by the United States
possessed, and which principle the Liberator supported. "This new diplomatic
instrument," declared Morton Fullerton, "decreased at the same time the proba-
bilities of wars and permitted, in the end, in a future more or less distant, the
constitution of a real Anglo-Saxon Amphticionic Council." *Great Problems of the
Political World.* 202.

[2]Consult the opinion of Doctor Roque Sáenz Peña. President of the Argentine
Republic. *Writings and Adresses,* I, 456. "This country pretended (the Saxon
Republic), declared, on the other hand, Olibeira Lima, "that the terms on which
the other European powers lived so as not to alienate the republican system of
Bolívar from the Holy Alliance, as well as pretending later that it nurtured its
sisters by preventing any other European country from harming it. Such a privilege
eventually came to be hers." *Pan Americanism,* 46.

[3]*August 16,* 1825. *Doc. X,* 74. *Vide* O'Leary, *Memoirs,* II, 637. *Edition* of 1915.

between the American belligerents and Spain."[1] The Congress did not welcome the imperial deputies.

Chile declared, at the last moment, that the consent of the National Congress, which was not then in session, was absolutely necessary in naming the plenipotentaries; and, as for Bolivia, she, too, was unrepresented.[2]

The Assembly was installed on June 22, 1826, with the assistance of delegates from Colombia, Guatemala, Mexico and Perú. Great Britain and the Netherlands were represented respectively by Mr. Dawkins and Colonel Verveer, being instructed "to listen diligently and to give a full account of what was going on" and to aid the Congress "with their counsels when these were requested."[3] The conferencies terminated the 15th of July following and the Assembly voted, for reasons of health among others, its removal to the city of Tacubaya, in Mexico. The delegates signed: First: a treaty of alliance, confederation, mutual guarantee and arbitration between the four signatory States, to which treaty the remaining American States might adhere within one year. Second: an agreement on the formalities for the meeting of the Congress, which was to be effected every two years in time of peace, and every year in time of war. Third: a convention and an agreement relative to military matters, the one on the respective contigent for each nation, the other the employment and command of the contingents. The bases of the treaty are those indicated by the Governments of Colombia and Perú, at the beginning of the discussion for a meeting of the Congress. The military conventions stipulated the creation and maintenance of an army of sixty thousand men and a navy of twenty-eight ships of war for the defense of the Confederation.[4]

The results of Panama did not arouse any enthusiasm in the Liberator. He critized those of a military character as defective, and wrote to Briceño Méndez: "The removal of the Assembly to Mexico will put it under the immediate influence of that power, already too preponderant, and also under that of the

---

[1]*Doc. X*, 132.

[2]*Vide* Gil Fortoul, I, 383.

[3]O'Leary, *Narrative*, II, 548. The author of the present book had the curiosity to ask Doctor J. A. Nederbragt, Chief of the Division of Economics of the Ministry of Foreign Affairs in Holland, if the papers relative to the mission of Colonel Verveer to Panama were in the archives. From the answer of this distinguished official it was found that the "observer" from Holland received instructions from his Government more or less vague and which, on his return, were reported orally. The Colonel wrote several letters from Panama "in which he told of his impressions of the Congress and the interviews with the Mexican and Brazilian delegates." (*Sic*). Verveer believed that the plan of Bolívar to establish "a system of co-operation between the States of Central America, in the form of an offensive and defensive alliance" was practical. Letter from Doctor Nederbragt to Para-Pérez, December 9, 1926.

[4]These papers may be consulted in O'Leary, XXIV, 352 *passim;* and in Restrepo, III, *Illustrated Notes*, 634 *passim*.

United States of the North. These and many other reasons compel me to say that you should not proceed to the ratification of the treaties before I arrive in Bogotá and before I have examined them carefully with you and with others. I will say the same to General Santander, and you tell him the same."[1] Bolívar abstained from discussing the conclusions of the Peruvian delegates, who, it is true, were named at his suggestion; and moreover, as he considered the results of the Congress illusiory, he suggested to the representatives of Colombia the desirability of a military agreement between this last Republic, Guatemala, and Mexico. Disappointed by the politics of the countries of the South, the Liberator tried to draw within his orbit the peoples located farther to the north from the Isthmus. The League gave Spain four months in which to recognize American independence, and to raise twenty thousand soldiers and thirty warships to attack the Spaniards in Cuba and Puerto Rico and even on European territory.[2] The letter which contained this vast and audacious program, absolutely opposed to the policy of the United States, arrived late in the hands of the addressees. Bolívar ratified, on September 14, 1827, as President of Colombia, the treaty of alliance concluded at Panama.

The Congress did not achieve the benficial result which Bolívar anticipated because of the anarchy reigning in America, because of the enormous distances, of the uncertainty created by the lack of support from Great Britain and the United States, of the incapacity of our peoples to understand the lofty character of the Bolivarian thought. In America the only man who possessed the idea of continental solidarity was Bolívar. The diplomacy of the Saxon States did its best to prevent this idea from spreading and from being realized. The rivalry, ignorance, and poverty of our people determined its failure. The Liberator himself announced the failure of his beautiful scheme. "The Congress of Panama," he wrote to General Páez, "an institution which would be admirable it if were more efficacious, is no other thing than that which the insane Greek who pretended to direct from a rock the ships which were sailing. Its power will be a shadow, and its decrees, opinions—nothing more."[3] Never, on the other hand, has any man treasured more tenderly a loftier ideal. The irrepresible convulsions, the social chaos, the quarrels of our peoples. convinced him that it was still impossible to bring about an alliance or federation between our countries;[4] but these circumstances also served in his great soul to revivify generous il-

[1]O'Leary, *Narrative*, II, 560.

[2]*Ibidem*, 561.

[3]*The Liberator to General Páez, Lima, August 8*, 1826.

[4]*Diary of Bucaramanga*, 143. The judgment which General Perú de Lacroix attributes to Bolívar on the Congress and the motives which brought it about, seem trivial, considered its anticedents.

lusions. And at the end of his life, when the restoration of his system in Bolivia, the reaction in Perú against Lamar, and his own ascent to the dictatorship in Colombia seemed to revive his hopes, the Liberator recognized also the surpeme remedy: The alliance of Colombia, Perú, and Bolivia becomes each time more necessary, in order to cure the gangrene of the revolutions which becomes constantly more malignant and complicated."[1]   The diplomacy of the Dictatorship will always be inspired by the eternal ideal of a Spanish American Confederation, and will seek the support of a great power to assure the political and social stability of this organism.

The attempt of Bolívar to "assure the moral and intelectual unity of America"[2] was in reality a program of a supreme political policy, and the most interesting concept of our diplomacy. This work was in the mind of its initiator the ideal compliment of the emancipation and the indispensible guarantee of peace and progress. Under other aspects, its importance did not escape those spirits, which, in Europe, followed with attentive admiration the dazzling career of the Liberator and this negotiation "as vast as new" inspired, among others, the pen of de Pradt. "The Congress of Panama," wrote the Archbishop of Molinas, "will give birth to a new era, principally in that which concerns the right of public of the nations. From this point of view, the act of Panama is not isolated, private, but universal, an act of the social order. It is not merely American, but an act of humanity."[3]

---

[1]*The Liberator to Marshal Santa Cruz, Quito. June 23,* 1829.
[2]García Calderon, *Contemporary Perú,* 31.
[3]*Vide The Study of the Archbishop, Doc.* X, 80 *passim.*

Valencia

IN the old Captaincy General of Venezuela, divided into the departments of Venezuela, Zulia, and Orinoco, symptoms of political disease began to manifest themselves before the end of the war, with the capture of Puerto Cabello on the 10th of November, 1823. This was caused by the ambitious rivalry of military chiefs, the autonomous tendencies of certain leaders, the intrigues of others, and the propaganda which attributed all existing evils to the distant administration at Bogotá. The Supreme Government in the hands of Vice-President Santander did its utmost to gain the sympathies and respect of the Venezuelans. Caracas soon became the center of an opposition, which, although it had at times acted within the limits of legality, or at least of justice, did not delay in overthrowing constitutional forms to become, in 1826, a real revolution. The municipalities were a constant center of dissension, and the tool used by the Venezuelan oligarchy to liberate itself from the central power. In the year 1821, the subterranean work began, installed for the first time in Valencia and determined, in 1830, the constitution of Venezuela as an independent State. Little by little the personality of General Páez became the pole of the regional hopes, and his ambition led to the fatal sequel. There is no place here to examine how and why the legionary plainsman, surrounded by an illustrious oligarchy, succeeded in incarnating during twenty years the political aspirations of his country. Suffice for our purpose to name his as the first who manifested dissatisfaction formally with the institutions and insinuated the need of a reform in the law of Rosario. Hating the Government of Bogotá, exasperated with the intellectuals whom he abhorred, and seconded by various men in his conference, Páez, Commandant General of the Department, sent, in October, 1825, as deputy to the Liberator, Antonio Leocadio Guzmán, to Lima, to describe to him the bad condition of the country, earnestly urging him to return to Colombia, lost in the hands of the intrigants. Páez sought, by an 18th of Brummaire, to induce Bolívar to suppress the Constitution, and the mirage of a discretional authority, in this or that form, was presented to the Liberator by the men who, shortly afterwards, succeeded with the demagogues of Cundinamarca in accusing him of aspiring to tyranny and to a crown. It was the first effort of the malcontents of Caracas to provoke disturbances and to create difficulties for Bolívar and the Government. Months later, the decrees of the Executive on conspirators, the national militia, and the violence of Páez in enforcing the last brought about open rebellion. If the conduct of the guilty municipalities be studied, and if the march of events, extraordinary complicated,

118

are followed, it will certainly be found that the promoters of the revolt exploited every means to discredit the Government and that they took advantage of the most unforeseen circumstances. Páez's zeal is scarcely comparable to that displayed by Santander and the Bogotans to offend Bolívar and Venezuela. It is unquestionably true that a reform was necessary.

The Liberator rejected with energy the project suggested to him by Caracas and wrote to General Santander:[1]

> In these last days, I have received letters from different friends in Venezuela suggesting Napoleonic ideas. General Páez is at the head of these ideas, suggested by his friends, the demagogues. A private secretary and editor of the *Argos* has brought me the project: you will see it in the letter which I enclose as originally received, which you are to guard with infinite care so that no one will see it. The writer of this letter is Carabaño. General Briseño wrote to me telling me that he has had to restrain those who wished to strike in Venezuela, and that he counselled them to consult me. General Mariño wrote also, and others of less importance, but more furious than democratic. Of course, you may guess what my answer will be. My sister tells me that in Caracas there are three parties: monarchists, democrats, and mugwumps. I should be *Liberator* or *dead*, is her counsel. This will be what I will follow, even though I know that in following it all mankind may perish. . . . I shall send my plan of a Constitution for Bolivia to General Páez, as a definite answer, so that he may consider my ideas on stability, unity, and liberty, and conservation of the principles which we have adopted. . . . I shall say to General Páez that I will lead opinion toward my Bolivian Constitution, that I shall unite all the extremes and all the goods, for even the federalists find in it all their desires, in a great measure; and in the Year 31 a reform could be made favorable to the stability and conservation of the Republic. . . . This and much more I shall say to remove from his mind so fatal a plan, so absurd, and so inglorious. A plan which would dishonor us before the world and before history; which would bring us the hate of the liberals and the contempt of tyrants; a plan which would horrify me by principles, by prudence, and by pride. This plan offends me more than all the attacks of my enemies, for it attributes to me a vulgar ambition, capable of making me like an Itúrbide, and other such miserable usurpers. According to these men, no one can be great except in the manner of Alexander, Caesar, and Napoleon. I wish to be superior to all of these in disinterestedness, if I cannot equal them in deeds.

Six days later from Lima he wrote to Briseño Méndez that he had sent the Bolivian Code to General Páez.[2]

The force of events was to convert Bolívar into the first revolutionist of Colombia. The Constitution of Cúcuta had never pleased him. To it he attributed the weakness of the political organism. On the other hand, the general discontent and the intrigues of Santander convinced him that a reform was necessary and that this movement must be anticipated to avoid a dissolution of the Republic. Thus a curious phenomenon is presented of Bolívar, President of Colombia, guardian of the laws and champion of the principle of authority and order, manifesting publicly his sympathy for the reform of the Constitution and insinuated as a remedy for the political disturbances the adoption of the Code of Bolivia. From that moment the Liberator was virtually divorced

---

[1] *The Liberator to General Santander, Magdalena, February 21,* 1826.
[2] *The Liberator to General Briceño Méndez, Lima, February 27,* 1826.

from the Government of Bogotá and then there remained but two alternatives: resign the command, or assume the dictatorship. All the people still loved and admired him. His name was still considered as a paladium in the social revindications, and for some time his authority served as a link in the cries for reform from Caracas to Guayaquil. But the number of his enemies increased unceasingly, and the distrust and hate crystallized behind him. His autocracy was exploited by those who wished to succeed him, and the motives of the revolts was clearly discerned, the difficulties increased, and he was scarcely able to save himself from the final catastrophe by his glory and the prodigious example of his energy and honor.

Bolívar wrote to General Páez in answer to his proposition:[1]

> He (Guzmán) tells me that the situation in Colombia is like that of France when Napoleon returned from Egypt, and that I should say with him: the intrigants are about to destroy the country, let us save her. In truth nearly all your letter is written with the pen of veracity, but the truth is not enough for your plan to succeed. You have not judged, it appears to me, impartially the nature of things and of men. Neither is Colombia, France, nor I Napoleon. In France they think much and they know more; the population is homogenous, and what is more, the war brought it to the verge of the precipice. No other republic was as great as France and France had always been a kingdom. The republican government had become discredited and defeated to a point where she was about to fall into an abyss of execration. The monsters who rules France were equally cruel and inept. Napoleon was great and unique, and besides inordinately ambitious. Here there is nothing similar, neither do I wish to imitate Caesar, much less Itúrbide. Such examples seem to me to be unworthy of my glory. The title of Liberator is superior to those which human pride has received, so much so that it is impossible to increase it. A throne would frighten as much by its loftiness as by its brilliancy. Equality would be destroyed, and the Colombians would see their rights lost to a new aristocracy. Finally, my friend, I cannot persuade myself that Guzmán's project is sensible, I believe also that those who have suggested it are like those who elevated Napoleon and Itúrbide in order to enjoy their prosperity and to abandon them in danger. Or if good faith has guided them, they are confused individuals, or partisans of exaggerated opinions. . . Under what form or principle it may appear, I tell you frankly that this project does not become me, nor you, nor the country.

The Liberator declared that when the time for reform should arrive, the Bolivian Constitution, in which "will be found united all the guarantees of permanence and liberty, of equality and order: if you and your friends should wish to approve this project, it would be most appropriate that you write on it and recommend it to the opinion of the people. This is the service that will be admired by all those partisans who are not extremists, or, rather, who desire true liberty." And Bolívar concluded with delicious irony: "For the rest, I do not counsel for you what I would not do

---

[1] General Páez denied categorically having sent Guzmán on the mission to Perú to offer the crown to the Liberator and declared that he never received the letter from which we have quoted. *Autobiography*, I, 490. Gil Fortoul declared that this document was inserted in O'Leary and that it did not reach its destination since Santander intercepted it in Bogotá. *Narrative*, I, 453.

[1] Or "degrade it" (*"degradarlo"*), as this phrase is generally used when this celebrated phrase is cited.

for myself; but, what is more, if the people wish it and you accept the national vote, my sword and my authority will be used with infinite pleasure in supporting and defending the rights of popular sovereignty. This protest is as sincere as the heart of an old friend."

The propaganda for the adoption of the Bolivian Code in Colombia continued during the years following, and later we shall see which part of the conventionists of Ocaña was partisans of that idea. In the earlier period the Liberator, harboring great hopes and faith in the efficacy of his institutions, made him recommend them personally to his friends. "I send you a copy of my Constitution for the Republic of Bolivia," he wrote to General Lamar; "in it I have secured the welfare and the stability of a nation which has been willing to give up its early name and give mine to future generations."[1] And to Briceno Méndez: "In Venezuela I shall attempt to evict the spirit of partisanship, and at the same time I shall spread among my friends the gospel of my Constitution for Bolivia, in opposition to federation and the empire. This Constitution combines the extremes and presents a means for securing domestic peace with liberty to the provinces. The Year 31 (the date designated by the Constitution of Cúcuta for eventual reform) may mean something in the negotiation of the reform. . . . Observe that my plea is definitely republican and also very much that of a philosopher in religion: the first has been necessary in order to silence the idea of *empire* which some attribute to me and others ask for as a means of salvation. In Buenos Aires and in Chile they *attack* (*atoliendran*) me under this pretext."[2] "You will see," he wrote to Fernando Peñalver, who defended in Angostura the idea of the presidency for life, rejecting the institution of the hereditary senate, "the Constitution which I have presented to the legislature of Bolivia. I do not know if my address will please you, but it certainly contains the expression of my political sentiments. Read it and have your friends appreciate it."[3] Finally, Bolívar wrote to General Lafuente: "All the world tells me that my Constitution may be very valuable, because it unites all distances and all parties. As far as I can see all have set their hopes on it because they see preserved in it liberty and equality, accompanied by stability and order."[1] Again: "At last I have finished the Constitution of Bolivia, and a messenger carries it to General Sucre so that he may present it to the Congress of Upper Perú; The moment has now come when I may say that this Constitution is going to be the ark which is to save us from shipwreck, which threatens us everywhere."[2]

---

[1]*The Liberator to General José de Lamar, Lima, May 30*, 1826.
[2]*The Liberator to General Briceño Méndez, Lima. May*, 1826.
[3]*The Liberator to Don Fernando Peñalver, Lima, June 1*, 1826.
[4]*The Liberator to General Gutiérrez de Lafuente, Magdalena, June 3*, 1826.
[5]*Idem., id., id., Lima, June 17*, 1826.

There was in England a man whose admiration particularly pleased Bolívar, and whom he wished to advise correctly on American politics, above all, during the last years of his life, when the eyes of liberal Europe followed anxiously the progress of events and scrutinized the thoughts of the Liberator. Sir Robert Wilson, like the great Irishman O'Connell, sent his son Bedford to serve in the Colombian army, and was, in London, the propagandist of the glory of the hero. Bolívar wrote to him: "Permit me, General, to offer you a copy of my project for a Constitution for the Republic of Bolivia. I well know the impossibility of realizing such high aims: but I must attempt, in some manner, to deserve by this small service some part of the immense glory that this Republic has conferred on me in taking my name. May I ask you to look with indulgent eyes on this effort of my zeal for the welfare of Bolivia."[1]

The events of Venezuela, in the meanwhile, assumed a character of gravity. The faction of malefactors which joined with the royal banner kept the people in alarm. The authorities of Caracas fought each other. The central Government, obtuse and hated, was incapable of counteracting the autonomous and separatist tendencies which increased daily. The municipalities prepared to usurp the political powers and to serve in turn as tools for all the bands, with the idea of creating disorder and precipitating, no matter how, the reform of the Constitution.

The city of Caracas began the conflagration, denouncing General Páez before the House of Representatives as violator of the laws and public security, in forcing the citizens to enlist in the national militia, in conformity with the recent decree of the Executive. The accusation was accepted, the Commandant General was suspended from the army under his command, in which he was succeeded by General Juan de Escalona, and received the order to appear at the bar of the senate to justify his conduct. Páez apparently was prepared to leave for Bogotá, when, on April 27, 1826, the Municipal Council of Valencia passed a resolution in which it expressed "its bitter regret" for the measures taken against the Commandant General and its hope that he would soon return invested with the command. Once the preparatory steps were taken, the municipality resolved that, in view of the popular discontent, General Páez should reassume the command. A detail which indicated the extent they wished to give to their initial movement was that "the other authorities of the departments and provinces of the territory forming ancient Venezuela were ordered to take part in this action."[2] From the very beginning it was intended that this movement should be given a general and solid character in the whole of the Captaincy.

Three days later, General Páez, in open rebellion, proclaimed

---

[1] *The Liberator to Sir Robert Wilson, Lima, June 1*, 1826.
[2] The action of April 30, 1826.

that he assumed the command,[1] and then the municipalities began to adhere to the acts of Valencia, directing the movement toward a constitutional reform. The municipality of Caracas, accuser of Páez, pronounced in favor of the revolution on May 5, in spite of the upright Mendoza who, Intendant at the time, declared that he would not authorize the violation of the laws. The cynical conduct of the Caracas Municipality was not unique as an example of contradiction and shamelessness in those days. That of Guayaquil showed the same, if not a greater inconsistency, by the expulsion of the Colombian functionaries, and other occurrences in the middle of this year and at the beginning of the following. We have seen how the Venezuelan federalists of 1826 flooded the Convention of Ocaña with acts contrary to the federalist system. "The explanation of this change of tactics," declared Gil Fortoul, "is that the party formed in Caracas in 1821 and with branches in other cities soon understood that supporting the rebellion of Páez would increase its power to fight against the Cúcuta Constitution and in favor of its reform throughout the whole territory."[2]

The Municipality of Valencia invested General Páez with the title of Civil and Military Head of Venezuela, and agreed that the Liberator should be called to remedy the evils of the country. The City Council of Caracas, which had sent two deputies to this session, ratified the agreements on the 16th of May. The revolutionary effervescence spread. "In the southern limits of the Republic, Guayaquil asked for the same reform, and Quito imitated it. Maracaiba expressed the same desire. At the same time the more frank and open Puerto Cabello pronounced, on August 8, for the federation, which the Council of Caracas rejected on the 21st. In the meanwhile, Colonel Macero, followed by the batallion *Apure*, left Caracas and approached Barcelona, proclaiming obedience to the Government. Supported by General José Tadeo Monagas, the city of Aragua asked for the Convention, Cumaná also asked for the Convention. . . . It had become fashionable to perform these acts and to make these pronouncements: every province, every city believed itself obliged to express its opinion in the exercises of its primitive sovereignty, the consideration of which brought about a general overthrow of authority. Some declared for a federal system, others for the central; some conceded extraordinary powers, while others resorted to arms to support their pretentions."[3] Baralt wrote that "no act was ever less approved by the majority of the sane people of the country." It is unquestionably true, however, that the majority of the leading men of Venezuela approved and supported

---

[1] "The events enveloped me like a helpless straw in the furies of a hurricane." Páez, *Autobiography*, I, 292.
[2] Gil Fortoul, I, 402.
[3] Baralt, *A Résumé of the History of Venezuela*, II, 145. Paris, 1841.

in the end, the revolt of Páez and there were to be seen respectable patricians like Cristóbal Mendoza supporting the new order, provisionally at least. It is a mistake to affirm that this question of Velencia originated wholly in the ambition of Páez and the unruly councils of Peña, even though it was welcomed by the disturbing element like Mariño and others. When the rôle and influence of the municipalities in our history are studied it will be possible to indicate certain factors apart from those generally known which characterize the Revolution of 26 which made it inevitable and prepared with it the dissolution of Colombia.

The Government of Bogotá refrained from taking military measures against the rebels and several declared that it was necessary that the Liberator should come and settle the question. He, on his part, advised Santander not to take "any strong or violent measure, nor of a nature capable of making what has occurred up to this time assume a dangerous character before my arrival."[1] Bolívar summed up the deplorable state of the Republic with exactitude on the following words: "You must know that the parties divide Colombia; that the treasury is empty; that the laws are violated; that the officials grow rich with the spoils of the treasury; and, finally, that in Venezuela they clamor for an empire."[2] On the 4th of June, he sent, for the sixth time, his resignation as president to Santander and congratulated him on his own reelection, with an irony which coming events will show: "Although a soldier may save his country, he is rarely a good magistrate. Accustomed to the rigor and cruel passions of war, his administration partakes of the asperities and the violence of an office of death. You alone are a glorious exception to this terrible rule."[3] The Vice-President, partly through fear that the coming of the Liberator would reestablish an order which he did not desire, knowing full well that he might assume the dictatorship, depriving him of his power, wrote to Lima, by July, that the presence of Bolívar in Bogotá would be productive of bad results. Santander wished the Liberator to lead an army aginst Venezuela.

Bolívar contemplated precipitating the reforms, abrogate the Code of Cúcuta, and establish his Constitution. Santander put himself at the head of the direction of the liberals of Colombia, of the anti-Bolivarians, exploited the rivalry of the provinces and the faults of Bolívar, and gave consistency to the formidable opposition which arose from the propaganda in the press and the obstruction in Congress and in Ocaña up until the crime of September. In the struggle which began then, General Santander appeared as the champion of liberty, and raised the banner of Pompey before the advancing Caesar. He began the war to the death against the Liberator. In the frightful struggle, many

---

[1] *The Liberator to General Santander*, Lima, August 25, 1826.
[2] *The Liberator to General Gutiérrez de Lafuente, Lima, June 17*, 1826.
[3] *The Liberator to General Santander, Lima, June 4*, 1826.

chieftains will cover themselves with ignominy, few will guard their name in purity and their heart with honor. Bolívar will preserve his grandeur.

While he prepared for his march to Bogotá and put in order the affairs in Perú, he did not forget to write to his friends in support of his Bolivian Constitution, and sent Guzmán to propagate his ideas.[1] The position of the Liberator was as clear as ever. The Government should not count on his aid to maintain legality, sensibly, because Bolívar made common cause with the reformers. He took his retaliation on the Constitution of Rosario, and believed that the moment had arrived for him to establish his system and the confederation, "establishing a beneficiary" not only for Colombia but also "for the Republics of the South which received it with avidity."[2] "In twenty or thirty days," he wrote, "I shall begin the march for that city: I shall return for the salvation of the country and hope to find all its sons disposed to the same end. In the meanwhile, my friends may, from now on, publish my views because they are of a public nature. The Bolivian Code is the résumé of my ideas and I offer it to Colombia as to all America. To my eyes there is evident no other means of salvation and all the rest seems to me absurd."[3] Or better still: "I write to Venezuela and to all parties that they may work to induce public opinion to adopt the project of the Constitution of Bolivia and I urge upon them, in the meantime, union and harmony until my arrival. I beg of you to write on these principles for the world to see and to prevent all evil until I arrive."[4] In announcing his views to Don Cristóbal, Mendoza the envoy of Guzmán to Venezuela, as the carrier of his ideas, Bolívar declared to the austere Intendant: "If you and the other persons of influence will busy yourselves in aiding them, the fire that now burns will be quenched on all sides. I propose, likewise, the Bolivian Code, which, with some slight modifications, seems applicable to all the situations which Colombia may need."[5]

It is not necessary to play upon the senses or to read between the lines to find shadowy projects or imperial aspirations in the politics of the Liberator, because this is of diurnal clarity. Bolívar wanted the dictatorship because it gave him the means of ending at once and for all time the vices of administration and to establish order with the Constitution of Bolivia.[6] This seems clear from his instructions communicated to his agents and of the enforcement of these throughout Colombia. The Liberator never permitted himself to believe, in reality, that he aided ideas favorable

---

[1]Colonel Damarquet received a mission to go to Ecuador for the same purpose.
[2]*Circular of the Liberator to his Friends, Lima, August 3, 1826.*
[3]*To General Tomás Cipriano de Mosquera, Lima, August 1, 1826.*
[4]*To General Briceño Méndez, Lima, August 8, 1826.*
[5]*To Don Cristóbal Mendoza, Lima, August 6, 1826.*
[6]The note of Buchet-Martigny to Baron de Damas, *Bogotá, September* 14, 1826, confirms this opinion. Villanueva, *The Empire of the Andes, 178.*

to the institution of a monarchy which he opposed at that time. The opposition, however, did not forget to make use of such a weapon in the future.[1]

There was no duplicity in Bolívar. He declared that to save the Republic he will only exercise discretionary and effective power. "From now on," he wrote to General Páez, "what is most needed is to maintain the public authority with vigor, in using force to calm the passions and to punish abuses, sometimes by the press, sometimes by the pulpits, and sometimes by the bayonets. The theory of the principles is good in periods of calm; but when agitation is general, these theories which pretend to rule over passions by ordinances from heaven which, however perfect, have no connection whatever, sometimes, with the applications." The monarchical projects which resulted were, as always, unrealizable. "I have been informed that many thoughful men desire a prince with a federal constitution, but, where is the prince? and what division would establish harmony? All is ideal and absurd. You tell me that my poor legislative dream is of little use except to encircle all evil. I know it, but something must be said in order not to remain mute in the midst of this conflict."[2] Bolívar believed, nevertheless, that his poor legislative dream will be the one likely salvation, as the circular to his friends previously cited will show: "I consider that the project of the Constitution which I presented to Bolivia," he declared,

can be the bond of union and firmness for these governments. More popular than any other, it will consecrate the sovereignty of this (people), conferring on the electoral body the immediate exercise of its most delicate acts. Firm and robust with a life president and an hereditary vice president, it will prevent oscilations, the parties (should read personalism), and the aspirations which frequent elections produce, as has recently happened in Colombia. Its chambers with duties so detailed and so extensive prevent the president and other members of the government from abusing their power. Depositories of as much as the ambition of the inhabitants desire, they strip the executive of the means of making them satilities, but leave him vigorously strong in the important branches

---

[1]*Vide* the interesting details on the monarchist propaganda in *The Empire of the Andes*, 167, *passim*.

[2]*The Liberator to General Páez, Lima, August 8,* 1826. A communication from Buchet-Martigny to Minister of Foreign Affairs of Charles X confirmed the ideas of Bolívar on American politics which are well known: "On this particular point he expressed himself with all clarity in the presence of the Vice President, who received them in silence, as he declared that the republican system did not conform to the customs, education, spirit and necessities of the inhabitants of South America; that he believed that there was nothing new in it, as he had explained in his address to the Congress of Angostura. . . . A monarchy would be even less convenient for the country, because of its poverty in supporting a king and a royal government. Only a dictatorship could suppress these two inconveniences. The only way of governing America is through the personal element. The laws mean nothing in the eyes of our people who do not know what they mean." *Buchet-Martigny to Baron de Damas, Bogotá, November 20,* 1826. *The Empire of the Andes,* 285. The objections of Bolívar to the establishment of a monarchy were known, many of which it would have been useless to relate in the presence of an agent of the king of France.

of war and finance. In no pact of representative government do I see such popular liberty, such direct intervention by the citizens in the exercise of sovereignty and such power in the executive as in this project. In it are united all the charms of federation, all the solidity of a central government, all the stability of monarchical government. All interests are bound together and all guarantees are established.

From August to October, a great municipal movement was under way in the country. Guayaquil, Quito, Panamá, Cartagena, Maracaibo, and other cities proclaimed, under the influence of Bolívar and his friends, political reform and the dictatorship of the Liberator. Caracas decided to adopt the federal system, which shortly before it had declined. Santander and the Government voted through various municipalities the inviolability of the Constitution. In Venezuela, the rebellion of Páez became more complicated thanks to the Commanding General who frightened the Republic. Only the return of Bolívar could prevent anarchy from becoming dominant. The district officials of Bogotá feared his return from Egypt and sought to mould public opinion, attributing to the Liberator absurd monarchical plans.

A decree of Páez, the 13th of November, fixed January, 1827, as the time of the meeting of the Constitutional Congress of Venezuela. The return of Bolívar brought an end to the separatist movement.

In the meanwhile, the Liberator continued to cherish great ideas this realization of which he judged necessary to save his work: the enforcement of the Code of Chuquisaca, and the establishment of the Bolivian confederation. He suggested to Marshal Sucre the necessity of working as far as Buenos Aires "to establish our sound principles," and hoped that Chile, the La Plata, and Guatemala "may enter our project as allies." At the proper time he would announce his voyage to Colombia "which presents a combination most lamentable because of an excess of force badly managed, and an absolute sobriety in the government is the only remedy."[1] Before leaving Perú, Bolívar arranged, on July 1st, for the meeting of the electoral colleges, to examine the project of the Constitution, which that of Lima adopted, naming him president for life. Marshal Santa Cruz was designated as president of the Council of Government "which will exercise all the attributes of the Executive Power by delegation of His Excellency the Liberator Simón Bolívar." Two months later, a new decree gave the Council the right to exercise the command and prorogued the legislative body until the following year. A proclamation to the Peruvians, on the 3rd of September, announced "my love for the President and the Council of Government, worthy depositories of supreme power: my confidence in the magistrates who rule you; my dearest political thoughts in the project of the Constitution; and the custody of your inde-

---

[1] *To the Marshal of Ayacucho, Magdalena, May 12,* 1826.

pendence in the victors of Ayacucho. . . . You should fear
only one evil, and I offer you the remedy. Conserve the fear of
anarchy; such a generous terror will be your salvation!" On the
12th of the same month the Liberator arrived at Guayaquil,
where his first words were a condemnation of division: "We
have no longer a Venezuela, no longer a Cundinamarca: we are
all Colombians, or death will cover the deserts which anarchy
creates."

The personal acts of Bolívar in Perú were many and prolific.
He exempted the Indians from service without previous agreement and he regulated the pay of parochial duties, a fountain of
abuses; he abolished the title and authority of the caciques: he
settled the question of the disposal of the goods of the enemies
who had not emigrated; he directed the redivision of lands to the
natives; he extended liberty of commerce to foreigners; he ordered
that the mines abandoned by their owners because of the war
should revert to the State for their development: he founded hospitals and schools; he arranged for the construction of roads and
the organization of the army and the militia; he created a commission instructed to prepare projects of civil and criminal codes.[1]
A decree of the Liberator which may be considered as an application of the powers which he had given to his moral chamber, in
Angostura, to prepare lists of vicious citizens and of those who
were worthy of public duties, is also worthy of mention. This was
a *Junta of Qualifications* which was "charged to attest circum-
stantially the honesty, aptitude, and services of those who
might be public officials." This Junta should submit to the
Government monthly "a list of the qualified persons, expounding
simply the merit of those for the office for which they were considered worthy, so that the Government may choose from among
them without compromising the skill which it desires."[2]

The difference of the criteria between Bolívar and the Government of Bogotá was accentuated by the answers which both
gave to the reformist municipalities. "The Liberator has made
his profession of political faith in the Constitution presented to
Bolivia," wrote Secretary Pérez to the Municipal Council of
Guayaquil. "In it are recorded all the principles and the individual rights of the peoples; and in it are united in a most convenient fashion the guarantees of government with the widest
extension of liberty; never will there be found a greater measure
of social and individual security in any other political system
whatsoever."[1]   The Government, on its part, censured publicly
the initiative of the municipalities, which it called unconstitutional, declared that the executive power was powerless to revise

---

[1]Consult the list of the decrees promulgated by Bolívar during the year 1825.
Doc. X, 112. Consult also Larrazabal, II, 303.
[2]11th of January, 1825. *Doc. IX, 518.*
[1]*Lima, August 1,* 1826.

the laws, and declared that the events in Venezuela and Ecuador were not sufficient to bring about the reform of the Constitution, a reform besides, which would establish a dangerous and anarchical precedent.[1] In a note to the Intendant of Ecuador, Minister Restrepo impugned the vote of certain municipalities which sought to invest the Liberator with dictatorial powers. In it he declared that General Santander, "faithful to the sentiments and promises which he has made to the Colombian nation and to the liberal world, to support the political code which the people freely adopted and to enforce it during his magistracy, without permitting any violation whatever, will support the Constitution and will not attempt reforms and variations which solely affect him in his character as a private citizen." The Vice President wrote personally to the Liberator, confirming the ideas of his minister and begging him to support the Constitution and save the Republic. "The nation is not in anarchy," he declared, "the National Government exists and the law exercises its proper domain."[2] A long document which contained the account of the political events and a criticism of the plan to establish the Bolivian Constitution in Colombia, signed by the members of the Government, the courts of justice, by senators and deputies, army men, priests and other public officials were to be presented to the Liberator with an appeal to democratic sentiments. Let Bolívar be great, but let Colombia be free! was the synthesis of this document.[3]

For the moment the Liberator thought that it would be well to maintain the *status quo* as far as the departments of the South were concerned. His Secretary announced his approaching journey to Bogotá to the Government and added: "The Government is already established by the acts taken in the departments of Azuay, Quito and in this one. His Excellency has ordered that in them the administration shall continue on the same footing and under the same principles, without the least alteration, except that all must comply with what the State has decreed since the establishment of the constitutional régime."[4] But in spite of this, Bolívar persisted in believing that everything could be saved by the dictatorship. "In the South there exists complete uniformity," he wrote, "all the departments have named me dictator. Perhaps Colombia will do the same. The path toward a complete solution of affairs will then be unobstructed."[5]

---

[1]The reply of the Secretary of the Interior to Captain Montúfar commissioner of the Municipality of Quito. *September 5*, 1826. Consult also the note of this functionary to the Intendant of Guayaquil, *September 6*, 1826.

[2]*General Santander to the Liberator, October 8*, 1826.

[3]*Doc. X*, 688.

[4]*Guayaquil, September 18*, 1826. But in spite of this, the Liberator dictated a series of measures contrary to this declaration. *Vide* Restrepo, III, 549.

[5]*The Liberator to Don José de Larrea, Guayaquil, September 14*, 1826.

On November 14th, the Vice President received the Liberator
in public session, congratulated him on his return and his triumphs
in Perú, and offered him, for the support of the laws, "the most
sincere loyalty" ("*la lealtad mas acendrada de su corazôn*". "I
have concecrated my services," replied Bolívar, "to the independence and liberty of Colombia, and I shall always concecrate
them to the unity and supremacy of the laws."[1] In spite of these
protests, we shall see that the Liberator exercised illegal powers
from the first moment of his arrival in Bogotá. In a resolution
of the 19th of November, Bolívar declined to accept the resignation
of the Cabinet, "although I am not charged with the Executive
Power at the present time," believing that its members were
"experienced in the business of the Republic for the crisis for
which the said Secretaries nor the Executive Power itself are
responsible."[2] The action of the ministers in taking advantage of
the grave irregularities to present their resignations to one who
was, as yet, only President-elect of the Republic, is inexplicable
unless we have in mind the immense personal influence of the
Liberator who was considered the unquestioned arbiter of Colombia at the time.

Bolívar assumed the command of the army on the 23rd of
November and invested himself with the extraordinary powers
provided in the Constitution, "desiring on the one hand to act in
accordance with the confidence of the people, and, on the other,
to preserve the actual Constitution until the nation by legitimate
and competent means provides for its reform." The Vice President
was to exercise extraordinary powers in the part of the country
where the Liberator could not exercise them.[3] It was the first
step toward the dictatorship, the war against liberal opinion, the
accepting of the pronouncements of municipalities which desire
novelties.   The only "legitimate and competent" manner in
which to reform the fundamental law was to wait for the completion
of the ten years specified for such contingencies. It is equally
certain, also, that the situation did not permit one to suppose
that one could wait calmly for 1831, and Bolívar did not wish to
confound his cause, which was that of the people, with the banner
of a legality without prestige. In this circumstance is revealed one
of the characteristics least understood in the personality of the
Liberator. Without ceasing to be an aristocrat, he always sought
to lead the popular will, through instinct, identifying himself
with it. It is a phenomenon which has enabled Doctor Arcaya to
see in Bolívar a providentialist (*providencialista*). "If one studies
the history of Bolívar impartially," wrote this judicious author,
"it will be found that he believed in the doctrine that a government should possess unlimited powers, a tutelage exercised over

---

[1]*Gaceta de Colombia*, No. 266.
[2]*Doc. X*, 706.
[3]*Doc. X*, 724.

the nation in order to save it, in his opinion, from anarchy and disorder. In a word, in his own dictatorship, since he considered himself as called to a providential mission, fundamentally, the the same as the old conception of the Spanish monarchs."[1] And the English historian, Lorain Petré informed us: "He began to consider himself as a predestined saviour of the Republic. He understood his country. He found it lacking in capable rulers both in politics and in administration. As time passed, he seems to have become more and more attached to the idea that he was indispensible to the independence of South America."

It is difficult to admit that Bolívar was a providentialist in the ordinary sense of the word, that is to say, that he believed himself sent by God to fulfil a mission on the earth.[2] He considered himself Voltairian, and General Perú de Lacroix put these words into his mouth: "Let us leave to the superstitious the belief that Providence has sent me or destined me to redeem Colombia."[3] The patriotic mysticism of Bolívar, however, touches, at times, the boundaries of religious mysticism: we know his remarkable phrase to the dictator Alvarez: "Heaven has sent me to be the liberator of the oppressed peoples."[4] Bolívar believed in destiny, which he did not dare to call fatality, and which he considered in spite of his materialism, Providence. "Lamar has forever lost his senses," he wrote on a certain occasion, "they say that he is delirious; Foley has died mad; and all become mad when they seek to make war against me, for it is evident that there is a special Providence for me."[5] "My doctor has told me," he wrote to Briceño Méndez, "that my soul must cure itself of sickness in order to conserve my body, in the manner that God in creating me permitted this tempestuous revolution that I might live, engaged in working out by special destiny. If Madame de Stäel would lend me her pen, I might say with her that I am the Genius of the Tempest, as she applied this phrase to Napoleon."[6] In more than one page of this book it has been indicated that contradiction was frequent in Bolívar, and the lines which have just been cited are not in entire accord with the philosophical and religious ideas which it is customary to attribute to him. His political principles, his temperment, and the historical atavism explain, better than those mystic wanderings, why the Liberator believed himself the exponent of his race, the active force of the people, who labored for stability and progress. The conscience of his genius and the mediocrity of those who surrounded him transformed the instinctive stimulus into a concept, and Bolívar was convinced that, by

---

[1]Arcaya, *Libro citado, Bolívar*, 27.
[2]*Vide* the note of Blanco-Fombona on the assertions of Lorain Petré in his book *Bolívar by the Greatest Writers of America, Madrid*, 1914, 350.
[3]*Diary of Bucaramanga*, 87.
[4]*December 8*, 1814. Larrazabal, I, 345.
[5]*The Liberator to General Urdaneta, Quito, May 11*, 1829.
[6]*To Briceño Méndez*, June 4, 1828.

word and arm, it was his duty to lead his people into the future
through the destructions which he considered necessary. "I am
the pivot for those who love the national glory and the right of the
people," he wrote to Mendoza and to other friends during this
period when, as usual, the popular cause was combined with his.
And from Caracas, some time later, he exclaimed with great
dominating voice: "Venezuela is a hedgehog and my name is a
talisman. I know the ways of victory and the people live through
my justice."[1]

Taine, who found in Napoleon the emperor of Rome, would
likewise have found in Bolívar a Caesarian type. The democratic conceptions of the Liberator approached the Roman
principles and the influence which historical writings seem to have
filled his temperate spirit sensibly with the absolute idealism of the
Revolution and the philosophical postulates of the eighteenth
century. Bolívar took from Sulla—whom he resembled through
some of the conditions under which he legislated and through
his ideas on the function of the aristocracy—the patician pride and
the hatred of demagogues; as he took from Caesar, with a mutliple
genius, a broad and generous comprehension of popular rights and
the tendency to regularize them. The Napoleonic interpretation
of the sovereignty of the people, which is a Roman doctrine
fortified by the theories of the Revolution was, undoubtedly, of
great significance in the mind of the Liberator. When popular
acclaim placed him above the Fundamental Law of Colombia and
gave him the dictatorship, Bolívar would have been able to
justify himself saying, as did Napoleon III: I have abandoned
legality to enter into the right. The logic of such reasoning was
contumacious. For the Liberator there could not be, nor should
there have been any intermediary between him and the people; to
oppose his will was an act of disrespect to the national will; and as
the popular will may not seek anything but the social good, as
Rousseau put it, only the enemies of the people were the adversaries of Bolívar. The Liberator could have been the greatest of the
Greek tyrants, tutelary and magnanimous, who protected democracy and established order in equality. Many reasons promptly
showed him the convenience of neutralizing the elements of
anarchy with oligarchical institutions, but his spirit always cher-
ished the dream of a great equalitarian and stable democracy,
governed by his genius. A notable act, which showed the faculty
of adaptation of the man superior to all necessities and circumstances, was that which presented to us Bolívar, an unknown
entity to the average American, changed into the man of America
par excellence, reuniting the scattered elements of those societies
to manipulate them energetically and to attempt to give them
consistency and organization. The aims of the Liberator were
unattainable. His dreams, realized in another manner, crumbled

---

[1]*The Liberator to General Urdaneta, Caracas, Adril 11*, 1827.

because free peoples cannot be made from elements of slavery, according to the phrase of Simón Rodríguez.[1]

On taking upon himself the supreme power, Bolívar began a series of decrees on politics, administration, finance, and justice. He confided the direction of the provinces of the South, which today form the Republic of Ecuador, to a superior chief; under the pretext of economizing, he combined the civil command with the military in the provinces where the Government believed it useful; he prohibited juntas and assemblies without express legal authorization; to prevent Spanish espionage, he adopted severe measures for strangers who entered Colombia; he ordered the national militia organized. A circular of the Minister of the Interior recommended to publishers "a discreet and moderate exercise" of the liberty of the press. José Rafael Revenga passed from the Foreign Relations to the Secretarist General of the Liberator, in order to accompany him to Venezuela, on the 25th of November.

"The national vote," declared Bolívar to the people, "has obliged me to assume the supreme command; I abhor it mortally, for through it I am accused of ambition and of desiring a monarchy. What! Do you believe me so foolish as to descend? Do you not know the destiny of the Liberator is more sublime than the throne? . . . . Colombians! I again submit myself to the insupportable burden of the magistracy, because in moments of danger my disinterestedness would be cowardly, not moderate; but do not count on me for anything except that of giving back to the people their law and their sovereignty."[2] This sovereignty could not be recovered, according to Bolívar, except through a reform of the Constitution, weak and impotent, and not in the year 31, but in the following year, that is to say, as soon as the electoral colleges could decide when and where a convention might be held to draw up a new statute.[3] The ideas of immediate reform were strengthened, in the mind of the Liberator, by the deplorable state of affairs in Colombia, in the social and economic as well as in the political and the administrative. Certain provinces, in particular, presented a sad spectacle, Boyacá and Zulia, for example. When giving an account of it to the Government, through the medium of his Secretary, Bolívar took advantage of the opportunity to again criticise the existing institutions. "This examination of a part of the peoples of Colombia," declared Revenga, "made by a man of such penetration as the Liberator,

---

[1]The poet Schiller has said of the Duke Bernardo of Weimar, one of the most illustrious figures of the Thirty Years' War: "His spirit, noble and just, possessed an object almost beyond attainment; but we must not forget that those men of that temple were ruled by other laws than those which govern the actions and desires of the masses, and which arrest them and deny them liberty of action, authorize them to hope that which nobody dared to desire."
[2]*Bogotá, November 23,* 1826.
[3]*Decree of Marcaibo, December 19,* 1826.

and that which we say in another chapter of the three departments of the South, observations which could be extended to the
whole of the Colombian territory, prove a sad truth. The same
is true of the whole system of institutions and laws adopted by
our newly created republics when we do not confuse them with
the principle of the whole. We give them constitutions taken in a
large measure from the French Republic and the United States.
We copy laws which nations older and more highly civilized than
ours have adopted, who are weak, without considering our habits,
usages, customs, religion, preoccupations, and other local circumstances; we wish to make philosophers of Indians, negroes,
mulattoes, and white creoles who make up the ignorant mass of
our peoples; the result was a general inquietude and discomposure
with the new order of things. The same thing can be said of all the
republics born from the Spanish colonies. We have not even seen
in any of these philosopher-legislators, whom we elect for guides,
who considered what exists in our countries, and who did not
teach French politics or what the Constitution of the United
States of the North might show. As a result of this came inquietude
and discontent of the masses which were not diminished with time
after such great trials: from this came those periodic revolutions
in the new republics, where some ambitious politicians moved the
people by their will because they have no faith in the good of the
institutions and laws which rule us, and never love them: from
this came that frequent changing of constitutions, which often
makes them worse and brings no happiness to the peoples.   .   .   .
from this.   .   .   .   but it would be copious in the extreme to
complete the picture of the evils that our political and legislative
errors have produced. But what will be the remedy and the system
we ought to adopt? In no way do we consider ourselves capable of
assuring it: the problem is hedged in by difficulties under whatever
aspect it be considered, since the evil is already very old.   It
seems, however, that we ought to adopt some other method than
that of copying foreign laws, in general unadaptable to our
conditions, taking for bases deeds and experiences modified
through the republican principles of a moderate and rational
democracy."[1] Bolívar insisted on the need of adopting an American system, *his system*, without expressly stating it, on account of
the opposition which his Code found in Colombia he had become
cautious; and not the monarchy so considered by the keen eye of
certain historians, nor the illusory democracy from which our
countries have suffered for a century. The Liberator continued
disapproving of the monarchical proposals which, shielded by his
name, showed a lack of confidence among the republican elements,
and tended more and more to identify his cause with the popular
cause. He seemed to renounce the propoganda in favor of his
Constitution and proclaimed that he would submit to the national

----

[1]*Doc. X,* 678.

will freely expressed. His letter to Páez was decisive: "You know very well that Guzmán only went to Lima to propose to me, at your request, the destruction of the Republic, in imitation of Bonaparte, as you yourself stated in your own letter which, in the original, I have in my possession. Through Colonel Ibarra and Urbaneja you have proposed for me a crown which I have properly refused. Likewise, General Mariño, Carabano, Ribas, and others of these gentlemen, have written to me in the same sense, insisting that I make myself a sovereign prince. Everybody knows this in Perú and Colombia, and for this reason, it is a crime to attribute to me such a diabolical project, which I have shunned as the fever of vilest ambition of some satelites. After these proposed perfidies, the affairs occurred which have placed the Republic in its present condition. Then, these gentlemen of the conspiracy spoke of federation, and Guayaquil requested of me, in Lima, such a system. I replied to Guayaquil that my political views were given in my Constitution for Bolivia."[1]

But the conservation of extraordinary authority was, in the mind of the Liberator, the only guaranty of safety. He went to Venezuela to attempt the reparation of his great work of unification, attacked at the time by the revolt in Valencia and by the tortuous politics of Bogotá. The Liberator, abandoning the legal formulas, which he considered useless or even dangerous, for the time, personally assumed the formidable task of conserving Colombian integrity, and risked his reputation and the splendid glory of his life in the enterprise. One may censure Bolívar for having, before he and Santander had been chosen by the electoral colleges and before they had taken the oath of office, ordered the latter to continue as vice president, at the same time that he took for himself the supreme command;[2] but it is worth noting that Venezuela did not wish to give obedience to the Central Government, and that only the prestige and personal authority of Bolívar could suppress the dissenters. One may censure him because, knowing, as he did, the results of the politics of Santander and the intrigues of his friends, he left them the power and the opportunity of endangering the Republic; but Bolívar could not evict them from the national palace. On the other hand, it was impossible for him to place himself in opposition to so powerful a party, capable of causing numerous difficulties for the Government. Some have attributed the magnanimity of the Liberator toward Páez to weakness, forgetting that Bolívar, attacked by the Granadians and without constitutional aid, needed the chiefs of Venezuela, the men who had made independence and had the sympathies of the army and the people, to defend himself and carry

---

[1] *The Liberator to General Páez, Cúcuta, December 12*, 1826.
[2] *Official Note to General Santander, Cúcuta, December 12*, 1826.

out his projects.[1] In 1826 the Liberator pardoned, a good stroke
of politics, a rebellion which under other circumstances he would
have punished with death. Nine years before, Mariño escaped
the gallows because the Bolivarian clemency could be exercised
without danger to the cause of the Republic. General Páez now
enjoyed a pardon that necessity demanded, and of which the
glorious plainsman soldier was personally the creditor. Bolívar
tried to save national unity, patronizing the oligarchical separatists
of Venezuela and the Santanderian separatists of Bogotá, and it
was here that his task was particularly difficult.

---

[1]"Only the activity of Venezuela should be laid to the demagogues of New
Granada," declared, in 1828, General Brisceño Méndez. *The Diary of Bucaramanga*, 242.

Bolívar and Venezuela

THE sequence of events in Venezuela and their effect upon the rest of the country during the year 1826 showed that the "profound misery" and the "sad consequences" of which General Santander,[1] twelve months before complained, came from a cause more abstruce and complicated than the caprice of the conspirators, or the sordid ambition of General Páez. The Republic of Colombia concealed, under its opulent appearance of glory, a precarious vitality. It is puerile to condemn Vice President Santander for his "hate" of all that was Venezuelan, and to attribute to his Machiavellianism the preparation for the separatist movement. It is also puerile to place on the shoulders of the "poor centour" of Las Queseras the heavy weight of the dissolution, even when the robust talent of Eloy Guillermo González was engaged in it, or to place it on the aversion of the political adversaries of Páez. Fragile armor was that of Colombia when the dangerous designs of Santander succeeded in piercing it, when the blow of the lance of the plainsman was sufficient to demolish it! No one man can lose or save a people, when that people is not capable by its own virtue of losing or saving itself. The laws of the collective evolution dominate every personal act, according to the proved principle of degenerate psychology. It is not possible to deny the influence of the superior man in political and social phenomena, but the action of the personage requires, as in the case of Napoleon, a country constitutionally disposed to approve the initiative of a genius. I submit that that influence is not sufficient when Bolívar exercised it in our America, whose social state was an almost absolute anarchy, the inevitable struggle between great detrimental elements. The Liberator was hardly great enough not to fall with his work, and to conserve, in the disaster, the moral elements of which Mitre spoke.[2]

When Bolívar returned to assume the presidency, in November, 1826, the Republic was in a sad condition. On the verge of bankrupcy, education abandoned, politics and administration served as an instrument of vile personal quarrels. New Granada, discontented, Venezuela, revolutionary, Ecuador, in ferment. The Constitution of Cúcuta enjoyed no national prestige. The Liberator, whose name was still the banner of the peoples, had, in order to save Colombian unity, to disinterest himself from what in that supreme moment was not the public interest; and believed that such interest was divided equally among all the factions, those that

---

[1]Gil Fortoul, I, 390. *Vide* the *Official Note of General Santanper to the Senate*, *January 28*, 1825. *Doc. IX*, 525.
[2]*Obra Citado*, VI, 235.

137

supported the laws to preserve the command and those who rebelled to usurp it.

Of the men of the Independence, the illustrious were supporters of Bolívar. Urdaneta, in Zulia, always observed a worthy and powerful conduct. He did not mix his name in the tumults and in disturbances. His admiration for the Liberator and his convictions induced him to work candidly to give him a crown that he judged necessary to reestablish order in the State.[1] Bermudez, head of the department of the Orinoco, prepared early against the revolt of Valencia and came at the beginning of the war to the defense of the Constitution. The restless oriental awaited the coming of Bolívar. Flores, in the South, was Bolivarian, as was Soublette, at that time Minister of War. Montilla remained loyal in Cartagena. Mariño promised in November to support the integrity of Colombia in Cumaná. Sucre, President of Bolivia, was the loving son of the Liberator and the most brilliant hope of the country. Even General Páez, unexpected chief of the oligarchs of Caracas, was fundamentally a supporter of Bolívar and his influence on the Apurean epoch permitted him to meet the separatist movement of Venezuela, established by the lawyers and the jurists who had the virtue of inducing the picturesque fury of the hero of Carabobo. The adversaries of the Liberator were, on the other hand, General Santander and other Granadian militarists. As for the civilian chiefs, those of New Granada sympathized with Santander, calling him the champion of legality and the real center of the particular interests of Cundinamarca. In Venezuela, illustrious men like Peñalver and Mendoza, gravitated in the Bolivarian orbit. In short, dissensions and intrigue extended farther and farther, weakening the Republic in the crisis.

The people, those who could be called the people, in Colombia were the toy of the factions, and meekly lent its name to the most contrary intentions. However, in the heart of the masses there was a profound sentiment of admiration for the Liberator, developed through fifteen years of flashing glory.

Bolívar finally took the last step to preserve his popularity and with it the integrity of Colombia. He proclaimed that the will of the people would be the norm of his conduct, and as I have said seemed to renounce his plan of imposing his Constitution, which shortly before he considered the only means of salvation for the country. The Liberator wished to practice in Colombia the politics which he outlined to Santa Cruz for Perú, where the reaction was raging. "I counsel you," he wrote to the Marshal, "to abandon yourself in the torrent of patriotic sentiments, and in place of being sacrificed by the opposition put yourself at its head."[2] The Liberator went to exploit his prestige for the benefit

---

[1]Vide Villanueva, *The Empire of the Andes*, 193.
[2]*To Marshal Santa Cruz, Popayán, October 26*, 1826.

of the country, and his aim placed him immediately into conflict with the defenders of the Constitution. Restrepo explained how they received the decree of Maracaibo, which was declared as illegal and anti-political. In fact, Bolívar never governed constitutionally. Whenever Congress elevated him to the presidency, in Augostura, in Cúcuta, in Bogotá, he hastened to turn over the civil command to the vice-presidents and, under the pretext of conducting war, always maintained his character as supreme chief, in accordance with his autocratic tendencies and the necessities of the situation. In 1813, in giving to Don Cristóbal Mendoza his instructions for governing Mérida, the Liberator told him: "The republic being in complete dissolution, the Government of the province is fully authorized to work according to the circumstances, without considering the letter of laws and constitutions, having for its only principle and rule of conduct: the safety of the people is the supreme law."[1] After Boyacá Santander was named vice-president of Cundinamarca: "My instructions and the law which invested me," he wrote, "contain only one rule: to free the country from Spanish domination at all cost."[2] In Guayana, the famous Council of State did not delay in falling into disuse, and when it was convoked to arrange regulations for the conduct of elections, for some time the honorable body was good for nothing.[3] In Perú, Bolívar was dictator. In Colombia, on first coming in contact with the Constitution, he took from it what he wanted: extraordinary powers. "He never sought monarchy," affirmed Restrepo, "in spite of which fact he loved the life of power and the command without being subject to laws."[4] The question then is whether the dictatorship of the Liberator was not more useful to those people than the constitutionality which his enemies defended? I should not dare to say that Bolívar did not favor laws. On the contrary, no one felt the need for respectful and effective legal organization than he. For the Liberator, however, there could be no order with out his dictatorship and no stability for the future without his system. Bolívar can never be accused of having placed his personal interest before the superior interest of society.

---

[1]*Doc. IV*, 577.

[2]*Suggestions for the Memoirs of General Santander. Archivo Santander*, I, 49

[3]Restrepo, II, 482. *The Diary of Bacaramanga*, 143.

[4]Restrepo, IV, 416.

[5]Samper believed that the all-absorbing Caesarism of the Liberator was the cause and the origin of our military régimes during a century. "Bolívar," he wrote, "was the founder and the chief of the school of dictatorships which has been the bane of Spanish Colombia. He inaugurated the rule of the sword where the greatest need was the rule of law, and the Revolution, facinating to the ardent dreams of the Liberator, receded disorganized, lost its moral force, its faith and its convictions and degenerated into those tortuous paths of military imperialism." *Obra citada*, 192.

On the absolute tendencies of Bolívar, consult also Ezequiel Rojas, *The Oath of the 25th of September*. A great many have studied attentively the policito-

In Maracaibo, near the scene of events, the Liberator offered
"to call the people to deliberate calmly on its welfare and its
own authority. . . . Very soon, this year, you will be
consulted about when, where, and under what circumstances you
wish to hold a great National Convention. There the people will
freely exercise its omnipotence, there it will decree its fundamental
laws. It alone knows best its own good, and is the master of its
lot, which is not true of a leader, a party, or faction. He who
seeks to put himself in the place of the poeple is a tyrant and his
control of power a usurpation."[1] Note, once more, the care which
Bolívar took to flatter the people with whose representation he
believed himself invested and to whom, at least, he left the
illusion of sovereignty. Convinced that in America the people
was not a conscious and efficient entity, and considering opinion
as an artificial product, manipulated by a group of individuals,
arbiters of Roman-like factions, the Liberator, however, spoke
as a revolunionist of 89, imbued with the doctrines of popular
sovereignty, the last phase of his own Caesarism, and flattered
the multitude with the language that an orator employs before an
illustrious democracy. "No people is," he declared in September,
1826, to the inhabitants of Guayaquil, in rebellion, "culpable,
because the people do not desire anything but justice, repose, and
liberty. The dangerous or false sentiments ordinarily belong to
their leaders; they are the cause of public calamities."

To the insurrectionists of Venezuela, the Liberator presented
himself as an emperor. "The national vote," he wrote to Páez,
"has been one alone: reforms and Bolívar. No one has challenged
me, no one has degraded me. Who, then, will snatch the reigns of
power from me? Only your friends, yours! What does not the
whole of Venezuela owe me? You yourself, do you not owe me
existence? . . . . I want to know whether or not you obey
me, and if my country recognizes me as its chief. God does not
permit them to dispute my authority in my own home, like
Mohammed, whom the country adored and his compatriots
fought." He repeated his newest intentions, which the political
condition of Colombia and the tendencies of the enemy groups
required: "Believe that I do not desire nor ever shall desire to
have one party triumph over another, neither in the Convention

---

social evolution of America, and know how emperical is the opinion of Samper.
The brilliant professor at the Sorbonne, which one encounters under the pseudonym
of Jean Pérez, believed, on the contrary, that Bolívar "has reduced the period
of the greatest power of the militarists in America, has reduced the rivalries of
politicians generally, and, not desiring to follow their example, which his superior
ability justified, did not use this method as a pretext for his ambitions. He felt
that nothing was more easily done than to establish a monarchy, the frequency
of the movement of which, during a long time, has served to accept the dictatorship in the South American republics." *Bulletin of American Bibliography*, October
1, 1915, Paris.
[1]*Proclamation of December 16*, 1826.

nor outside of it. I shall oppose the federation; neither do I prefer to establish the Bolivian Constitution. I wish only that the law shall unite the citizens, that liberty will let them work, and that wisdom will guide them, so that they may accept my resignation and let me go away, very far away from Colombia."[1] And as Bolívar had brought several divisions from New Granada and the people of Venezuela rose up, acclaiming him, General Páez submitted and the separatists applauded his revindication. The revolutionists, Carabano among them, began to believe that the movement did not have popular support.[2] In truth, the name of the Liberator and his skillful politics averted civil war.

The decree of Puerto Cabello conceded general amnesty to the disturbers, and named Páez Superior Chief of Venezuela and Mariña Commandant General of Maturin.[3] "I do not know what has happened," declared the Liberator. "Colombians! Forget what you know of the days of sorrow and let silence root out your memory of them." A little later, Bolívar wrote an equivocal phrase: "General Páez, far from being culpable, is the savior of the country," and gave the rebel chief, in Caracas, definite proof of his confidence by giving him the sword that had redeemed his brothers. The will of the Liberator moved suddenly from Bogotá to Caracas, the axis of the defense of the unity of Colombia, because the former was determined to help itself with force which Venezuela could give it against the pernicious tendencies of its Granadian enemies. In Venezuela, the revolutionists attacked the Government of Santander, but put their fate in the hands of Bolívar; in New Granada, the inviolability of the Constitution was preserved, but it plotted against the power of the Liberator, and to destroy it the integrity of Colombia was impugned. The methods of Bolívar reestablished peace in the seditious departments, but exasperated the hatred of his adversaries. The Santanderian press redoubled its attacks, and from then on the two enemy bands fought without quarter. Some one has lamented the fact, perhaps with reason, that Bolívar should have permitted himself to be carried by circumstances to the point of becoming the "rival" of Santander. The Liberator, however, always remained in the moral zone which suited his character. "The country and its welfare," he wrote to Colonel Blanco, "take from me the time which Santander uses in arousing passions very foreign in a magistrate."[4]

It is possible that the conduct of Bolívar, who protected the conspirators of Venezuela, without disguising his sympathies for

---

[1] *To General Páez, Coro, December 23,* 1826.
[2] Austria, *Report to the Government, October 13,* 1826.
[3] January 1, 1827.
[4] The break between Bolívar and Santander dates from the reply of his to Bustamente. "'The great and frank soul of the Liberator,'" declared Restrepo, "condescended to busy itself by writing articles for the papers and in other ways what the qualities of General Santander were." IV, 23.

the cause of reforms, lent himself to the reproach of the constitutionalists; but, on the other hand, it is evident that the
means which put an end to the agitation were most fortunate.
The Minister of the Interior recognized it in his report to the
Congress. "Order and law have reestablished their position in all
the departments of the Republics, as the President Liberator
himself has said. The frightful danger of a civil war has been
averted and from one extremity of Colombia to the other we have
now only brothers. This happy termination of so dangerous a
crisis as this which the Republic has suffered is due to the favorable
influence and power the Liberator President."[1] It is the voice of a
prudent and of circumspect citizen like Restrepo, which justifies the
Bolivarian politics in the name of the interest of the national
peace.

While his enemies poison their politics in Bogotá, Bolívar, in
Venezuela, repaired the public administration. The condition in
those provinces was deplorable. In giving an account of it to the
Central Government, the Secretary of the Liberator ingeniously
declared: "It is incomprehensible how in such a general disobedience of the laws, that there should be any to complain of
their effects."[2] Bolívar established councils to improve agriculture, improve the administration of justice, to found hospitals,
create an organization to direct manumission, increase the
revenues, benefit commerce and industry, and, above all, to
reorganize and endow public instruction.

The Liberator always gave especial attention to the education of the people, and his measures, frequently dictated on the
day following a victory, prove his interest in civilization and
social reform. In Santa Fé, after Boyacá, he made the convent
of the Capuchins over into a school for orphans and paupers, and
prepared a great many similar measures. He did the same in
Quito, and when in Trujillo del Perú, he was organizing the army
of Junín, he took time to establish a university and a large number
of schools in cities and towns. "But above all his measures by
which he established, in the capital of each department, a normal
school on the Lancastrian system, were then as always, as I have
already said, based upon his great desire for the education of all
social classes, and to this end he ordered that the children of the
poor should receive free instruction at the expense of the government."[3] The system of education that Lancaster, whom Bolívar
knew in London, in 1810, tried to establish in America, won the
approval of the Liberator and "the first sum of money that the
Peruvian Congress appropriated for the benefactors of the
country was the twenty thousand pesos which it sent to the
famous Lancaster for furthering the education of the youth of

[1]*Report to the Congress of Colombia, February 16*, 1827.
[2]*Puerto Cabello, December 31*, 1826.
[3]O'Leary, *Narrative*, II, 328.

Caracas. This amount had to be paid, strangely enough, much later because the agents of Perú in London could not meet such large bills of exchange."[1]

"Write for me," declared Bolívar in his letter to his sister Maria Antonia, on the eve of leaving for Upper Perú, "to those in the North, charged with the education of young Fernando Bolívar, stressing carefully the attention with which I wish my nephew to be educated. Let him learn the classical and modern languages, mathematics, history, morality, the fine arts, etc. An uneducated man is an incomplete being. Instruction is the happiness of life, and the ignorant, who is always closest to be immersed in the mud of corruption, invariably falls soon into the obscurity of servility. "And in this same period, in the instructions he gave to the executives of Perú, he likewise revealed his desire of instructing and civilizing our youth. "The Council of Government," he ordered, "will send ten youths to England with commissioners or alone, so that they may there learn the European tongues, public law, political economics, and whatever subjects a man of the state must know. These youths should be from twelve to twenty years old. They should be chosen from the most distinguished for native talent, application, good conduct, and intellectual aptitude. They ought to present also a good figure as one of the qualities necessary in persons who are to be employed in the foreign service."[2]

On his trip to Upper Perú, which had just established itself as an independent State, with the name of the Republic of Bolívar, the Liberator was accompanied by his old master Don Simón Rodríguez, to whom he gave the title of Director General of Education and Charity, and to whom he intrusted the task of establishing schools in cities and towns.[3] In addition, he assigned to Don Simón thirty thousand pesos in order to found a model school at Chuquisaca. Unfortunate, declared Sucre, Rodríquez committed, in spite of being a good man of talent and wisdom, many absurdities. The Marshal could never know what his plans of instruction and charity were.[4]

[1]*Ibidem*, 348. *Vide* the letters of Lancaster to Bolívar from July 1, 1824 and from Bolívar to Lancaster from March 16, 1825. O'Leary, *Doc. VII*, 242.

[2]O'Leary, *Narrative*, II, 353.

[3]Lozano y Lozano, *The Teacher of the Liberator*, 95.

[4]Nihilist and revolutionary, of a disgraceful socialism, by which all authority was tyranny and all rules oppression, Señor Rodríguez, by the extravagence of his life, has been declared partly insane by Grasset. Pollyglot, philologist, subject to hallucinations and fits by reason of his views and his belief was sceptical. Influenced by the educational methods of *Émile*, as Mancini has it, improved upon the system of Lancaster and sought vainly to put into practice his own theories. Don Simón confessed his failure. "I thought I knew something, but when I talk on strange subjects no one understands me, and I pass for one who is mad." Recently Doctor Vicente Lecuna, in the *Archive of the Liberator*, found some pages which contain certain pedagogical ideas of Bolívar. It is claimed that it is not difficult to detect the influence of Rodríguez in the spirit and point of view in

The arrival of the Liberator in Caracas coincided with the selection of the rector of the University, a position for which, according to the Statutes, there should be chosen a theologian, a lawyer, or a physician. On January 23, he decreed the repeal of this regulation, and the celebrated Vargas ascended to the Rectorship. From that event dates, in effect, the University of Caracas. Negroes, mulattoes, Protestants, Jews, foreigners as well as nationals were admitted to its halls. The studies were organized on a liberal and scientific basis. The study of experimental science was begun; and the Institute was provided with its own revenues. All reforms were effected through the interest of the Liberator, whom "Vargas informed almost daily of the minutes which were being edited."[1]

In the midst of this, Bolívar observed the political events. On February 6th he sent to the Congress his resignation of the presidency in these words.:

"The suspectors of a military usurpation demand my head and trouble Colombian hearts. The jealous republicans know me only to consider me as a secret terror, because history tells them all men of my kind have been ambitious. In vain does the example of Washington seek to defend me. I grieve between the agonies of my fellow citizens and the judgments that may await me in posterity. Even I cannot feel myself innocent of ambition. I wish to free myself from the claws of this fury to liberate my countrymen from inquietudes and assure myself after my death of a memory that liberty may deserve."

Santander then asked Bolívar to free him from the burden of government because he was ill, disgusted, and calumniated. It disturbed him to be charged with authority for the purpose of attacking "this insidious plots of his enemies and of those dissatisfied with the constitutional system to add to the incision of the Republic discord between the National Government and Your Excellency."[2] Although General Santander did not possess the grandeur of the Liberator, both excelled in political caution.

The Vice President cannot be defended, even though his conduct with respect to Venezuela, and general Páez, the original source of the disturbances, was moderated and guided by constitutional precepts, and judging him by his letter of June 12, 1826, which certainly was a severe rebuke for the disturbers. Santander, who condemned the revolutionists of Venezuela through the mouth of Restrepo, Minister of the Interior,[3] approved in person and through the means of Soublette, Minister of War, the act of Bustamente in Lima, who destroyed military discipline and the prestige of Colombia.[4] In fine, the Granadian

methods of teaching and training of the youth. A decree of May 8, 1829, by Bolívar, in Quito, made several changes in the plan of organization of the University of Caracas.

[1]Laureano Villanueva, *Biography of Doctor José Vargas*, 82.
[2]*Santander to the Liberator, Bogotá, April 30,* 1827.
[3]*Manifesto of July 12,* 1826.
[4]Letter of General Santander and the Report of General Soublette to the Commandant José Bustamente, March 15, 1827. Santander declared that the

general did not possess the exceptional ability with which his friends credited him, and it is probable that neither did he have the diabolical perversity which the Bolivarians attributed to him. His position was notable because circumstances placed him in opposition to the Liberator, as representative of the liberal tendency, at the head of a powerful party, exploited by rhetoricians and orators. History will, without doubt, note the falsity of his conduct toward Bolívar and the subtilties with which he defended him before posterity. Inspirer and supporter of the press which in Bogotá insulted the President, calling him hypocrite and tyrant and attributing to him the discord and the lack of discipline, General Santander, on renouncing the magistracy, did not hesitate to say to the Congress: "The gratitude which I owe to my country, to its representatives, and to the Liberator will forever be dear to my heart. The liberty of Colombia shall be while I live the object of my political cult, of my struggles, and of my sacrifices; Bolívar will be the object of my profound affection and admiration."[1] In all his public documents, Santander showed himself reconciled to the man whose creature he was, and proclaimed his good intentions to reestablish order and to preserve Colombian integrity.[2]

Bolívar suffered, at that time, from a crisis of Venezuelanism. Before the diaster of Colombia, there was born in him, so genuinely American, a paternal love for his land, for his own dear country, which had given him glory to inundate the Continent, and whose sons he believed would be the last to adandon him. "There are really only Venezuelans," he declared to General Salom, "and unfortunates are we if we venture more than an opinion."[3] He thought that only a god could remedy things and wrote with sadness:[4]

"You shall then see if I were the cause of the public unhappiness and if I were culpable and if I were prejudicial to the Republic. Then it will be seen

---

official note to the rebel was "examined in the Council of Government and approved unanimously." *Representation to the Liberator President*, January 25, 25, 1828. Restrepo confirmed the act and condemned it "as a grave error." IV, 19.

[1] *General Santander to the Congress of Colombia*, April 25, 1827.

[2] *Vide* the measured judgment of Gil Fortoul on General Santander, I, 442. It would seem almost extraordinary that the Vice President, whom Don Miguel Antonio Caro called with a grain of disdain, "a mixture of Venezuelan military and of a Granadian lawyer," found, like Páez, odium in the lawyers, which he reproved later in his struggle against the Liberator. The "man of laws" became singularly "general" when he wrote to Bolívar: "Do you fear serving among some ingrate men, interested and enemies of the red coats. I have here six or eight of such men whom with pleasure I will turn over to you to be hanged." *Archivo Santander*, III, 19. And more, tolerance and the love of liberty were qualities common to all the liberators. With reference to the attacks of Rafael Diego Mérida, in 1829, Urdaneta wrote to Páez: "Here there is nothing new, except the papers of the one-eyed Mérida who has come to us from Caracas. These serve to molest and I desire to have you deny them a salary at least. They ought to be given another good drubbing." *Bogotá, May 7, 1829*.

[3] *To General Salom, Caracas, April 17, 1827*.

[4] *To General Urdaneta, Caracas, April 18, 1827*.

whether the administration of Santander has sown all the seeds of crime and evil. I think only of saving Venezuela: if I achieve that I shall have done enough."

Bolívar declined to propose a plan for the reforms which were to come, and as for the division of Colombia into seven departments, preserving the unity, as recommended he replied; "I cannot approve it (the plan), nor any other, because I am quite determined to do only what the people may itself wish, as I have more than once declared."[1]

Soon, however, the sedition of Lima by the third Colombian division and the attitude of the Government of Bogotá stirred his old energy to reproach the chief officials and to write to the Minister of War that "the Liberator has been alarmed by such overwhelming evidence of the decay of the morality of the Government"[2] and to General Santander that he, Bolívar, "must hasten to prevent the dismemberment of the Republic and the ridicule of its laws, and is resolved to march against the traitors, who, after having established the splendor of the Republic, seek to ruin it. . . . The Liberator, then, will march upon that city and will not believe that he has completed his duty as a soldier of the country until he sees it again tranquil and capable of freely exercising its destinies."[3] And in the execution of such proposals, Urdaneta and Solom received orders to move with their troops, the first toward Cúcuta, the latter toward Cartagena. The Vice President had asked the Congress, in his message of the 25th of May, pardon for the guilty in the insurrection of Lima and in the events of Guayquil which were its results.

In the midst of the anarchy which reigned supreme throughout the territory of the Republic, from the provinces of Venezuela, which had attained a true autonomy, to the South, nearly segregated, according to the expression of Bolívar, the only hope of salvation was the personal prestige of the Liberator. In fact, the influence of the man whom the country admired and whom La Fayette identified, at that time, with liberty itself, was considerable. In Colombia, his power and his glory weighed upon the most embittered detractor and Doctor Soto declared in the Senate: "I am not so lacking in sense as to try to make myself notable as the enemy of the Liberator, because my memory can never forget the ingenious fable of the struggle of men against the gods. . . ." But Bolívar was discouraged and ill. He never had confidence in the stability of these peoples, but the picture he then saw was frightful and filled his soul with unalloyed bitterness. One after the other he abandoned, as useless, the ideas which they believed for the moment capable of saving Colombia. At the time he thought of the Great Convention. "If my resignation is not accepted," he wrote to José Rafael

[1] *To General Urdaneta, March 6, 1827.*
[2] *Secretary Revenga to General Soublette, Caracas, April 18, 1827.*
[3] *Secretary Revenga to General Santander, Caracas, June 19, 1827.*

Arboleda, "I could submit to the public will, but not because of that could I cease to insist that the differences be settled that agitate the people by means of the Great Convention, and that certain reforms be undertaken for those who claim they will establish a new order of things, which, though not absolute, at least will satisfy the opposing interests that are now fighting and would eventually tear down the Republic."[1] At intervals he exclaimed: "I see no elements with which to build, and consider the Republic fallen. If I desert, I shall feel very sad, and if I remain, it will be to attend the funeral of Colombia. What a misfortune!"

The Liberator confided his desolation and his fears to Sir Robert Wilson: "Our Americas cannot always go well because they belong to half of the planet: when one part does well, another is out of harmony, and you know that liberty ordinarily finds itself sick from anarchy. My constancy, however, is not dismayed and is even fortified by adversity, but there are difficulties not to be conquered by one citizen. A monarch enjoys privileges and rights of sufficient authority to punish evil and promote the welfare of his subjects: a republican magistrate, constituted a slave of the people, is nothing but a victim. Laws, on one side, entangle him, and circumstances, on the other, arrest him. So it is that which disturbs me. I could overthrow them, but I do not wish to pass on to posterity as a tyrant. Bad laws and a bad administration have broken the Republic: it is ruined by war: after blood has poisoned us, corruption has come to leave us with barely enough hope of betterment. . . . A dictatorship would be capable of saving the country, but a dictatorship is the danger of the Republic."[2] Given the impetus and authoritative nature of Bolívar, these reflections have an enormous merit and are sufficient to confound his detractors. Let them explain, besides, the vacillations, the weakening of the formidable energy of the Liberator, and the abandonment of the projects which until then he had believed the means of saving the country. Bolívar knew how difficult and grave was the problem of rescuing Colombia and America from the abyss to which the fascinating mirage of democracy had carried them, and confessed his impotence, also to Wilson: "They do not know in Europe how hard it is to maintain equilibrium in some of these regions. What might be said of my services would seem a fable, for I am like the wretch condemned to carry an enormous weight to the top to have it fall with him again into the abyss. I find myself struggling against the combined forces of a world: I am alone on my part and the struggle, by the same token, is most unequal: so, I ought to be conquered. History

[1] To José Rafael Arboleda, Caracas, April 20, 1827.
[2] To Sir Robert Wilson, Caracas, April 30, 1827.

itself shows me no example able to encourage me, nor does the
fable teach us how to solve this prodigious problem. What they
tell us of Bacchus and Hercules is in reality less than is demanded
of us. Can one man alone succeed in constituting half a world?
And a man such as I?''[1]

America was convulsed with anarchy. Liberal opinion and
ambitious politicians attributed to the Liberator projects for
continental domination, and the propoganda in the press took on
extraordinary breadth and violence. Perú and the Argentine
brought pressure to bear on the Government of Chuquisaca to
compel it to remove Colombian auxiliaries from Bolivian territory.
Bolívar was accused of casting glances toward this Republic,
declared the Secretary of State of Bolivia to the Commandant
of the Auxiliary Division in September.[2] The press and the
Liman Government employed a language of invectives. The
Liberator wrote to Marshal Santa Cruz: "The Constitution of
Bolivia does not matter to me: if they do not want it, let *them
burn it*, as they say. I do not care for the author when grave
problems weigh down humanity."[3]

On the same day, he wrote to the Marshal of Ayacucho: "This
New World is nothing more than a restless sea which will not
become calm for many years. Some attribute part of the evil to
me, others all of it, and I, so that they may not blame me more
culpable, do not wish to enter into it any further. I shall conform to the part they assign me in this diabolical division."[4] A
new letter which he sent to Wilson was pathetic and dolorous:
"I shall avenge myself according to the tactics of the parties: I
shall flee from them so that they may perish in following me.
Then they will know whether I was useful to my country and
whether I preferred liberty to everything else. . . . .Up until
now, I have been blind to prayers, but I think I shall be so no longer, because I cannot bear to suffer the opprobium of hearing myself called tyrant and usurper. I know how to endure everything,
except that. The horror that I have of oppression does not permit
me to be a victim of this sacrifice. This is my dominating passion,
and I cannot forget it, and my greatest weakness is my love of
liberty: this love will lead me to forget even glory itself. I prefer
to pass for everything, to succumb in my hope, to pass for a
tyrant and even to appear suspicious. My impetuous passion, my
greatest aspiration is to win the name of *lover of liberty*. The rôle
of Brutus is my delirium, and that of Sulla, though saviour of
the Roman Constitution, seems to me execrable. I have dis-
coursed much on this point because my beloved aide-de-camp,
your worthy son, has asked me to tell you what are my thoughts.

---

[1] *To the Same, Caracas, May 26*, 1827.
[2] *September 29*, 1827.
[3] *To Marshal Santa Cruz, Caracas, June 8*, 1827.
[4] *To the Marshal of Ayucucho, Caracas, June 8*, 1827.

What you were pleased to write me with respect to the Bolivian Constitution fills me with satisfaction: this is my youngest child, I love it with tenderness and sorrow because it is unfortunate: I entreat you to protect it, as a victim, from the fury of the soldiers. It may be blameworthy, but its punishment exceeds cruelty: not even good faith has saved it, its innocence and artlessness have led it to torture."[1]

The National Congress considered, the 6th of June, the resignation of the Liberator, and twenty-four voices were raised to accept it. The historians find that there did not exist the unanimity which acclaimed his glory and his name in the days of Ayacucho. Neither was the resignation of General Santander accepted, and the Congress called on Bolívar to take charge of the command. From that day personalisms sprang up in Parliament, which divided the country.

The Liberator decided, at last, to leave Caracas and by decree of the 3rd of July conferred on Páez the civil and military administration of the departments of Venezuela, Maturín, and the Orinoco, with the title of Superior Chief of Venezuela. Two days later, on leaving for Bogotá, "where his friends awaited him," he notified the Venezuelans that he was marching to the South again and promised them that he would renounce the command when the Convention reconvened, to live on the soil of his fathers.[2]

After having pacified Venezuela, by the strength of his prestige and by his authority as President of the Republic, Bolívar went to subdue the departments of Ecuador and to dissolve the Granadian factions which, under constitutional forms, worked against the unity of Colombia. Complicated and difficult problems arose, leading to bitter censure and warm defense. The vindication of the Liberator and the excuse for his errors, if he then committed errors, consisted in the condition of Colombia and America during these years from 1826 to the dissolution of the Great Republic. Fighting alone against half of the world, according to his own words, the prodigious catastrophe was doubtless the highest eulogy to his genius. In the immensity of the struggle, there disappeared the obscure corners, the worthless detail, the suspicious lines, in order to leave an *ensemble* full of greatness and harmony, working with noble intention, in the midst of the heart-breaking pettiness of things and of the vileness of the men. No matter to which one he turned, to Caracas, Bogotá, or to Guayaquil, Bolívar brought with him the unity of Colombia crowned with his glory. Páez, rebellious, instrument of the rancorous factions and of an oligarchic power; Santander,

---

[1]*To Sir Robert Wilson, Caracas, June 16,* 1827.
[2]*Proclamation of July* 4, 1827. General Páez declared that Bolívar, on leaving, believing the dissolution of Colombia inevitable, counselled the cessation of opposition to the adoption of the federal system in Venezuela and recommended the Bolivian Constitution. *Autobiography,* 1, 375.

the old partisan of the life presidency, Bolivar's friend and co-worker,[1] seized suddenly with the delights of liberty and of power, who practiced Jacobinism in the presidential office;[2] the petty disturbances of Ecuador; the municipalities, usurpers, and the unruly: here we have the many-headed hydra which the heel of the Liberator struck unceasingly and without success, before a people ignorant, divided, without purpose, and without conscience.

The revolution of Venezuela obtained its object, as Gil Fortoul points out, and separated the country from the Colombian Union. "From that time on there allied themselves," declared the historian, "the two political forces which determined, from the last years of the colonial period, the constitutional evolution of Venezuela, to wit: the aspirations of the civil oligarchy to dictate the laws for a society in formation, and the will of a famous warrior, who represented, according to circumstances, the command *de facto* between two revolutions, or the dictatorship, or the autocracy. Both factors, sometimes in harmony and sometimes in opposition, pressed the popular mass during the whole of the nineteenth century, in paths which are yet undefined." The success of the revolution was assured by the necessity of Bolívar of compromising with its authors and, in general, with the active military element, in order to avoid civil war and to gain its support in order to rule in Bogotá. Páez was "no savage," as claimed by Doctor Laureano Villanueva, but an ambitious and vain spirit, lacking perhaps in the elevation of ideas and tendencies often given at birth or acquired by a good education, astute and tricky, capable of assimilating and using quickly any initiative, provided it served for his own personal advancement. He had brought to the inner circle of the councils of Valencia and Caracas the perspicacity, violence, and extraordinary wisdom for which the plainsman was noted. His attitude at this time was energetic and decided, and except for the respect inspired in him by Bolívar, he would have called to arms the troops who were approaching, and only the popularity of the Liberator prevented counterrevolutionary blows by the distant and faithful Apure.

And General Páez represented, above all, the most powerful military force in Colombia. With the organization which he gave to his provinces and to those which obeyed Mariño, with his character, quick to hear suggestions, capable of being used by clever control, the lancer was a very dangerous adversary. Bolívar understood him, and took the part which would avoid at all cost a tremendous war which would have exposed the Republic to the attacks of the Spaniards and for which he could not depend on the Government of Bogotá, which acted much like Páez. The

---

[1]Baralt, *Résumé of the History of Venezuela*, II, 178.

[2]*Vide* Restrepo, on the proposition which caused Santander to renounce the vice presidency, in order to lead a separatist revolution. IV, 55.

efforts of the Liberator served to prevent his enemies from making use of the ambitions of the chiefs of Venezuela, of whose qualities he had an exact opinion, and we saw him persist in this line of conduct when he wrote with his own hand to Doctor José Angel de Alamo: "It is great of you and the good ones not to abandon General Páez. An opposite conduct would have allowed the wicked to gain. For God's sake, do not leave him alone, even when he errs, for in every case honorable men will serve the country and him in undeceiving him, and in not flattering him with lies."[1] Bolívar was about to assume the dictatorship and required a Venezuela united, powerful, under the direction of a man who eighteen months before offered him the crown and who, resolved not to deal with Bogotá, who could promise and support the personal authority of the Liberator, who was the unity of Colombia.[2]

[1]*To Doctor José Angel de Alamo, March 26,* 1826.

[2]Villanueva cited a letter from the Liberator to General Páez, dated November 15, 1826, from Bogotá, which confirmed this opinion. "You," Bolívar wrote him, "who are the first soldier and the first representative of the army of brothers, has the first right to all my cares and solicitudes after that of our sacred land." *The Empire of the Andes,* 273.

The Great Convention

THE march of the Liberator to Bogotá was slow. It might be said that he hoped for the arrival of the troops which he had sent from Venezuela, in order to present himself in the capital sufficiently strong to impose his will. To the official note of Santander, who claimed to have still "the most profound respect for his authority, his virtues, and for his most distinguished services," Bolívar replied, from Cartagena, on the 12th of July, that he would arrive in Bogotá "as soon as possible."

The opposition, in the meanwhile, worked openly and forced the elevated spirit of the Liberator onto the reactionary path.[1] Bolívar was disgusted with the Constitution, with the Congress, with everything which in his mind prevented him from giving the Republic a strong Government, capable of crushing anarchy. The decrees of the Congress which prohibited the Executive from adopting extraordinary measures without the consent of that body, when in session, and which established the public order of Colombia "in all its force and vigor," as it existed before the 27th of April, 1826,[2] was contrary to the plan of Bolívar, who desired discretionary authority to reestablish order. The Great Convention was his favored thought, but Santander objected because he considered it illegal. "The inability supposed to exist on the part of the Executive," declared the Vice President on the 28th of July, "to reestablish peace and ordered progress of the system and which is also implicity attributed to Congress does not arise, in my opinion, from lack of means, of energy, nor of co-operation on the part of a considerable portion of the Republic, but from *the enormous counterbalance imposed by the persuasion of the Liberator, which implies the anticipation of the Great Convention*, independently of the hatreds and personal vengeances against the actual control of the Government." The Congress decreed, nevertheless, the convocation of a National Assembly for the 2nd of March, 1828,[3] and, some days later, passed an act governing the elections.

The Liberator, on his part, wrote to Aboleda:[4]

"Tell the Congress and your friends that I shall not take charge of the Government tied hand and foot, to be the laughing stock of the traitors and of the enemies of Colombia. The army should be increased (a recent law reduced it to nine thousand men) to reestablish the morals and to prevent the Republic

---

[1]The *circles* (*circulos*) "whose principal object was to undermine the reputation of the Liberator and to create a disbelief among the different sections which composed the Colombian Union" were already working in New Granada. O'Leary, *Appendices*, 129.

[2]*July 19*, 1827.

[3]August 3, 1827.

[4]*To José Rafael Arboleda, La Carrera, August 24, 1827.*

from being overwhelmed. Let me be given the power to save the country, in such a manner that the confidence of the Congress will give me authority with the people. I speak generously. The Republic will be lost if it does not confirm on men an immense authority. I do not trust the traitors of Bogotá, nor those of the South. On the other hand, the whole of the North is in commotion, from one extreme to the other there is not a single individual who does not find himself involved in this general commotion, and you know that to cover such immense distances and to subject to the law of duty such irritated passions, it is necessary that a colossal authority be established which is backed by public opinion and by public force. The Great Convention will never meet if I do not first destroy the passions. Let the Congress do what the people ask of it, that is to say, command me to save the country."

Santander protested before the Senate against the presence of the troops of Urdaneta in Magdalena and Boyacá, where they had been directed by the order of Bolívar, and in general "against every unconstitutional act ordered by the Liberator as Supreme Chief, before having taken the necessary oath prescribed by Article 186 of the Constitution." Secretary Revenga advised the Indendant of Venezuela that the proximity of those troops to Bogotá "has been to calm the parties." The differences between the Liberator and the Vice President were aggravated.

The situation in Colombia was grave, internally as well as externally. A profound anarchy shook the country. The provinces of the South were "almost independent." Several municipalities proclaimed the federal system; others, the greatest number, the dictatorship of Bolívar. In Maracaibo and Maturín the troops protested against the decrees of the Congress, acclaiming Bolívar and liberty. In Perú the opposition was preparing, concentrating troops on the frontier,[1] and intriguing in Bolivia. At the end of the year the Government of Lima, in which "increase daily alarms with respect to the ideas of the most Excellent President of Colombia," demanding as a condition for cordiality in its relations with the Cabinet of Chuquisaca the withdrawal of "the armed foreign intervention," that is to say, the auxiliary Division.[2]

The Liberator, in the midst of such difficulties, was disposed "to do everything that he can do for the welfare of the nation, as I have told this very Congress," even when "the epoch of performing miracles has passed."[3] On September 10th, he assumed charge of the authority, after having taken the oath to defend the Constitution, and decreed the prorogation of the extraordinary

---

[1] *General Flores to the Minister of War, November 29,* 1827.

[2] *Decree of October 1,* 1827. O'Leary explained that there was born in the extreme South of the Continent the suspicions and fears because of the supposed intentions of Bolívar, above all "in Chile and in Buenos Aires, where the Governments, in opposition to the people, criticized with exaggerated force the acts and also the words of the Liberator and they continued to arouse fears concerning his conduct in which an impartial observer would only have found things to admire." *Narrative,* II, 512. This lack of confidence soon extended to Bolivia and to Perú and later even to Colombia.

[3] *The Liberator to Peñalver, Bogotá, September 15,* 1827.

sessions of the Congress. Bolívar arranged his forces to pacify the
spirits, predicted concord and confidence in the coming Convention,
inspired respect and faith in the institutions, and quieted the
ambitions of politicians. He judged from the moment in which the
Government, the Congress, and he himself had accepted the idea
of the reforms and promised their realization, the motive of revolt would cease and all would enter into an orderly state and
patient expectation. Unfortunately, the agitation in Colombia
was not calmed by futile constitutional causes, but only became
more profound and incurable, of the sort that no human power can
detain or arrest.

The constitutionalists and the demagogues continued their
bitter press campaign against Bolívar, attributing perverse intentions to him, and he suffered from such injustices. "Those
dogs say," he wrote to General Páez, "that I came to repeat the
scene of the Five Hundred in this capital. Can there be greater
insolence, a more atrocious calumny?"[1] Bolívar was, like Napoleon
particularly sensitive to the insults of the newspapers. "Many
times," declared O'Leary, "I saw him full of rage, or rather
suffering indescribable torments from reading an article written
against him in some despicable rag. This cannot be characteristic
of a great soul, for it manifests great respect for public opinion."[2]
To the attacks of the liberals the Liberator responded by drawing
nearer and nearer to the conservative elements. A series of reactionary decrees began the extraordinary politics of the Dictatorship, and raised liberal opinion against him forever. On October
24th, at a banquet to the several chiefs, Bolívar concluded his
toast with these words: "The union of the church with the sword
of the law is the true arch of the alliance." . . . . From
September, he had the Congress approve all the acts which he had
ordered done in Venezuela to reestablish order and improve the
public administration.

The Liberator hoped that salvation would come from Ocaña,
and wrote to Doctor Mosquera: "The Great Convention is
my hope, moreover, in favor of the Colombian people, because to
it they will bring their rights, their claims, and their needs,
united in a solemn manner. These will determine their future
fate."[3] But very soon the result of the elections in Bogotá,
which sent to the Assembly General Santander and his principal partisans, disconsoled Bolívar. "All this would matter
little to me under other circumstances," he wrote; "but now,
everything endangers us. I do not see any person who can save
Colombia. The Convention will do nothing worth while, and

---

[1]*To General Páez*, Bogotá, September 21, 1827.

[2]*Vide* also view of Gil Fortoul: "The Liberator, as far as concerned his autocratic will, was respectful of two things, the critisicms of the judges. . . and
the criticisms of the newspapermen." I, 417.

[3]*Bogotá, September 24*, 1827.

factions and civil war will be the result. To avoid this conflict they called for me. But what can I do when all the parts fail me, when they call me tyrant when I execute a law, and finally, when it has almost become a duty to swamp me with insults, and to call me ambitious?"[1] And some days later he wrote to Arboleda: "From Pamplona to Papayán, from Bogotá to Cartagena, all New Granada has confederated against me, and my enemies have sought to triumph over my opinion and my name. Santander is the idol of this people, or at least of those who represent it, and at least on those who have arrogated to themselves the right of popular sovereignty."[2] Bolívar sought, in this hour of anguish support from all his friends, in order to confess sadly his impotence. This man, who felt that his life was linked to the fortune of Colombia, had, however, an immense desire to go away, to leave the land which could not support the weight of his greatness and of his glory, to abandon to ambitious politicians who dispute the authority already useless in his hands. "I ought not to live any more in Colombia," he exclaimed, "and always far from her; however, I shall not go away until I am permitted, not because I fear future calamities, but because I do not wish them to attribute them to me, and I have to preside over the land of Colombia."[3] He feared the result of the Convention. "I tell you frankly, that from that time the federal system will, if adopted, destroy the remains of Colombia. It will be its sepulchre and the sign of death for the virtuous. For me, it will be the sign for my departure, and I shall go far away. If they divide Colombia, the evil will be less, but it will be nothing but a place of destruction."[4] "My ideas are very general," he confessed, "to fortify the constitutional Government only up until the Year 31. If not, I shall leave the country, for to divide and to federate it is the same as to destroy Colombia and its members."[5] He wrote to General Páez:[6]

"My opponents have succeeded in depopularizing me: the representatives who go there are my personal enemies: these, after having opposed the Great Convention, now come to be the arbiters of the reforms. I have told them, to satisfy my conscience, that things cannot remain as they are, for many reasons which I have indicated; that we should fortify the Government so that this vast country be not lost; that if this be not done, Colombia will be divided rather than placed under a destructive federation whereby all her essential principles and guarantees will be dissolved. I have insisted that I will not again take the command of Colombia for any reason, but I will aid the Government, if they fortify it as I wish; and if not, I shall go away with God, because I do not wish to live here a single day after they have divided the country or established a federa-

---

[1] *To General Mariano Montilla, Fusca, January 7*, 1828.
[2] *January 22*, 1828.
[3] *To Antonio Leocadio Guzmán, Bogotá, January 10*, 1828.
[4] *To José Rafael Arboleda, Bogotá, February 7*, 1828.
[5] *To Cristóbal Mendoza, Bogotá, February 16*, 1828.
[6] *To General Páez, Bogotá, January 20*, 1828. Santander and his friends worked very hard during the elections, which was quite a contrast to action of Bolívar and the Government, which took no part in influencing them whatever. Restrepo, IV, 592.

tion, since war will be the continuous result of this change. Yes, my dear General, this is my sincere confession and the cry of my conscience: it is my conviction, it grows thus, and no doubt causes me to vacilate. It is evident to me that Colombia will be destroyed if they do not give the Government an immense force capable of struggling against anarchy which raises a thousand seditious heads. . . . *division* is ruin in itself and *federation* is the sepulchre of Colombia; even at that, the first is perferable to the others, but more as a place than as a utility."

Bolívar appreciated his position in the Republic, and knew that his enemies fought him unceasingly. Santander, in announcing to the people that he would go as a deputy to the Convention, called him the most illustrious chief of Colonbia, but he promised to work for the establishment of a government "vigorous, popular, representative, responsible, and temporal." "I am no chief, nor do I beong to any party," concluded the Vice President, "my cause is that of Colombia."[1] There were two causes in Colombia: that of the Liberator and that of the liberals, which Santander represented.

For the purpose of exercising directly in that part of the country on which he must most count in the coming struggle, Bolívar declared himself invested with extraordinary powers in the departments of Maturín, Venezuela, Orinoco, and Zulia, because of foreign danger, as he declared.[2] At the same time the dispatch of public business was reorganized by means of four secretaries who remained in Bogotá, who planned a journey to Venezuela, accompanied by a fifth secretary, reserved to himself with extraordinary powers, the exercise of the Executive Power.[3]

The Liberator, on February 29, at the instance of his ministers,[4] directed a message to the Convention which was to meet in three days later in the city of Ocaña. In this document, Bolívar gave a desperate picture of the situation, in all aspects of the national life: anarchy, disorder, economic disaster, social chaos. In critizing existing laws, the Liberator knew that "he cannot do it without exposing himself to sinister interpretation, and through his words will be read ambitious thoughts," but as "he has not refused to consecrate his life and reputation to Colombia, he considers himself obliged to make this last sacrifice."[5] He did not fall into the error of attributing all evil to the institutions, but since the Convention was a political end, politics held, above all, his attention. He declared:

"Our Government is essentially badly constituted. Without considering that we have just begun our union, we allow ourselves to be dazzled by aspirations higher than those which the history throughout all the ages shows com-

[1]*Manifesto of January 13*, 1828.
[2]*Decree of February 23*, 1828.
[3]*Decree of February 26*, 1828.
[4]*The Liberator to Don Joaquin Mosquera, Bogotá, February 29*, 1828.
[5]According to what Restrepo confirmed, "the Liberator had abandoned but had not completely interred his project for the Constitution for Bolivia, which at other times caused a furious attack on his political profession of faith." IV, 84.

patible with human nature. At other times we have mistaken the means and
have attributed the poor success to our failure to approach near enough to the
deceptive guide which misled us, not listening to those who wished to follow
order and wished to compare the various parts of this Constitution, and all of
this with our education, customs, and inexperience, in order not to be engulfed
in a turbulent sea. . . . . Our various powers are not distributed as required by our social conditions and the welfare of the citizens. We have made
of the legislature alone the sovereign body, whereas it should be only one arm of
the sovereign; we have put the Executive under it and have given it a greater
part in administration than the general interest permits. As a culmination of
folly, we have placed all power in the public will and all flexibility in the movement and action of the social body. . . . The Executive of Colombia is not the
equal of the Legislative, nor of the Chief of the Judiciary: he is a weak arm of the
Supreme Power, because he is not allowed to participate in the totality which
should belong to him, for the Congress interferes with his functions in the administrative, judicial, eccesiastical, and in the military. The Government,
which should be the fountain and the motor of the public authority must look
for it outside of its own resources, and support itself on others than those which
should be subordinated to it. It is essentially necessary that the Government
should be the centre and the heart of public power without being subordinated
to any other. Having been deprived of its own nature, it falls into a lethargy
which is fatal for the citizens, and which brings with it the ruin of the institutions.'

The Bolivarian theories have been proved by the experiences
of the last years, and the Liberator persisted in demanding
a powerful executive power, with ample initiative, capable of
remedying with energetic action the rhetorical uselessness of the
Parliament. His system, which required a government of the
people by the people of an oligarchy of the best, is, as he has
declared, an example of political eclecticism, in which preponderate
the Anglo-Saxon elements with the aristocratic and paternal
tendency, covering the revolutionary ideas of France, which
lose their radicalism, but give to the combination, nevertheless,
an advanced liberal aspect. The Spanish tradition, on the other
hand, the creator of what has been called, perhaps incorrectly,
democratic Caesarism, tends to attenuate the absolute principle
of popular sovereignty, and to affirm among the factors of our
political evolution the individualism of the race, as a reactionary
force against revolutionary collectivism.[1] In the Bolivarian theory

---

[1] The eminent Venezuelan writer Don Laureano Vallenilla Lanz published
recently with the title of *Democratic Caesarism* (*Cesarismo Démocratico*) a book
which, as one of great worth, has been much discussed and also criticized in all of
Spanish America. When, in 1916, I referred to the peninsular tradition, qualifying
the immense improvement of the same domination, I found everywhere an acceptance restricted to these terms of political technology. The democratic Caesarism of Rome, when the democratic evolution, initiated centuries before with the
creation of the tribunate, reached its peak and took possession almost completely of
the authority of the aristocracy, it made a bulwark of the public liberties. Then
when Caesar incarnated democracy and, in the name of the people, attacked and
gradually destroyed republican institutions: Caersarism is, then, by definition,
democratic. The coming of Diocletian was necessary under the influences which
came from the Orient and in virtue of these means there occurred in Roman
society and in the general movement of the ideas provoked by Christianity, imperial authority, evolving, removing itself from the people and acquiring the
attributes and forms of the Asiatic monarchy. In Constantinople, the ruler de-

of government and of the State these diverse elements were noted, distributed with tact, in conformity with a genial observation of the means. The parliament proposed to absorb the government, to monopolize the administration, leaving the executive a shadow of ineffective authority. Democracy, through fear of tyranny, turned against the parliament, and worked to impede executive action. Bolívar tried to balance in the legislative power the revolutionary tendencies with the hereditary senate and the life censors. Finally, when he was convinced that Colombia desired neither the one or the other, he sought to endow the executive with energy and resistence and conceded to opinion and to fashion a parliament within reasonable limits, without the power to impede the action of the government. The Liberator more than once desired to be able to forecast the future of America, to avoid tyranny and fatal personalism, tempering the Jacobin system which, by destroying the conservative forces, and raising it above a rule of chiefs and of generals. Bolívar was, in reality, the defender of the people against future despots, but his thoughts were tortuously interpreted and gave occasion for the criticism of those who attributed to him absurd and ambitious plans.

Bolívar was, above all, a methodizer. He did not tolerate anarchy. Laws, politics, administration, should be entrusted to protectors, who are to function mechanically, without any sudden changes. The British Government gave him the synthesis for his system: civil equality and order. He loved liberty; and the humanitarian formulas of the French Revolution was of frequent use to him in dressing up his magnificent discourses, but, basically, he considered them as future postulates rather than as realities in his present political scheme. He desired practical laws, in accord with the conditions and the social necessities. "Our laws," he declared, "are made by accident: they lack unity, method, classification, and legal phraseology. They are contradictory, complicated, sometimes unnecessary, and even opposed to their aims. There is an adequate example of the destructive vices having been made indispensible to repress vigorous dispositions: law, then, which has been made purposely, has been much less adequate than the old laws, aiding directly the vices which it sought to avoid." He spoke against ideology and its

---

sired to be Caesar, so that we see across the marvelous and calumniated history of Byzantium successful generals raised by the army to the throne. The Middle Ages ignored Caesarism, as it did not care to give this name to the barbarous military monarchies of the early times, or to the German Empire whose chief was chosen by a diet of princes. A new element, the hereditary transmission of the power, broke, definitely the knot of the origin which united the monarch to the people, but the royal power is always in England, in Spain, in France an instrument of struggle in favor of the people against the barons and the nobles. Under the despotism, the people preserve equality; against the despotism, the nobility defined liberty. At the beginning of the Nineteenth Century, Napoleon returned to the Roman ideas and resurrected Caesarism: it is the plebiscitary Caesar, democratic *par excellence*. Note of 1922.

arbitrary applications: "To attain perfection, we adopt as a basis of representation a scale which our capacity as yet does not warrant." He asked for a vigorous and unrestrained authority, based on legal force, which might prevent tyranny and abuses. "All observe with sorrow the contrast which the executive presents, carrying a superabundance of force on the side of extreme weakness. He could not repel foreign invasion or prevent seditious attempts without being considered a dictator. The Constitution itself, convinced of its own fault, has exceeded itself in supplying with profusion the attributes which it had avariciously kept from him. As a result the government of Colombia is a weak force of safety or a devastating torrent."

As regards the administration of justice, Bolívar had become more narrow. . . . He did not then desire, as he had in Angostura or Chuquisaca, the absolute independence of the judical power and the inviolability of the magistrates. The abuses which have been committed made him regret that the executive could not exercise a repressive vigilance over this branch of the public power. He protested against the enlargement of the powers of the judiciary. "In no nation has the power of judging been elevated to such great heights as in Colombia." He considered military power indispensible and logical, now that he needed the army.

The Constitution of Bolivia did not establish municipalities, and as the influence of these bodies had been base and revolutionary of late, the Liberator sought to have them suppressed in Colombia. He declared:

> The municipalities, which should be useful as advisers of the governors of provinces, have hardly fulfilled their true functions. Some of them have dared to arrogate to themselves the sovereignty which belongs to the nation: others have fomented sedition: and nearly all their new acts have harmed, rather than improved the welfare, prosperity, and the safety of their respective peoples. Such corporations are not helpful for the purpose for which they were destined. They have become hated for the taxes which they require, through the disturbances which they cause the electors which compose them, and because, in many places, there is nothing with which to replace them. . . . And if I am to say what everybody thinks, no decree would be more popular than that which would eliminate the municipal governments.

The town governments, however, for the most part, favored reforms and the dictatorship of the Liberator.

A law of general politics was necessary, to repair the obvious inconveniences in the application of laws and regulations.

It was necessary to support legislation with military force in order to maintain discipline. The suppression of military courts had been fatal "for the passive submission and blind obedience which forms the basis of military power, an aid to the whole of society." The soldiers should not be permitted to marry without government license, nor to obtain substitutes from among the fathers of families, nor to complain directly against their chiefs by means of public writings. Bolívar declared: "To have

declared arbitrary detention a corrective punishment is to establish by ordinances the rights of man and to spread anarchy among
the soldiers, who are the most cruel as well as the most powerful
when they become demagogues." The rivalries between the
militarists of the different provinces and with the civil population
should be proscribed. The "vituperable indulgence" for military
crimes had brought unhappy results.

The public revenue demanded a vigorous reform. "The Republic has erred," declared Bolívar with sadness, "and it finds
itself pursued by a formidable army of creditors."

Agriculture "has not been able to conserve itself in the deplorable state into which it has fallen," and its complete ruin
"has contributed to that of other forms of industry, demoralizing
the rural community and decreasing the opportunity for increase:
everything has fallen into desolute misery."

Foreign commerce "has followed the same path as the industry of the country: it may even be said that we have hardly
enough to supply us with the necessities; so much have frauds,
favored by the laws and the judgments, accompanied by numerous
damages, undermined the confidence of a profession which depends so much upon credit and good faith."

"The maintenance and development of the foreign relations
requires unity, peace, proper respect, in order that friendly
nations, regretting that they have recognized us, may not bar us
from among the peoples that compose the human race."

And after having presented in somber colors to the members
of the Convention the spectacle of a dying Colombia, the Liberat-
or exclaimed:

> "Turn your penetrating glances on the secret thoughts of your constituents.
> There you will read the prolonged anxiety that torments them. They pray for
> security and respose. A strong government, powerful and just, is the cry of the
> country. Observe the ruins of the desert which despotism has left, paled with
> horror, weeping for the five hundred thousand heroes which died for her, whose
> blood, sown in the fields, has caused her rights to grow. Yes, Legislators! The
> dead and the living, the graves and the ruins, pray guarantees of you. And I,
> who am seated now in the home of a simple citizen and lost in the multitude,
> recover my voice and my right. I, who am the last to clamor for the end of
> society. I, who have made a religious cult of the country and of life, dare not
> be silent in so solemn a moment. Give us a government in which the law will
> be obeyed, the magistracy respected, and the people free: a government which
> will prevent the transgression of the general will and of the commands of the
> people. Consider, Legislators, that the power in public affairs is the safeguard
> of individual weakness, the threat which terrifies the unjust, and the hope of
> society. Consider that the corruption of the people is born in the indulgence of
> the tribunals and in the immunity of the criminals. Observe that without
> force there is no vitrue, and without virtue the Republic perishes. Observe,
> finally, that anarchy destroys liberty, and unity preserves order. Legislators!
> In the name of Colombia, I ask that you give us, in the image of Providence
> whom you represent, as arbiters of our fate, for the people, for the army, for the
> judge, and for the ruler laws inexorable!"

The situation continued obscure. Periodical disturbances
followed the events of Angostura (deposition of Colonel José

Félix Blanco) in the rest of Venezuela and anarchy in the South, threatened by the Peruvians. Padilla, by March, headed a movement in Cartagena. In Bogotá, the Santanderian press redoubled its attacks, to such an extent that Colonels Ferguson and Luque believed themselves justified in destroying a printing press by military force. Bolívar, who in Venezuela had recommended to newspaper writers "moderation and decency" because he did not believe "that liberty consisted in the capacity of offending" and had just repeated such counsels through Secretary Restrepo,[1] ordered Urdaneta, Minister of War, to institute an investigation of these militarists "for having attacked personal security and in such a manner that they had prevented the citizens from freely publishing their thoughts."[2] Without hope of remedying these evils, the Liberator continued to approximate the conservatives, grasping resolutely the forces of resistance in order to oppose anarchy. Disillusioned, the great man cast into the unploughed ground *the useless seed.* He wrote to Sir Robert Wilson:[3]

"All that they tell you of these unfortunate Republics, is more than certain, and even more inevitable. The influence of civilization produces an indigestion in our spirits which do not have enough strength to masticate the nutrative food of liberty. That which should save us, makes us succumb. The purest and the most perfect doctrines are those which poison our existence. The Great Convention of Colombia will give new testimony to this unfortunate and yet all too certain situation: there the spirit of partisanship will dictate *interests* and not laws; there will triumph in the end demagogy and the *canaille.*"

Toward the last days of the life of the Liberator, a tendency to pass suddenly from one extreme to another in the scale of his impressions became more pronounced: a tendency which was reflected in his politics and in his conduct in general. The copious correspondance of those years showed him voluble and capricious, partly due to the characteristic of his genius, which were agility and multiplicity, which were complicated by the morbid factors in an organism prematurely aged, and by the irritating condition of his liver. He was found, many times in the same day, alternately optimistic and weighted down by dark thoughts. The notice of a new rising, or the announcement of a favorable election, served to put him in a state of desperation, or to raise his spirit on the wings of hope. Notable contradictions in his letters are explained by this peculiar state of mind and health. The "inconstancy" and "the extreme pliability to the insinuations of his courtiers," with which an author reproached him, can hardly be expected to harmonize in this peculiar situation of a man who fought desperately, hesitating before the paths which opened up to his view, and of one who desired to please his last friends.[4]

---

[1]*Note to the Intendant of Venezuela, March 14,* 1828.
[2]*Vide Doc. XII.* 191. O'Leary, *Appendices,* 177. Restrepo, IV, 85.
[3]*To Sir Robert Wilson, Bogotá, January 22,* 1828.
[4]*Vide* Gil Fortoul, I, 430. "This variety in the humor of His Excellency,' '

Compare, in order to understand what is still to be written, the letters of the Liberator to Briceño Méndez and to Mantilla with that written to Wilson. On congratulating the former on his election, he declared himself "satisfied, because I see that most of the deputies who will go to Ocaño are like you animated with the best sentiments and aim for unity."[1] "My aide-de-camp Wilson," he wrote to the latter, "is bound for Ocaño, and I take the opportunity to write to you and to tell you that all Colombia has risen against the federation and detests the faction which wishes to involve it in anarchy. . . . The army and the people are united to save the country from the demagogues."[2]

The representatives of the people assembled at the Convention, indicating remedies to improve the state of the country. From Ecuador came votes for a central and strong government in the hands of Bolívar. General Páez explained that the opinion of the municipalities of Venezuela, of the military bodies, of the military chiefs as well as that of himself was "to centralize the power and to place in the hands of the Liberator the supreme power of the State, to which the peoples call him by unanimous acclamation, until when, the independence of the nation is assured there shall be established the form of government desired by the general will."[3] The plainsman was won for the Bolivarian cause, which was that of the integrity of Colombia, and so may be seen the result of the opportunist politics of the Liberator in Venezuela. The Department was transformed: the municipalities, the troops of the line, the militia, the university, acclaimed Bolívar as Supreme Chief. They attacked General Santander and the revolters. The military discipline was slackened with the new manifestations, as before through other motives and principles.

Such indications gladdened Bolívar who even believed that if in the Assembly his adversaries negated his designs, he would be able to count on his personal prestige to establish his policy. The Liberator considered civil war inevitable, if "the Great Convention does not conduct itself with widom and the people with prudence," and believed that "I can somehow remedy the faults of the people but not of the Great Convention," because "the former have a remedy and the latter none," according to

---

one reads in the *Diary of Bucaracamanga*, "may be attributed to a fault or inconstancy in his character, if the motive for it was not to divide the public business, which continued to occupy his imagination and caused his spirit to be bright or sad. His Excellency was always fluctuating between fears and hopes, to those who surrounded him or to whom he wrote he displayed this uncertainty, and it was easily known that he was sad because he was, generally of a jovial character." 110. Restrepo declared that Bolívar was always condescending to his friends. IV, 417.

[1] *To Briceño Méndez, Bogotá, February 22*, 1828.

[2] *To Montilla, Sátiva, March 24*, 1828.

[3] *Representation of General Páez to the Great Convention, Caracas*, March 15, 1828.

what he wrote to General O'Leary.[1] Bolívar was determined, in fact, to appeal to a plebiscite in case the decisions of Ocaño did not suit him. The people and the army, whom he believed faithful, ought to serve him in the last instance to conquer his enemies. He wrote to Doctor Castillo:[2]

"The country is all animated with a holy fear of anarchy and of the federation and is resolved, moreover, to establish national unity, if the Great Convention does not work in accordance with these general ideas. On all sides there are popular demonstrations against the federation and the weakenss of the government. Unity and strength is the cry of the Assembly: and you may believe that this cry will not be in vain because I see the spirits greatly inflamed. You ought, likewise, my dear friend, to write to the Great Convention, so that it may not equivocate."

On the same day he wrote to Brisceño Méndez:[3]

"Write me about everything with Wilson and do not be surprised if I do not express my opinions, because I have no other than a *powerful and just* government, provisional or not provisional, since everything is provisional in a revolution and for the same reason it is better that it is provisional than stable in order to avoid misgivings and fears. Tell the federalists not to count on the country if they triumph, because the army and the people are resolved to oppose them openly. The *national sanction* is in reserve, in order to prevent that which the people do not want."

This was, in fact, the Napoleonic theory of the call to the people.

The Great Convention met on the 9th of April. The Liberator, who from the 13th of March had extended to the whole of the Republic, with the exception of the canton of Ocaño, the exercise of extraordinary powers, came to establish himself in the city of Bucaramanga. The standards which were to make it fruitless, showed themselves from the very beginning in the Assembly. From that time, there existed a neutral group, formed of certain representatives who came to Ocaña with the idea of working according to their own conscience, without inclining to Caesar nor to Pompey. The Bolivians followed blindly the politics of the Liberator, judging that without his presence in the command, at the head of the central government, vigorous and powerful, the Republic would be lost. The partisans of Santander came to the Assembly disposed to attack Bolívar, to oppose themselves to his designs, to defend liberal principles against autocracy, local autonomies against centralism, the independence of the institutions against the powerful personality of the Liberator. They were "the free and determined men" of whom Victor Antonio Zerpa speaks.[4]

Bolívar did not find it convenient for his friends to organize "a Bolivian Party," in the Convention, and would have preferred to have had them associate themselves with the neutral

[1] *Sátiva, March 24, 1828.*
[2] *Idem, id., id.*
[3] *Idem. id., id. The italics are in the original.*
[4] *Biography of Don Juan de Dios Picón.*

group, to oppose in a mass the Santanderian faction. But he did not wish to take part in the proceedings of the Assembly,[1] and confined himself to observing its progress. General Montilla desired to resign his Cartagena command, because he was tired and was the object of violent attacks on account of his Venezuelan nationality. Bolívar wrote to him:[2]

> "I should perish a thousand times before taking personal views of my own case. I have fought for liberty and for glory and not for my own advancement, and this sentiment is common to you and to my generous friends who have followed me because I have followed the good cause. I see in our opponents nothing but ingratitude, perfidy, shame, and calumny: like monsters they are unworthy of our clemency, and we ought to punish them, because the general good demands it. Sacrifice, my dear Montilla, all your delicacies on the altar of the country which calls for this sacrifice."

Without hope in the result of the deliberations of Ocaña, he foresaw the future unhappiness of Colombia, and confided to Briceño Méndez the indignation which the exclusion of Doctor Peña caused him:[3]

> "I assure you that each day I despair more and more for the safety of the country, and I am resolved to leave it immediately the Great Convention decides its fate, which only a miracle can prevent me from doing. I say miracle, because I so consider the action of the Great Convention in the election and composition of the government. I am very certain that this body so opposed to my opinions will only fight and when more it will only compromise, leaving half of the evil with half of the good so that the only result will be a delay in the final downfall. That is to say, an existence of two, three, or four years before succumbing before greater disasters. You may believe me, Briceño, it will do nothing that is good, nothing, nothing."

And he continued disheartened:

> "You see my friends the Mosqueras how coldly they conduct themselves. You will, doubtless believe, that it is because of something I have done. What folly! What do I need of Colombia? The Colombians will be those who will pass to posterity covered with ignominy, but not I. No passion blinds me in this matter, and if passion of judgments of this nature would serve for anything it would be to give undeniable testimonials of my purity and disinterestedness. My only love has ever been for the country; my only ambition, its liberty. Those who attribute to me anything else do not know me, nor have they ever known me. So it is that the vile supposition that I have personal ambition torments me, so that I am resolved and even determined to go away to prove the contrary. And if necessary, I shall do even more. Perhaps, perhaps, I may go away sometime, and on my going depends the life of Colombia, I shall leave it to perish, and even though I condemn it to nothingness, so that it might be seen that I wanted nothing, so as to prove what has wounded my pride in the most delicate part."

The miracle that Bolívar invoked in order not to leave the Republic was realized with the dissolution of the Assembly and the people confirmed it, by proclaiming him dictator.

On the 16th of April it was decreed in Ocaña that it was urgently necessary to reform the Constitution, and that it would

---

[1] *Diary of Bucaramanga*, 36 and 37.
[2] *To General Montilla, Bucaramanga, April 13*, 1828.
[3] *To General Briceño Méndez, Bucaramanga, April 15*, 1828.

proceed to do so, holding in consideration the principles of integrity and independence of the Republic, the sovereignty of the nation, civil and political liberty, the form of government to be popular, representative, elective, and alternate, the responsibility of the magistrates and officials, and the division of the supreme power into the legislative, executive, and judicial.[1] It was done to denounce the fundamental principles of the Bolivarian system. When the President of the Convention announced to the Liberator the receipt of his message of February 29th, it was true that he had declared that "the voice of a magistrate experienced in the grave and complicated business of administration should be heard with interest in the conflict of such critical circumstances" and "that the widsom of the Liberator of the country was necessary, when they began to perform the difficult task of reforms."[2] Bolívar, on his part, spoke always of appealing to the people, or to force. "The entire nation," he declared, "has come out for ideas more sane, and will compel adherence to these. The people and the army have made energetic representations to serve as instruction for the legislators. If these depart from the public ideas, their deliberations will not receive popular sanction, which is perfectly in accord with my principles."[3]

Among the manifestations of which the Liberator spoke, one of the most noticeable was that which brought to the Convention by Colonel Leon de Febres Cordero, in which the troops of the South requested that Bolívar be given the supreme authority. The soldiers of Ecuador declared "against the delirious frenzy of continuing the fatal trial of theories which have damaged the nation in the name of a principle," and believed that "the Liberator, who is doubtless the divine anchor of our hopes and the only torch remaining in Colombia to illuminate the deeds which become lost in the obscurity of history, should assume the supreme command of the State, so that with his experiences and wisdom, he may effect the reforms which he considers necessary, reestablish public confidence, consolidate opinion, revive honor and virtue, so that the brilliance of glory and the lustre of liberty be not dimmed, that he may improve the different branches of the administration, and finally, that he with his omnipotent arm may make Colombia again Colombia."[4]

Less than a fortnight had passed since the meeting of the Assembly, and Bolívar was then sure that it would produce nothing useful. Santander, if not victorious, was at least able to prevent work from being done. The words of the Liberator re-

---

[1] *Address to the People of the Republic, April 17,* 1828. Beralt observed that this was the only act of importance in which all the members of the Assembly were in accord. II, 227.

[2] *Note of President Márquez to the Liberator, April 25,* 1828.

[3] *To Sir Robert Wilson, Bucaramanga, April 16,* 1828.

[4] *Frank and Respectful Manifestation, Guayaquil, May 1,* 1828.

sound with extraordinary violence. His impetuous character, his fiery imagination,[1] forced him into an insulting anger. He wrote to Briseño Méndez:[2]

> "Only to please my friends, I have offered to aid them, to save the country. But what country can be saved in the midst of so many monsters who control it? When virtue is called servile and a parasite liberal, and when the most atrocious scoundrel is the oracle of opinion and of principle? I do not wish to contest with such *canaille*. I do not wish to serve with them an instant. If you wish me to give my opinion with respect to yourself, I shall counsel you to retire from Venezuela, because you are a *suspect*, because you are supposed to be the organ of my ideas. These wretches should be considered as the finger of Providence, directing them to safety; but now that they outrage me and outrage you, may they keep their suspicion and let them rot in their own filth. Wretches! Even the air they breathe I have given them, and I am suspected, and my friends and my relatives are scorned."

The most atrocious of scoundrels was General Santander, Vice President of the Republic.

Joaquin Mosquera had communicated to him his ideas on the reforms he considered desirable, and the Liberator who knew the state of mind of the members of the Convention answered:[3]

> "Your opinions have seemed to me very good in the matter of what should be done in reform; but I am afrain that nothing of what you think and propose can be obtained. You desire that the senate be composed of great proprietors, and that the executive be given the suspensive veto and the initiative in the laws; I see this will be very difficult, because it leads to giving force to the government, which the opposition will not permit. I believe, also, that the federation will not be sanctioned, because all the people are opposed to it. Neither do I believe what you think will be done."

Bolívar wished to sound the opinion of the deputies, and suggested to his friends the project for dividing Colombia into three or four independent States, confederated "under the auspices of the Liberator" to avoid "the internal war which in the end would have led to the same result, if before that it shall not have become a prey of Spain, or of an ambitious and lucky chief." General Soublette, Secretary to the Liberator, wrote to Doctor Castillo, Chief of the Bolivarian Party: "Better to separate in peace and harmony than at the point of the sword, and not to waste our time and energy in defending ourselves against our brothers when we should use it in organizing ourselves."[4] Castillo rejected the project, replying that he and his friends were disposed to support Colombian unity. General Soublette then explained Bolívar's reasons: "The Liberator," he declared, "continues to demand an immense power to save the country." The Secretary wrote:[5]

---

[1]*Diary of Bucaramanga*, 168.
[2]*To General Briceño, Bucaramanga, April 23*, 1828. *Vide* also the letter of Bolívar to Montilla, April 24, 1828.
[3]*To Don Joaquin Mosquera, Bucaramanga, April 25*, 1828.
[4]*General Soublette to Doctor Castillo, Bucaramanga, May 2*, 1828.
[5]May 8, 1828. Consult also the letters of Bolívar of these days to Doctors Alamo and Vergara, to Martínez, to Colonel Mosquera, etc.

"I can well see that everything is difficult, because these petty nations are disgusting; but, if all their desires are satisfied, harmony may be reestablished and treaties concluded which may conserve the unity of power by which to resist the common enemy. I lose myself in conjectures, but I always return to the resolution of the President. He repeats that without adequate means it is impossible to do anything to the condition in which the country has fallen, and persuaded that he will not be given such means, he does not wish to undertake a work which he is certain he will not be able to carry out."

On the contrary, if the country should succeed in placing itself "on a column of granite and if its base be so firmly fixed that our political tremors cannot move it," then Bolívar "would agree to everything and give up his morbid thoughts[1]. . . . ."

The Liberator personally explained to Castillo that the proposition was the best proof of his sentiments, "that they have not been directed to do good but to avoid evils which I consider inevitable, because our horrible situation obliges us to choose from among those who are bad." And since his correspondent advises him to exercise resolution and audacity:

Let then our standard be *fatality for timidity*. When they speak to me of valor and audacity, I feel myself reviving, and again I am born for the country and for glory. How happy we should be if our wisdom were led by fortitude! Then I should propose even the impossible. Then would Colombia and the rest of America be saved. Then let all our friends unite under this sentiment, and may those unworthy words of danger, of fear remove themselves from our mouth. Let them send me to save the Republic and to save all America. Let them order me to destroy anarchy so that its memory may no longer remain. When law authorizes me, I know no impossibilities. These offers of my heart and of my patriotism are not boasts neither are they vain presumptions. No, my friend, he who has presided over many prodigies has the right to hope for everything.[2]

The Liberator aroused, sometimes, his old energy. His genius swelled and burned before America which he felt was omnipotent. But he saw himself fighting desperately and begged his new faithful ones to aid him, to invest him with an enormous power and which he did not wish to usurp. He gave up under the pressure of his friends the project of division with which he tried to conciliate public opinion. "They have accused me," he declared, "of wishing to abandon the country, and even to ruin it sacrificing my glory and the most sacred interests of Colombia."[3] He urged Brisceño Méndez to have patience, to guard the results of the works of his party, even when he maintained his fears, because "no intellectual power is capable of penetrating into the deepest abyss of my unfortunate conjectures. . . . I consider the New World as a globe that has gone crazy and whose inhabitants find themselves attacked by frenzy, and to contain this floating mass of madmen and transgressors, they should be

---

[1]*The Liberator to Doctor Castillo, Bucaramanga, May 8*, 1828.
[2]*To Doctor Castillo, Bucaramanga, May 15*, 1828.
[3]*To General Diego Ybarra, Bucaramanga, June 2*, 1828. *To Don José Rafael Arboleda, Bucaramanga, June 1*, 1828.

collected together by the keeper of the madhouse with book in hand, in order to teach them their duty."[1]

"After the rising in Valencia," he wrote to the same a week later, "I saw this country lost and each day I see it nearing the ultimate precipice. Each step, each instant, is a scale we descend, and if my desperation were not equal to the horror of our fate, I should have lost judgment; but I find myself in the tremendous moment of the calm of disorder."[2] Bolívar considered the dangers to which it was exposed, if it did not work according to his requirements, without a law which authorized him "to save Colombia," would destroy the country.

In one of his letters to General Urdaneta, Minister of War, he summarized the data for a knowledge of his ideas at that time:[3]

No one knows what will happen to Colombia; united or divided, it is ungovernable. I plan to go to Venezuela to improve its organization in some respects: but I await the resolution of my friends in Acuña to determine this matter. I have told them that the project of reforms which they have proposed will prove a futility, and I shall not charge myself with the government of the Republic with them: and that it would be better to divide the country, so that each part of it may do as it pleases. I agree with you that we can expect nothing from the Great Convention. Therefore, you should formulate your ideas on the basis of these words. I lose myself in conjectures without gaining a single ray of hope. One must indeed be shortsighted not to see infinite evils in the present state of affairs. I am of the same opinion as when they held the elections in Bogotá. I want to say that I am resolved to leave Colombia, if a miracle does not offer something else. I am burying myself alive in the ruins of this country, through complacency and docility, and by giving heed to the counsels of fools and of perverts. I must, therefore, go away, or destroy the evil. The last would be tyranny, and the first cannot be weakness because I do not have it. I am convinced that if I fight I shall triumph and save the country, and you know that I do not abhor fights. But why should I fight the will of those who call themselves free and moderate? You will tell me in reply that I did not consult the same good and free people, in order to destroy the Spaniards, and that I took the opinion of the common people for that. But the Spaniards were called tyrants, servants, slaves; and now I have to oppose those who call themselves, by the pompous names of republicans, citizens. I have here what detains me and makes me doubt.

As regards the exercising of the presidency without the powers of a Constitution unadaptable to circumstances, Bolívar believed that an impossibility.[4]

During this time, the factions were disputing with each other in the Convention. The Bolivarians in a proposition to which the Liberator considered as "impolitic and unattractive," wanted him to be called to Ocaña. The proposition was refused. No bases of an agreement between the constitutional projects of the two parties were found, one with federal tendencies with an executive the same as existed, the other, more centralistic, desired

---

[1] *To General Briceño Méndez, Bucaramanga, May 15,* 1828.
[2] *To General Briceño Méndez, Bucaramanga, May 25,* 1828.
[3] *To General Urdaneta, Bucaramanga,*
[4] *The Liberator to General Briceño Méndez, Bucaramanga, May 7,* 1828.

an eight-year presidency with ample powers, according to the ideas of Bolívar.[1] A group of Bolivarians signed, on the 2nd of June, as members of the Convention,[2] a document setting forth the reasons which obliged it to separate itself from the Assembly, whose labors, they declared, were useless and dangerous. Santander, Azuero, and Soto, in their turn, also expressed a desire to leave the Convention and their partisans presented, on the day of the 6th, a project of an additional act to the Constitution which wonld leave that in force, thereby frustrating the aspirations for reform, and weakening the executive power. Finally, on the 11th of June, the Assembly adjourned for lack of a *quorum*, because the Bolivarian deputies had left. The two groups blamed each other for the guilt of the failure, in manifestoes to the Colombian people.

According to Restrepo, O'Leary, Posada Gutiérrez, and Peru de Lacroix, the Liberator took no part in the dissolution of the Assembly, which he considered, on the contrary " as the worst calamity which could have come to the Republic."[3] But he could not disapprove the conduct of his friends, whose position in Ocaña was insupportable.[4] Doctor Castillo communicated the proposal for dissolution to the Liberator, and the latter judged that, as he could not prevent it from being realized, for lack of time, or believing the continuation of the sessions useless, it was desirable to so inform his partisans. He ordered the journey of Andrés Ybarra to Maracaibo for that purpose.[5] Bolívar tried to keep the fidelity of General Páez in Venezuela, on whom he could count. He was made uneasy by the fickleness of the plainsman chief behind which, the oligarchs intrigued, and in order to quiet him he commanded Colonel Carabaño that "he should suggest from time to time that I am wholly satisfied with his noble conduct, and, further, that he should take no notice of rumours because I prefer to leave the command and go to hell rather than bear the name of governor and not be it."[6] And when the fiasco of the Convention opened the path to the dictatorship, the Liberator wrote to his friends to prepare to support him. To Páez he wrote:[7]

"I have proposed to my friends a resolution which will conciliate all interests in the different sections of Colombia, which was to divide it into three *or four States which would allow them to ally themselves for common defense*, but

[1]Diary of Bucaramanga, 132. Vide also Gil Fortoul, I, 431. In a letter from Bolívar to O'Leary, March 31st: "I should like to know if I shall go to Ocaña and what impression my visit will make. . . ."

[2]*Vide* a résumé of these projects in Gil Fortoul, I, 432.

[3]*General Soublette to the Minister of the Interior, Socorro, June 16,* 1828. *Vide* Larrazabal, II, 434, and José Joaquin Guerra, *The Convention of Ocaña*, 490.

[4]*Letters of the Liberator to Diego Ybarra and Doctor Cristóbal Mendoza, Bogotá, June 28,* 1828.

[5]*Diary of Bucaramanga,* 190.

[6]*The Liberator to Colonel Carabaño, Bucaramanga, May 13,* 1828'

[7]*To General Páez, Bucaramanga, June 3,* 1828.

nobody has ventured to support this expedient and the whole world has accused me of wishing to abandon the country, sacrificing my glory and the most sacred interests of Colombia. . . . I await a horrible storm, and because of that fact, we should prepare to avoid it, taking all precautions, in order that disorders may not force us into the crimes of a bloody anarchy. For that reason, you should take such providential precautions against the external and internal enemies as may be necessary, for they will resort to the worst excesses in this horrible crisis."

In announcing his journey to Bogotá to General Salom, he declared that he expected that Páez "will support Venezuela and that friends like you will cooperate with him during this new crisis, so that the country may be best maintained. In the South the same will happen, because they have declared in an irrevocable manner for my continuance in command. Cartagena has done the same, and the departments of Cauca and Boyacá, with the exception of Pamplona have also expressed themselves in the same way."[1] As for the members of the Government, Bolívar is sure that they will accompany him in the coming contest, and thus wrote to Doctor Vergara;[2]

"I do not answer your letter on other points, because I have written to General Urdaneta a letter which he will show to you, in order that you may decide what seems convenient. Now that the bull is in the ring, we shall see who are the clever ones. I believe you are among them: I even believe you the best. Let us cast fear aside and save the country. You have seduced me and I am compromised: it is necessary, therefore, that you do your duty."

Not suddenly did the Liberator decide to follow the path of dictatorship which he knew was dangerous.[3] The situation was exceptional, for really the Constitution did not exist, which the people had condemned and whose reform was decreed at Ocaña. The Assembly, in addition, had dissolved without providing a statute, and the authority which maintained the Government was very precarious. From Bucaramanga, in the midst of his vacillation, Bolívar planned to call a congress; but, to do so, it would be necessary to assume an authority of fact, which offered many obstacles. In any case, he would take counsel of men of light and influence in Bogotá.[4] The course of events, nevertheless, facilitated the solution of the problem.

As a matter of fact, on the 13th of June, the civil and ecclesiastical authorities and many fathers of families of Bogotá declared that "the Liberator President be authorized to assume full control with all the authority corresponding to it, to work for the good and to put aside the evil, until the circumstances and when his wisdom suggests it, he may call the nation by means of its representatives."[5] Doctor Restrepo, Minister of the Interior,

---

[1] *To General Salom, Bucaramanga, June 5, 1828.*
[2] *To Doctor Vergara, Bucaramanga, June 3, 1828.*
[3] *Vide Guerra, Obra citada, 505 passim.*
[4] *Diary of Bucaramanga, 223.*
[5] *Pronouncement of Bogotá, Doc. XII, 625.*

in transmitting the resolution to the Secretary to Bolívar, informed him that the members of the Council of the Government were firmly convinced "that there is no other means capable of saving the country than a strong and energetic Government, exercised by His Excellency the Liberator."[1] The Council had correctly interpreted its duty which Bolívar had described to Doctor Vergara.

The Liberator announced from Socorro his march to Bogotá,[2] at the same time the Minister of the Interior presented the views of the Government. Restrepo declared: "Let the Liberator assume and exercise exclusively the supreme command of the nation, save us from anarchy, conserve the union of Colombia, and perform for the people all the good which can be conferred by a government which is at the same time just in its resolution, firm and vigorous to punish crime and elevate virtue."[3]

Bolívar arrived at the capital on the 24th of June and, replying to the speeches addressed to him, repeated his wish to serve the country and respect the will of the people, "supreme law of the rulers. . . . I shall always be the defender of public liberty, and the national will shall exercise the true sovereignty. . . . The people is the source of all legitimacy and knows best what is right and what is just." It was a plebiscitary program to which an immense majority of the municipalities of the Republic, adhering to the pronouncement of Bogotá, agreed.[4]

---

[1]*Minister Restrepo to General Soublette, June 13*, 1828.

[2]*General Soublette to Doctor Restrepo, Socorro, June 16*, 1828. Bogotá.

[3]*Minister Restrepo to General Soublette, Bogotá, June 16*, 1828. Perú de Lacroix declared the Liberator considered the pronouncement of Bogotá as one of those unfortunate accidents "which show the loss of public morals, the obedience and respect of the people, causing them to become accustomed to political inconsistancies, to seditions and to popular excesses." (*The Diary of Bucaramanga*, 239.)

[4]*Letters of the Liberator to General Diego Ybarra and to Doctor Cristóbal Mendoza*, June 28, 1828. From the residence of Bolívar in Bucaramanga date one of the most interesting works which we possess for the study of the psychology and life of the author. His master of the camp, General Peru de Lacroix, an old official of Napoleon, completes, in effect, certain data and references which we find in O'Leary, in the *Diary*, published recently, written by a neo-Colombian. Written in 1828, or years afterwards, mutilated as it is, it seems impossible to raise any questions as to its veracity, which contains nothing incredible. It is, of course well known, that the reserve which characterizes the discourses of the heroes, reminds one of the method of Thucidides. On the other hand, the judgments which the Liberator passed upon Páez, for example, for whom Bolívar had very great respect, or that on Soublette and on Wilson, his confidants of those days, were indisceet pronouncements in the mouth of a man, who, according to this same narrator, was guarded only in the secretariat of Colonel Santana, because he knew how to keep a secret. . . . The *Diary of Bucaramanga* is an imitation of the *Memoirs of Saint Helena*.

The Dictatorship

WHEN Bolívar again assumed the power, he did not imagine that Colombia could be saved simply by the mere deed of being freed from the faction of Santander and by entrusting to one man the responsibility of restoring the weak national organism. Bolívar feared, in fact, that the evils of his Republic would resist the most energetic measures and that one will would not be enough, even though it was the will which had liberated America, to annul the influences which were decomposing this society. As early as May, and while still at Bucaramanga, the Liberator confided his inquietude to General Brisceño Médnez:[1]

"I should like to know what we can do in a country where at each step the government dissolves or conspires against it. I do not know to what we aspire nor the end which we propose in our sacrifices. Imagine that I have served the Republic four more years, and that it has miraculously been maintained more or less peacefully. Given this case, which I do not see at all possible, in whose hands shall the country be put in order to maintain it in order and harmony? You may imagine that you would like to give it to General Sucre. But I tell you that Sucre could not maintain it. And I will tell you more, he would never accept it, because he is most tired of the ingratitude and the instability of things American. Every day he writes me he can construct nothing on a base of sand, of which the whole American people is composed. Do not doubt it. We cannot form a stable government, because we lack many things, and above all men who can command and know how to obey. Still less are we able to govern a vast and extensive empire with democratic laws. On the other hand, we shall never have any other laws, because each Convention will be worse than the one before."

And Bolívar continued condemning men and things, in the language which he himself, in terminating it, characterized as emphatic.

With an irremediable disillusionment in his soul, the Liberator entered the saddest and most tremendous period of his life. In Bogotá, the contact with the difficulties of public affairs did not help to lighten his mind in his struggle against disenchantment and illness. His pessimism at this time was pronounced, as was before, the formidable optimism which had guided him through the times of Revolution and had given him successes and victories. "Yes, my friend," he wrote to the poet Olmeda, at the beginning of his Dictatorship, "I have converted myself on the way to heaven. I find myself repenting my profane conduct. Tired of imitating Alexander, I go in search of Diogenes, to take from him his lantern, his barrel, or his house. Everything tires one in this life. It is the fault of nature, which I have not the right to improve or reform. It is time, then, for other heroes to enter to play their parts, since mine has terminated, because you

---

[1] *To General Brisceño Méndez, Bucaramanga, May 29, 1828.*

172

know very well that fortune, like all the women, enjoy changes, and as my lady finds herself tired of me, I have, also, become tired of her."[1]

Bolívar was vacillating, as we have seen, when, the legal government had been suppressed, about the convenient road, he entered into possession of a *de facto* authority, which the municipalities confirmed and which the factions seemed to accept provisionally. The popularity of the Liberator, however, outshone his last acts. The respect that his name inspired in the chiefs and the hope of the nation in his inexhaustible genius, did not resist the new and rude proof. Bolívar sick of the Dictatorship was not able to control the events which make him creep about, impotent and conquered, up to the eclipse of San Pedro Alejandrino. Like the ancient athlete of Crete, Bolívar buried his fists in the false trunk which delivered him to the beasts of the forest.[2]

The projects of the Liberator led as always, to the strengthening of the government, maintaining national integrity, giving the country flexible institutions, after the hard experience of the past. He would apply these ideas "when the Republic shall have pronounced its votes in this new epoch," that is to say, when the people to whom he appealed should confirm his powers.[3] "I shall form a Council of State," he wrote to Briseño Méndez, "composed of deputies named by each department, who shall pass the laws and decrees which are to be made, and at the same time guard the welfare of each individual in their respective departments. These individuals will be selected from among the most deserving and the most honorable."[4] According to the records of Don Joaquin Mosquera, the Liberator had the intention, in the middle of August, of giving Colombia a Constitution, consisting of the following bases: a life president; a life senate, composed of two senators from each department, designated by the Liberator President; a renewable house of representatives, formed by two deputies from each province. Bolívar gave up the project because of the observation of Mosquera; and charged Castillo, at the instance of Mosquera, with the task of formulating the Organic Decree of the 27th of August. Don Joaquin had brought out, among other reasons, the fact that the people had granted the Liberator the power of governing until he should have convoked a congress, but not the power of "constituting" the Republic.[5]

---

[1] *To Don José Joaquin Olmedo, Bogotá, July 6,* 1828.

[2] *Vide* the defense which Restrepo made of the Liberator in accepting the supreme command. IV, 108.

[3] *The Letters of Bolívar to Mendoza and to Briseño Méndez. Bogotá, July 20,* 1828.

[4] *To General Briseño Méndez, Bogotá, July 20,* 1828.

[5] *Don Joaquin Mosquera to Don Felipe Larrazábal, Popayán, August 4,* 1828.

After two months of preparation, signalized by reactionary and semi-repressive decrees, Bolívar decided to proclaim the Dictatorship, and announced it to the nation, presenting this act as an imposition by the sovereignty of the people, terrified by the mountain wave of anarchy. A definite program informed Colombia that the Dictator would protect "the sacred religion as the faith of all the Colombians and the code of the good"; that he would dispense justice, reduce the taxes, and that he would convene, within one year, the representatives of the nation. "Let us mutually respect one another," concluded this eloquent proclamation, "the people who obey and the man who governs alone."[1] The exercise of public power was organized by a decree which invested the Liberator with the supreme command, assisted by a Council of State, composed of the ministers of the cabinet and of counsellors from each department. The intendencies were suppressed, and the territory divided into prefectures. Courts and tribunals for civil and commercial cases, admiralty courts, and military tribunals were instituted. The Government appointed and removed all the officials. This régime was to continue as constitutional law until congress, convoked for the 2nd of January, 1830, should dictate the Constitution of the State.[2] The Liberator believed that with the decree and the proclamation he would see the people "assured of their interests at the same time that he flattered the hopes of the demagogues, offering them a national convention."[3] "A national congress will be convoked," he wrote to Doctor Alarmo, "so that the people may believe, or rather the demagogues, that I do not wish to govern without a congress."[4]

The policy of the Dictatorship was essentially reactionary and conservative. Bolívar, who never deceived himself about the application of democratic principles in America, cared little, once he was in control of complete power, to hide his disdain of the protests of liberal opinion. Prosecuting as the immediate object the order of the State, he did not hesitate to sacrifice liberty and the sonorous postulates of the Revolution. In the struggle against anarchy, the Liberator demanded the aid of all the factors of reaction. Unfortunately, the only forces that could serve him in a country whose political tradition had been lost in the formidable combat for independence, were, precisely, two forces haughty or dangerous for the success of his ideal: the army and the clergy. The army, on the one hand, represented by the ambitious generals who aspired to create for themselves feudal power on the ruins of

---

[1]*The Liberator to the Colombians, Bogotá, August 27,* 1828.

[2]*Vide* the text of the decree. *Doc. XIII,* 13. Consult also Gil Fortoul, I, 435, and Restrepo, IV, 110. Th rules for the regulation of the Council of State was issued September 20, 1828.

[3]*The Liberator to General Salom, Bogotá, August 20,* 1828.

[4]*To Doctor José Angel de Alamo, Bogotá, August 24,* 1828.

the national unity, for no one was of sufficient stature to seize as a whole the succession of Alexander, was of doubtful loyalty, practiced uprisings as formerly they realized victory; and the soldiers did not yet see the daily spectacle of the Bolivarian glory, prolonging itself in each battle, like a radiant wake through the skies of America. There remained the clergy, the religion of the upper classes, the fanaticism of the masses, and Bolívar resolved to exploit them. His decrees revealed the intention to combat liberalism, which he believed to be the fountain of the anarchy, and to fortify the army in which he saw the bulwark of the public power. With these elements, united through his personal authority, he believed, still, that he could save the country.[1] But the Liberator did not renounce without pain his old illusions. It might be said that he reproached himself for the decision to follow a new path. "You know," he wrote to Arboledo, "that glory and war are my weaknesses, and you will not doubt that I will use all my strength because the love of country and the desire of victory occupy the void left in us by the beautfiul chimera of social perfection. This chimera, as you say, is too seductive, but the painful picture of our deceptions is worth more than a chimera and a thousand hopes." Bolívar excused himself with historic fatality, threw on the law of social movements the responsibility for his conduct, and prepared an absolution for his acts. He declared:

---

[1]There were the principal decrees of 1828. On the 10th of July the convents were reestablished. The law of March 4, 1826, was repealed, which prohibited the admission of novices before the age of twenty-five years, and which Bolívar himself enforced in Perú. The posts of vicars and chaplains were reestablished in the army on July 28th. There were introduced, by decree of October 20th, which was completed on March 12th, certain variations in the general plan of studies of the University of Bogotá, ordered the study of Latin and the suppression of the chairs on the principles of legislation and of constitutional and administrative law, at the same time there was created "a chair of the principles and apologetics of the Roman Catholic religion, of its history and of ecclesiasticalism," in order that "the curates shall be grounded in the principles of our holy religion, and so that they may be able, on the other hand, to fight the sophisms of the impious and to aid them to better control their passions." On the 29th of November, the new colleges of Rosario and of San Bartolomé were opened. As for the army, the Liberator, in order to attend the war in Perú, to defeat the Spanish and to protect his power, ordered the army increased to forty thousand men and decreed the organization of the national militia on the 7th of August. On the 27th of the same month, an order of the Minister of War declared established the military tribunal for the men who composed the militia, giving to the military courts in this way an enormous amount of power and to the despoticism of the Government. Two days later, it was ordered that the old Spanish Ordinance of 1768 was to be enforced. The decree of the 8th of November should also be mentioned, which prohibited secret societies, strengthened by another decree of the Intendant of Cundinamarca, General Alcántara Herrán, which made conspiracy a crime and criminals of those who disobeyed it. The judicial power was reorganized in November. In October a special tax was levied and a tribute of three pesos and four *reals* annually was laid on all the natives of Colombia, from eighteen to sixty years of age, except those Indians who possessed a thousand pesos in goods or property, personal or real, who were then subject to the ordinary taxes.

This history of the world tells us that the movements of the people have had to submit to a strong stable order. You saw the French Revolution, the greatest event in the life of man, the colossus of the most seductive illusions. Yet everything fell at the end of eight years of painful hopes. Note that that Revolution was indigenous, was a property of the French and, yet, only eight years and one man put an end to it and turned it into an absolutely contrary direction. And if we need the double and much more time, it is because our man is infinitely smaller than that of France, and needs ten times as much time as Napoleon to do much less than he. But I believe that something will be done which will lead to the happiness of Colombia. . . ."[1]

As has been written, the Liberator, in promising the convocation of the congress, sought to silence the voices of the opposition, although he may have wanted no assembly of any kind, harboring the secret hope that the people "would authorize the Government to give them a fundamental law" and to prolong indefinitely the provisional régime, in order to work for the organization of the country. A letter to Brisceño Méndez is significant in this connection. The difficulties to be encountered in forming "a good congress" were great. "The men of ability will not attend it, the roads are horrible, and the distances immense. Only the fools or the intrigants will act as popular representatives. . . . Three individuals in the Great Convention decided the fate of Colobmia, even against the people, the army, and the government."[2] Bolívar hoped that a people in whom he did not believe would confirm and complete his power. That is to say, he requested the authority to constitute the country, and this disposition explained his vacillations and his fears. The fear of public opinion made him give up the project of which Mosquera spoke. According to his words to Brisceño Méndez: "The Council of State wished to give a permanent constitution, with an irremovable house and a life president; but the congress embarrassed us, on the one hand, from working with effect, and in the naming of the executive, on the other. The project was very bold, and might have prejudiced public opinion against me. I resolved at last to let myself be guided by it and this is my last resolution."[3] On the 19th of the same month he repeated these views to Colonel Tomás Cipriano de Mosquera: "For my part, I have no other law than that of accomplishing the public will. I certainly shall not forget it, not even for its own good, my motto being *obedience to the people*."[4]

The new régime was immediately accepted by General Páez, who announced on the 15th of July, to the departments of Venezuela, that the Liberator, acclaimed, would save the country. Caracas adhered to the proclamation of Bogotá, and on the 4th of September an assembly of the citizens of the city, Bolivarians,

[1] *To Don José Rafael Arboledo, Bogotá, July 20,* 1828

[2] *To Brisceño Méndez, Bogotá, September 5,* 1828.

[3] *To Brisceño Méndez, Bogotá, September 5,* 1828.

[4] *To Mosquera, Bogotá, September 19,* 1828.

among whom were some members of the municipality, declared that "the municipal bodies had done very little for the welfare of the people," and asked that they be suppressed. Valencia and other cities formulated identical requests. Páez accepted the Liberator as the Supreme Chief of Colombia. With these acts the automony of Venezuela was confirmed, under the domination of the general of the plains, to whom, as Gil Fortoul has declared, federation, centralism, or dictatorship were indifferent, provided always that he was at the head of its government. Venezuela was a State within a State,[1] and the powerful feudal lord intended, as we shall see, to be free in his own dominion, showing only in the public papers and in certain letters a vassalage to Bogotá, as troublesome as it was illusory. In the full Convention of Ocaña, Bolívar showed himself uneasy over the proceedings of the Supreme Chief. "General Páez," he wrote to Carabaño, "has no more power than to watch over the intendants and military chiefs, to control force and the resources in order to maintain internal order and to defend the country. Nevertheless, he does what he pleases. If he proposes what is right, I will do it; but it is impossible to have two Governments in the Republic."[2]

But it was so, in effect. A decree of Páez suppressed the municipalities in Venezuela, and another created in place of these magistrates, for the economic organization and for justice.[3] An earlier decree by Bolívar on this same matter was declared suspended. The Government did not dare to oppose the measure of Caracas, which used and abused its powers. The Minister of the Interior recommended to Soublette that he inquire cautiously whether Páez would accept the change in his title from Superior Chief to that of Prefect General, instituted by the decree of the 23rd of December, 1828.[4] The laws were not applied to Páez. He was consulted so that he might say whether it suited him to obey them. We are in the period of the manifesto of the Colombians of the North, in which epoch the baron apologized for the Liberator, proclaimed his own public sentiments, and promised to support Bolívar for all time.

As for the provinces of the South, anarchy continued to disturb them, stimulated by the Peruvian Government which, headed by the Guayaquilanian Lamar, sought to dismember Colombia. The foreign relations also complicated the internal situation. In Lima, the Congress had passed a decree in preparation for war "against the present head of Colombia and Bolívia," for the boldness of "General Bolívar in carrying forward his plan

---

[1]Gil Fortoul, I, 445.

[2]*To Carabaño, Bucaramanga, May 13*, 1828.

[3]*Doc. XIII*, 119. Bolívar approved these measures March 5, 1829.

[4]*Minister Restrepo to Soublette, Bogotá, March 16*, 1829.

of domination, attacking the independence of the Republic."[1]
The Liberator, on his part, called the people to the national
defense, enlarged the army, and, on the 15th of July, broke off
diplomatic relations with the Government of Lima. Desirous,
no doubt, of resorting to peaceful means, he sent Colonel O'Leary
to Perú charged with the task of proposing an armistice and to
negotiate for peace.[2]

To the decree of Bolívar, assuming the dictatorship, the
demagogues replied with the act of the 25th of September, which
provoked the Government to take retalitory measures. "Gene-
rosity," declared the Liberator to General Páez, "has given us,
up to this time, nothing but backsliding. Then let justice pre-
vail." And on the day following the crime, he invested himself
with "the authority that the national vote confided in me,"
that is to say, he annulled, for an indeterminate period, the decree
of August 27th. He encouraged the prelates to instruct their
priests to teach the people the duty of supporting the Government
"as a rigid obligation of conscience" and "a great service to
God and to the State."[3] Fourteen conspirators were executed,
as a result of this. General Santander owed his life to the policy
of the Liberator, but lost his military rank, and was condemned
to perpetual exile. The Liberator determined before hand the
fate of the Vice President, to judge by a letter written to General
Salom. "Of General Santander I cannot even tell you what will
happen. But there are signs that he will be expelled at least,
although if we were rigorous in judging him, and if he had been
my most bitter enemy, I could not see myself compromised by
being generous with him, there being quite sufficient cause for him
to perish."[4] His own pride and the high concept of his personality,
induced Bolívar to be merciful. "You will already have known
the worming out of the conspirators," he wrote to Doctor Peña,
"and the extraordinary clemency which I have exercised. More
than my own life, I care for the remains of a reputation acquired

[1]On the 3rd of March, 1828, the Government of Colombia sent to that of
Perú an ultimatum through the Minister of that Republic in Bogotá, in which it
was given six months to return the provinces of Jaén and Mains, which they
occupied at that time; to pay Colombia 3,500,000 pesos, an amount equal to the
cost of the war of independence of Perú; and to withdraw or decrease the number
of troops on the frontier. *Vide Doc.* XII, 506. On the 29th of May the Peruvian
representative received his passports. The Governments of Buenos Aires and of
Chile offered their good offices to prevent war.

[2]O'Leary, *Appendix*, 409.

[3]*Circular of the Minister of the Interior. September 27*, 1828.

[4]*To General Salom, Bogotá, October 16*, 1828. The military tribunal condemned
on the 7th of November, Santander to death, which sentence was commuted by the
Liberator. The extraordinary volubility of Bolívar in this period contributed
to intensify the feeling against him shortly after this act of clemency. "Each day,"
he wrote, "it seems more imprudent to have to save Santander. This man will be the
ruin ultimately of Colombia. Time will tell." *To General Urdaneta*, December 14,
1828. *Vide* also his letters to Briseño Méndez, of November 9 and 16, of the same
year.

at such cost and voluntarily wounded by enemies of an authority which no one else has wielded with greater moderation."[1]

The reaction followed energetically. The municipalities were suspended and the political power given to the political and military chiefs. The political and economic régime was organized on the 23rd of December, in accordance with the Organic Decree of the 27th of August. The domination of the prefectures was given to the intendants; the prefects supervised, also, the police and, when the Government thought it proper, the military authority in their districts. The governors of the provinces were given the powers of the police, and were assisted by a lieutenant, experienced in law, to take charge of legal matters. The political chiefs were changed into political judges, and all the officials placed under the immediate control of the Supreme Government.[2] Centralism, so dear to Bolívar, was accentuated, losing him the confidence of sincere republicans and firing the ambition of revolters, who were swarming about in Colombia. In order to calm the uneasiness, the Liberator called a Constituent Convention in Bogotá to meet on January 2, 1830, to dictate a constitution "in conformity with the theories of the century, as well as with the habits and the needs of the country."[3]

Córdoba was sent to Pasto to quell the rebellion of Obando and López. The Liberator appointed the Marshal of Ayacucho Superior Chief of the Departments of Ecuador, Guayaquil, and Azuay, to repell the Peruvian invasion, granting him "all my powers, good or bad." He wrote: "You wage war; you make peace; save or lose the South. You are the arbiter of its fate, and in you I confide all my hopes."[4] Bolívar was seized with a panic of comfortlessness, at this time, as a result of this whole situation. And his voice resounded throughout the Continent, after a fearful night, some say, like the clamor of a prophet. "Neither in Colombia nor in Perú can anything good be done," he exclaimed, "neither is the prestige of my name worth anything. All has

---

[1] *To Doctor Miguel Peña, La Mesa, December 6,* 1828.

[2] There was a special régime in Venezuela, decreed by General Páez.

[3] Decree of December 24, 1828. On this same date the regulations governing the elections were issued. These regulations laid down the following conditions for voting; a man should be twenty-one years of age, or married: should be a citizen of the country, or a public official: should have an annual income of not less than 180 pesos: and should be in full possession of civil rights. The assembly of voters should choose an elector for each canton. This elector should know how to read and write, should be thirty years of age, and should have an annual income of 380 pesos. The electors of each province, the number of which should not be less than ten, should meet on the 1st of July, 1829, and should be presided over by the governor. After having "heard a solemn mass and a religious exhortation on the duties and responsibilities of the high office to which they had been called" should choose the delegates to the Constituent Convention, on the basis of one for each 40,000, and another for each 20,000 inhabitants. The deputy should have an annual income of 500 pesos. This was the system of the Constitution of Cúcuta with bit slight variations.

[3] *To Marshal Sucre, Bogotá, October 28,* 1828.

disappeared for ever. . . ." To General Flores he added:
"Renounce the chimera of hope. Instinct alone makes us live,
but without purpose usually. And what object can there be in a
people where neither glory nor happiness stimulate the citizens?"[1]

His enemies in the meanwhile accused Bolívar of aspiring to
the crown and this rumor acquired a certain degree of importance
in Cauca, and in the eastern provinces of Venezuela, where the
Castillos raised a revolutionary party and left for the war against
usurpation. In vain did the Liberator deny such stories, because
the general situation and the means which the Government took
to preserve order favored the seditious conspiracies and the pro-
pagation of anarchy, because of the fear which the secret proposals of Caesar inspired in the republicans. The words of Bolívar
were, nevertheless, catagorical. He declared to Doctor Vergara:

> "You know that the mail has brought me nothing of great interest. The
> war of opinion waged in Cauca by Obando and López and in Maturín by the
> Castillos requires directing the opinion of justice and truth. Nothing else is
> heard than that I am a tyrant of my country, and that I only aspire to erect
> an imperial throne on the ruins of the liberty of Colombia. Although my friends
> laugh at these calumnies, and my friends include all men of good judgment.
> The calumnies influence the innocent public; they thrive in the shadow of
> partisanship; and when least we may think these impostures would appear in so
> colossal a form that they would become masters of public opinion. The English
> newspapers, those of the United States, and who knows what others, speak in
> the same vein of a monarchy. It is of prime importance to refute these false
> opinions; to give the lie to these imposters with bitterness, precision and energy
> which they deserve; to undeceive the nation and promise it that next year will
> see the national representation assembled with full liberty. Arrange that there
> be published in the Gaceta and other papers the desired object, and that these
> be written with candor, but with the fire of indignation which calumny and
> demagogy excite.

On the same day he wrote to Salom, Urdaneta, and Montilla,
that they might destroy "the calumnies which my enemies
propagate, more especially that I wish to be crowned." To Páez
and Briscẽno he wrote that "it is necessary that you issue a
manifesto sufficiently clear and energetic, persuading the people
with the language of truth and making them see that there is no
intention of establishing an empire."[2] Bolívar, besides, declared
through the Gaceta de Colombia' organ of the Government:

> Do not tell us now that the Liberator has a different opinion on the form
> of government which is most suitable for the Republic. He has held it and mani-
> fested it publically and privately, always advocating the same ideas from the
> Assembly of the Congress of Angostura until today. This frankness, at the same
> time that it is the best proof of his patriotism and honor, is the best guarantee
> that he does not aspire to this throne, for everybody knows that for this class
> of undertaking there is no better path than dissimulation and hypocracy."[3]

Such protests did not bring the results hoped for by Bolívar,
that is, the reestablishment of peace and confidence in the people.

---

[1]*To General Flores, Bogotá, October 8, 1828.*
[2]*To Briscẽno Méndez, Bojacá, December 16, 1828.*
[3]*Gaceta de Colombia. No. 392. January, 1829.*

And when, in the following year, the projects for the establishment of a monarchy became a principle of execution in the bosom of the Government, the campaign of insults and discredit against the Liberator gained such strength that it came near causing the ruin of Colombia, and disappearance of him from political life. Even the events of the South, which were about to break out, could not occupy public opinion on matters of a foreign nature.

Bolívar, after delegating to the Council of Ministers the exercise of his authority for the conduct of ordinary business, reserved to himself the sanction of all administrative acts, and marched to Cauca, which was still in rebellion.

The war with Perú was decided at Tarqui, where the Marshal of Ayacucho, after a campaign particularly laborious, because of the extraordinary blunders of the adversary,[1] gained the victor over President Lamar, on whom he imposed the Convention of Girón, not ratified by the Government of Limá.[2] Obando submitted at the beginning of March. The pacification of the country seemed well under way and his triumph against the foreigner gave new glory to the declining lustre of Colombia. The Liberator installed himself in Quito, in the midst of those people whom he believed had "conserved their primitive enthusiasm," and in a proclamation full of moderation announced that he would refrain from prosecuting great military operations against Perú, in order to dissipate the legend of his "conquest."[3] After having secured this indispensible triumph, Bolívar desired peace. He wrote to Urdaneta that "steps should be taken with the friendly governments" with the object of obtaining peace, because "I do not wish to displease the people of Colombia with new sacrifices, nor that my enemies may justify the ambition which they have attributed to me" and this in spite of the fact that "we do not lack the means of conquering Perú." Chance, more than policy, or as much as it, inspired in him these sentiments of an incurable disillusion: "I assure you," he concluded, "that, although I am prepared to see such horrors, I am frightened on contemplating the future picture that this country (America) offers. Even now it is horrible; later it will be worse. No restraint, no duty is respected; everything is involved in chaos of disorder."[4] "There is no faith in America, either between men or between nations. Treaties are scraps of paper; the constitutions, books; liberty, anarchy; and life, a torment."[5]

---

[1]*Official Report of the Chief of the Staff of the Major General of the Colombian Army, Colonel León de Febres Cordero.* The battle was fought on February 27, 1829.

[2]The definite treaty of peace was signed on the 22nd of the following September, in Guayaquil. The Chilean Government was designated as arbiter and conciliator to regulate the difference that might arise in its enforcement.

[3]*April 3*, 1829.

[4]*To General Urdaneta, April 6*, 1829.

[5]*A View of Spanish America (Mirada sobre la America Española), Quito, April,* 1829.

Anarchy presented, among its thousand forms, something which disquieted Bolívar particularly. The federalist phenomenon grew day by day more noticable all over the Continent, which the Liberator compared to medieval feudalism, and which was, in effect, the work of the unruly barons born of the Revolution. Bolívar fought these tendencies toward federation, which continued in attributing, each time for politics, the usurpation of sovereignty, realized in Colombia by Santander and his partisans;[1] but by reason of the irresistible course of events which even he felt himself drawn to a belief in local autonomy. The differences of customs, and aspirations, as well as the political necessities of the character, diverse departments, drew from him, perhaps unconsciously, a true autonomy as in Venezuela, or a favorable, but very dangerous, attitude, as in Quito. The decree of the 11th of April, created a junta entrusted with the task of presenting to the Supreme Government the solicitudes which were judged useful for the people of the South, relative to reforms in the administration, in finance, and in municipal government; and for which institutions Bolívar declared that "I desire to consult public opinion and to hear the petitions from the Colombians of the South on the matters concerning them in the administrative, economic, and municipal branches, and the interests of each province." This decree was, in fact, the recognition of the formidable pretensions, in one way or another, of the Ecuadorian departments, from their annexation to the Republic.[2]

The question of the monarchy, agitated simultaneously in Perú, where the reaction against Lamar increased the prestige of Bolívar, and in Colombia, whose own Minister of War took the initiative in negotiating with Páez the foundation of a throne, definitely compromised the authority of the Liberator and his popularity. It was at this time that General Gamarra proposed to Flores that Bolívar proclaim himself emperor of Colombia and Perú, "which Flores refused with reflections full of moderation and strength."[3] The Liberator judged that, in this matter as in

---

[1]*The Liberator to General Montilla, Quita, March 26,* 1829.

[2]On the autonomy, more or less effective, which the different provinces of Colombia enjoyed, see Restrepo, IV, 201. The federalist tendency in America had its source in the colonial period. Doctor Estaban Gil Borges, wrote to us in this vein, in February, 1916: "There was an interesting and original aspect of this epoch (the colonial) which has not yet been studied, and that is the feudal character of the American institutions. The elements of colonial feudalism are to be found in the economic organization, in the life of the family, in the structure of the political institutions. It is a large field unexplored which leads to rational explanations of the phenomena of regionalism, of unitarianism, of personalism (*caudillismo*). You know that an explanation of these phenomena had, up to this time, been sought in the surface of history. I believe it is necessary to look deeper, to find their origin."

[3]*The Liberator to General Brisceño Méndez, Quito, March 26,* 1829.

that of federation, all was usurpation of the sovereignty and that "no one had seen the will of the people written."[1]

The condition of America in general, and the unwillingness of Perú to conclude peace, gave in Bolívar an idea which had grave consequences, because of the interpretation which the official circle in Bogotá gave it. He desired that England, or the United States, or France, should serve as arbiters in our differences and to interest themselves sufficiently in our affairs, in order, if that were possible, to establish internal order and peace without. He thus expressed it to Urdaneta:

> "The Government of Bolivia has declared itself for the league of Perú, as was natural, and has even threatened us with Chile. I laugh at all these forces of the *canaille*. Buenos Aires has had, in five days, three presidents, having killed two of them. Chile is in very inept and vacillating hands. Mexico has had a major scandal and had committed the gravest crimes. Guatemala increases its difficulties. All this makes me believe that this world of anarchy needs foreign intervention which may serve as a mediator in our differences and our madnesses. May the United States do something with Perú which has chosen them as guarantees in order to make a joke of them."

Later the Liberator ordered his Minister of War to demand of Campbell "that he should make England see that our enemies (the Peruvians) are implacable, and that the anarchy of America will be eternal, if means to stop it are not adopted."[2] The Secretary-General of the Liberator had transmitted, two days before, to the Cabinet, a communication to the Minister of Foreign Relations. Bolívar desired to defend Colombia against external danger, "characterized by the finger of vengeance and of resentment," threatened by an alliance in formation. He desired an honorable and permanent peace, soliciting, in order to secure, the *mediation* of the United States, or, in order to repel any possible attack, the *protection* of a European power ,that of Great Britain particularly. The Liberator authorized the Council of Ministers to study this matter on which "depends the fate of Colombia," and to sound out the English and American representatives in the matter, in order eventually to have the negotiations take on an official character.[3] The Liberator insisted, months later, that the Council consider the project. Espinar declared to the Minister of Foreign Relations:[4]

> "His Excellency does not have the remotest interest in this business, outside of Colombia, outside of America. He does not consider the form; he looks for the thing. Call it what you will, so long as the result corresponds to his desires, that is that America puts herself under the custody of a safeguard, meditation or influence of one or more powerful States, which will preserve her from destruction to which she is heading through anarchy developed in her system and the colonial régime with which she is menaced."

---

[1]*The Liberator to General Montilla, Quito, March 26, 1829.*
[2]*To General Urdaneta, April 6, 1829.*
[3]*Secretary Espinar to the Minister of Foreign Relations, Quito, April 4, 1829.*
[4]*Secretary Espinar to the Minister of Foreign Relations, Buijo, July 6, 1829.*

Bolívar could hardly have imagined the extensive notice that was given to his thought, nor the harm which so vague an insinuation would cause his reputation.

General Urdaneta, on his part, informed Páez, before receiving these impressions, that the envoy of Austria would advise him by word of mouth about "the general ideas of sensible people, of persons of rank, by fate, by family, or by interest of the clergy and of the army," who wished "to save the country from the convulsions to which it had been exposed."[1] Urdaneta showed himself "tired of waiting for the resignation of the Liberator, resolved not to count on him in this matter, because I know he will say 'no' ", and proposed to change the form of government, because Colombia could never be consolidated itself with the existing one. To this General Páez replied that in the matter of reforms he considered it better to elect the Liberator president for ten years, with veto power and the right to present laws, to command the army, and reform the Constitution with the approval of Congress, according to the circumstances. Páez rejected the plan to establish immediately the monarchy.[2]

Urdaneta appeared to be in agreement with these ideas,[3] but, some months later, he wrote again to the Chief of Venezuela: "You will tell me that the Liberator rejects the monarchy because a thousand times he has told you so and has told everybody so. It is true. I know that he has always opposed consideration of this matter; but I also know that this has been because the matter being intimately related to his person, it was not decent, nor could he admit the idea. But ask him apart from himself, if he believes this step necessary, if he believes it the only way to save the country, and he will answer that it is."[4] In the course of these negotiations with Páez, General Urdaneta fell into certain contradictions which should be noted. The meritorious Zuelan knew, as did the whole world, what the ideas of Bolívar were as to the monarchy. A year before the Liberator spoke to him of "a trifle which even seems dangerous," on giving the order to publish The Friend of the Country (El Amigo del Pais) a refutation of the propositions of The Echo of Azuay (El Eco de Azuay) on an American monarchy, Bolívar wrote:[5]

"They will say that this project is mine, therefore, I wish my friends to write against it, stating what the project deserves, and attributing it to whomever may be responsible, because they may say that it is I, it is necessary to say that it is they. . . . After that, you might mention me and the hate I have of the imperial system, and on that head many important references could be made."

---

[1] General Urdaneta to General Páez, Bogotá, April 3, 1829.
[2] General Páez to General Urdaneta, Caracas, May 3, 1829.
[3] General Urdaneta to General Páez, Bogotá, May 30, 1829.
[4] General Urdaneta to General Páez, Bogotá, September 9, 1829.
[5] The Liberator to General Urdaneta, Bucaramanga, May 8, 1829. Vide also the exordium written by Bolívar, which was published in O'Leary. Appendix, 300.

It is quite certain that Bolívar anticipated a change of régime, inspired by the disorder that was increasing. Any accident aided him in propagating his ideas. He told Montilla that he should take advantage of the usurpation of Lavelle, who "is governing liberally in the Tartar way" in Buenos Aires, and that he should write "with observations very strong and with what illusions he could to demonstrate the irregularities and embarrassments of our system."[1] He spoke in similar words on the same day to Briseño Méndez, to Doctor Vergara, to Restrepo:[2]

> "I am in entire agreement with you in that there is an imperative need of a change in the constitutional system in America, formerly Spanish, so that we may be consolidated, and I believe also that, although there be difficulties, they are not insurmountable, the more so if men of judgment would attempt to overcome them, being, as I consider them, wholly undeceived by the hypocracy and the wickedness of the demagogues. We have more reason every day to deplore the diabolical ideas which are given birth in this situation of things."

What meaning is to be given to these words? The logical thing, evidently, is to believe that they comprehend the immutable Bolivarian ideas, confirmed by recent declarations on the creation of a "stable government suitable to our actual situation,"[3] that is to say, the adoption of his system, whose restoration in Chuquisaca gratified the Liberator. "There has been established in Bolivia," he wrote, "the Bolivian Constitution, and the life incumbents are ruling everything very favorably for us."[4] It is the same thought which we find confirmed in the letter to Marshal Santa Cruz:[5]

> "I give thanks to Velasco for the restoration of the Bolivian Code, and I ask that you do not permit, if it be possible, the change in the nature of the executive and the legislative of this Constitution. The other powers permit of a thousand betterments and in part the exectuive may need to absorb them. . . The Congress which I have convoked will assemble and give a strong government, according to the public spirit which rules. Colombia has returned to its illusions, so that the Bolivian government appears to it a trifle. Its executive will be given more power than yours."

General Urdaneta came to know just exactly what the political principles of Bolívar were or his actual wish, not only in his letter to the Cabinet, addressed on the 13th of July to Doctor Vergara, but also from the catagoric and direct concepts which, on the same day, the Liberator issued: "There is no question about the project for a monarchy, for I do not wish and no foreign prince wishes to ascend a king's scaffold; and if I should forget at any time what I said to Bolivia, I have at my side Itúrbide who will

---

[1] *To General Montilla, Quito, May 6,* 1829
[2] *To Doctor Restrepo, Quito, May 6,* 1829.
[3] *View of Spanish America, Quito, April,* 1829.
[4] *Vide* the letters cited for May 6, 1829.
[5] *The Liberator to Marshal Santa Cruz, Barranca, June 23,* 1829.

remind me of it every day."[1] This did not prevent the illustrious
defender of Valencia from writing to General Páez: "The Liberator
has shown himself sorry that you did not welcome my proposal,
and has said so to me. . . ."[2] The chief was convinced,
perhaps, that Colombia needed a monarchical government,
tried to overcome the resistance of Páez by calling on the authority
of Bolívar, because it seems incomprehensible since the latter was
"always opposed to this being considered," should not have
been ensnared in a proposition of this kind. Bolívar, on the other
hand, was in Ecuador during nearly the whole of the year 29,
and it would be difficult to find a document to prove his communications with Urdaneta.

It was later that the affairs of Venezuela took a certain turn,
and the Minister of War appreciated the error which he had
committed in involving Bolívar in the project. He hastened to
rectify his asservations in a letter to Páez, in which he honorably
turned to the truth, and refrained from making use of his phrases,
in the future, to accuse the Liberator. In the last analysis, there
might be reason to challenge the testimony of the great soldier,
who fell into contradictions. "Read anew my correspondence,"
he wrote, "and in all you will see that the Liberator has been
very far from taking part in the project. . . . You told me
in one of your letters that you would do nothing unless the
Liberator ordered it,[3] because you did not wish to act in any matter
without his approval, and I replied that the Liberator could tell
you nothing about a matter which he disapproved, and if one
believes it proper for Colombia, it should be done by the nation,
absolutely apart from the Liberator, who never could approve it,
never could recommend it to you. . . . If, finally, it appears
from all my correspondance that the Liberator has been opposed
to this project, why is he attacked? Why so insulted?"[4]

A circumstance which prejudiced Bolívar in this matter was
his letter to Colonel Patrick Campbell, chargé d' affaires of His
Britannic Majesty in Bogotá. Urdaneta pointed out to Páez
that his document was a proof of his acquiescence, and that the
principal obstacle was overcome. The Liberator presented the
objections of the project to Campbell, concluding by saying that
when he should know definitely what France and England thought
of the matter, "he should renew his forces" for the purpose of
aiding in the "reorganization of Colombia in accordance with the

---

[1] The Liberator to General Urdaneta, Buio, July 13, 1829.

[2] General Urdaneta to General Páez, September 9, 1829.

[3] Páez, in effect, had told him that he would not separate himself in "the
slightest degree from what the Liberator ordered." Caracas, October 14, 1829.

[4] General Urdaneta to General Páez, Bogotá, February 9, 1830. It is probable
that there are those who can prove that Bolívar issued such an order to Urdaneta.
It would be necessary in addition to prove it, since the whole character of the
Government does not support this theory.

institutions which the experience of a wise Europe preferred."[1] Bolívar knew for a certainty that the nations named would never, either separately or jointly, undertake the extravagant venture of *imposing* a prince on the country, so that the question was not that of selecting a candidate for the throne. The United States and the American peoples in general were, also, experiencing grave troubles, and the Liberator could not be ignorant of this. In the event that they might be disposed to cooperate in the establishment of a monarchy, not at all probable, their aid depended upon a hypothesis not realizable: the agreement between France and Great Britain to *impose* a king on Colombia. Is it likely that if the agreement had been made, that Bolívar would have lent his aid to the operation? Neither the character of the Liberator, nor his ideas, nor his scruples before a liberal world, permit one to pronounce in favor of the affirmative.[2] Besides, death would have torn him away from a task which immortalized Warwick, but was unworthy of the Liberator of America.

In reality, Bolívar was advancing with great strides toward the tomb and his illness was incurable. He had come to a point where he hoped for nothing from presidents or from monarchs. He believed America was lost, fated to live on revolutions and usurpations for a long time, to be the prey of "petty tyrannies." In terrible and choleric words he repented of his work and complained of his fatigue. No, the Liberator would not have sacrificed his concept of glory in the adventure, and there would have been lacking the tremendous vigor of former times to accomplish it. Dissect this spirit:[3]

"There is not a day, there is not an hour, in which those abominable people do not make me drink the dregs of calumny. I wish no longer to be the victim of my consecration to the most hellish people which have occupied the earth, America, which after I have liberated it from its enemies and given it an undeserved freedom, they daily tear me to pieces with all the furies of its vile passions. No, friend, I will no longer be a martyr; and although it will cost me much to abandon my friends, it is impossible for me to endure the ridicule of all liberals of the world, who prefer the things of anarchy to the welfare of repose. They call me tyrant, and the sons of our capital have tried to punish me as such. Besides, no one loves me in New Granada, and nearly all the military

[1] *To Colonel Campbell, Guayaquil, August 5, 1829.* Gil Fortoul observed with much skill that "the ambiguous terms of this letter are explained, in part, by the desire not to reveal to a diplomat from abroad the discrepancy which existed already between his own mode of thought and that of his Council of Ministers." I, 461.

[2] "To elevate or not to elevate a throne—Secretary Espinar told the Government—is a matter with which the Liberator must not meddle. And what is more, he must not cooperate in its establishment, nor affirm, for the same reason, the inadequateness of the present form of government." Japio, December 18, 1829.

"But, to support monarchies of domination and the Spanish vice-royalties, was not to give the lie to his mission? The pure glory of the emancipator prohibited it, and, without doubt, also philosophical ideas." Jean Péres, *A Great Hispano-Latin Man (Un Grand Homme Hispano-Latin).* A work already cited.

[3] *The Liberator to Doctor Castillo, Quito, June 1, 1829.*

detest me. A hundred high grade men judge me necessary for the conservation of the Republic, considering me rather as a necessary evil than as a positive good. This is certain, evident, infallible. Why should I render services to him who does not appreciate them? Why should I sacrifice myself for an enemy people, who have been obliged by force to defend their rights, and still force is necessary for them to do their duty? In such countries there cannot arise a liberator, only a tyrant. Consequently, anybody may be better than I, for in in spite of myself I have had to degrade myself sometimes to this execrable duty."

Bolívar was convinced that no system would succeed in America.[1] He did not believe in the ability of the forthcoming congress, which might draft a constitution which "will not please everybody," which nobody would guarantee, because no one could answer "for my life, nor for my success, bor for popular waves, nor for the traitors."[2]

It has been said that the Liberator showed himself very susceptible to the opinions in Foreign countries on his political conduct, and this is among the elements to be considered in explaining his vacillations and fears. Sir Robert Wilson received more than once his confidence, with the hope that his friends "may justify my conduct and the principles which guides it," and "remember me in this time of unrest, in order to place me in contrast with the effects of anarchy and do me the justice which I have desired."[3] The attacks of Benjamin Constant caused Bolívar profound pain and he expressed himself thus to the British General: "You should consider me sorry enough for the yoke I have undertaken, and then to have fought for liberty and glory, they call me tyrant and reward me with vituperation. All America resounds with denunciations against me. The only hope that remains to me is that Europe will do me justice; but now this has deceived me, judging by the disenchantment which Constant has just caused me. De Pradt defends me with praise, but not with reasons and sound fundamentals."[4] In the hope of fighting off the calumnies and throwing light on what Benjamin Constant called usurpations, Bolívar ordered General Montilla to send to Leandor Palacios in Paris the documents bearing on his politics and life, and begged the latter to defend him. "In Bogotá," he declared, "they believe that changing the government will do much; but I am sorry to say that I hope for nothing from any form of the American system. This America is a New Guinea and must remain so because of its principles and social elements. . . . You will also give La Fayette my respects for his venerable opinions on which a part of my liberal glory rests."[6] O'Leary, appointed minister of Colombia in Washington, bore the mission to vindicate the Liberator before American

[1] *The Liberator to Urdaneta, Buijo, July 5, 1829.*
[2] *The Liberator to Urdaneta, Buijo, July 5, 1829.*
[3] *The Liberator to Restrepo, Buijo, July 7, 1829.*
[4] *The Liberator to Sir Robert Wilson, Quito, April 27, 1829.*
[6] *The Liberator to Sir Robert Wilson, Guayaquil, July 28, 1829.*

public opinion,[1] which was adverse to him, lamenting "that we may not achieve the happiness of Colombia with the laws and customs of the Americans, "because one can not "govern China like England.["2] Fears of the opinion in the United States were reflected in the official circles, as was proved by the words of President Jackson, in his Message to Congress, at the beginning of the following year. "The powerful influence which in the affairs of his country," declared this magistrate, "the heroic deeds and sacrifices have given General Bolívar, makes all lovers of liberal institutions anxious about his future conduct."[3] There were necessary besides "your patriotic message and the first resolutions of the Congress" to restore "confidence to many minds in Europe. . . ."[4]

By September, the Cabinet of Bogotá began conversations with the diplomatic agents of France and Great Britain[5] to whom they declared expressly "that the Council did not depend on the consent of the Liberator, for the eventual establishment of a monarchy in Colombia.[6] The bases of the negotiations were: the selection of a French prince to succeed Bolívar, the latter exercising the power during his life; the practical aid of France, in case the United States, or other American States should become hostile to Colombia. According to Restrepo, the Government believed itself authorized by the communications of the Liberator, dated April 4th and July 6th, to take the initiative. "Its members,"

---

[1]*The Liberator to General O'Leary, Guayaquil, August 17,* 1829.

[2]*The Liberator to Colonel Wilson, Guayaquil, August 3,* 1829.

[3]*President Jackson to the American Congress, January 19,* 1830.

[4]*General La Fayette to the Liberator, June 1,* 1830.

[5]One of the sons of Generalissomo Miranda and of Sarah Andrews went to see Colonel Campbell, who tells of it in a note to Doctor Vergara, from which it appears that a communication of the English representative to the Count of Aberdeen, dated September 7, 1829, which the author of the present work has extracted from the archives of the Foreign Office. Campbell writes:
"I have received a visit from Mr. Miranda, Sub Secretary of State for Foreign Affairs, who was born and educated in England. . . . Since Mr. Miranda is my intimate friend his visit did not suprise me; but after a general conversation he touched upon the question of a change in the form of the government of Colombia, and asked me what I thought of the opinion of the British Government was and if it inclined toward approving for Colombia, the establishment of a hereditary constitutional monarchy under a European prince, after the renunciation of the Liberator (Bolívar). I replied that he knew very well my own private and individual views on this particular point, that is to say: that, in the actual condition of Colombia, which is, as I think it is, the sentiment of the country, and if it can realize it easily, as I think it can, in that which concerns Colombia herself, without any internal commotion, the establishment of this form of government would contribute more than anything else to the consolidation of the country; but that I had no right to speak the opinions of my Government. . . . Mr. Miranda said, however, that he was very anxious to know what I thought of the matter, because he had received a note from Mr. Vergara in which he had explained the wish of the Government on this particular point, with the request that it be communicated to the Government of His Majesty." (The Note of 1927).

[6]Restrepo, IV, 226.

declared this historian, "know in general the opinions of Bolívar on the convenience of this form of government, for the countries of Spanish America which have been erected into republics; however, they do not know his method of thinking and the undesirable features he may find in applying the monarchical system to the reorganization of Colombia."[1] This insinuation of the Minister of the Interior deserves consideration, not with the purpose of defending the Liberator against trivial accusations, but to fix the historical criterion of the question. Restrepo expected the Liberator to place his influence at the service of a foreign prince, and he so expressed himself in treating of his plans when he returned from Perú. On the same page, however, he contradicts himself. "Bolívar believed, at the time, that the Constitution should be modified, not at once but within one or two years. He desired that the project used in Bolivia should be adopted, as far as was proper, for Colombia, in order to give it the permanent character that its government needed, for he feared above all the sanguinary wars, believing it impossible for any of the governments established in America, previously Spanish, could not maintain themselves against the storms and reverses of the periodic elections, without having a president and a senate serving for life."[2]

But where the honorable historian of Colombia is catagorical and knows Bolívar's views concerning the establishment of a monarchy, he assures us, in commenting on a letter by Bolívar to General Páez, that it "proves evidently the decided aversion of the Liberator to the plan of replacing the democratic principles which reigned in Colombia for those of a monarchy. But in spite of these undeniable deeds and of the repeated expressions published by Bolívar against the partisans of the plan to establish a throne in our Republic, he did not succeed in removing the distrust which many jealous republicans had formed concerning his intentions."[3] The ambition of Bolívar", he wrote on another occasion, "and his aspirations for a monarchy in Colombia and even in other parts of America, which his enemies attribute to him, have been gratuitous calumnies without any foundation whatever. His thoughts were always noble, elevated, and republican."[4] It is evident that, in the present case, there can be no question of the personal ambition of Bolívar for a crown, but of a project for "a constitutional monarchy after the days of the Liberator."[5] that the latter, also, decided "when he knew it,

[1]Restrepo, IV, 227.

[2]Restrepo, III, 557.

[3]*Ibidem*, III, 528.

[4]*Ibidem*, IV, 231. Vide the larger statement of the affirmations of Restrepo, in the same vein, on page 204, volume IV, of his work.

[5]Minister Restrepo to General Soublette, Bogotá, May 24, 1829. It is interesting to restate the testimonials of two foreign historians on this point:
    "That Bolívar desired a life dictatorship cannot be doubted. He considered

disapproved it confidentially, and afterwards did so officially and with more severity."[1] Several historians, Groot and Larazábal among others, prove that the Council of Ministers could not have been deceived for a moment of the views of Bolívar and all that is necessary is to compare the dates of the documents which we possess to be convinced of this. On the 13th of July, as we have seen, the Liberator wrote to Doctor Vergara, Minister of Foreign Relations, pointing out the principal objections to the project: the difficulty of finding a foreign prince who would care to ascend a throne without guarantees; poverty and debts for the country; the fears of the lower classes; the ambition of the generals. Bolívar declared that, in view of an inevitable civil war,[2] the best thing to do would be to divide Colombia, or, in the final analysis and after a conscientious investigation of the national will, to establish a life government, with an hereditary senate, even though he had no faith in the efficacy of any institution and considered as chimerical the union between Venezuela and New Granada.[3] This letter considered anarchy as the future fate of America. "Our country, unable to support either liberty or slavery, a thousand revolutions will make necessary a thousand usurpations. . . ."

The Liberator repeated, in a letter to General Páez, that his views on the political régime were those which he had always published and that he would add nothing to them, in spite of the fact that the "thinking people of Bogotá" were asking him for advice.[4] And further, on the other hand, to O'Leary—to whom he had formerly suggested the idea that the Congress might name a successor to him, retaining the powers of Generalissimo[5]— confirmed his arguments against the project for a monarchy which he believed impracticable, and insisted on the solutions which he had presented to Vergara, namely, to separate Venezuela from New Granada, or to create a permanent and powerful

---

it as the only means of affecting the liberation of America, believing it indispensible for the success of his plans and for the greatness of his country. In this matter he was on the way, fatally, leading to despotism. But we will persist in believing in his sincerity, in his good faith, and in his patriotism." Alfred Deberle, *History of South America*, Paris, 1897. "Nor is it to be presumed, on the other hand, that, during his last days, when he had lost hope in the great federation of the peoples, he aspired to a crown of Colombia for himself. . . . Bolívar may be thought of as absolutely above desiring a crown for himself." Lorain Petre. Cited in the work *Bolívar by the Greatest American Writers (Bolívar por los más grandes escritores americanos). Madrid*, 1915.

[1] *The Liberator to José Fernández Madrid, Bogotá, February 13*, 1830. *Vide* also the letter by Bolívar to Colonel Bedford Wilson, Guayaquil, August 3, 1829. Consult Larrazabal, II, 493, *passim.*

[2] The rebellion and the death of General Córdoba took place two months later.

[3] *The Liberator to Doctor Vergara, Buijo, July 13*, 1829.

[4] *The Liberator to General Páez, Guayaquil, September 5*, 1829.

[5] *The Liberator to General O'Leary, Guayaquil, August 6*, 1829. *Vide* also the etter of Bolívar to Vergara, Guayaquil, September 20, 1829.

régime. Colombia, he declared, "exists only because it is held together by my authority, which must fail now or later, when desired by Providence, or by men. . . . Let two governments be formed, allied against the common enemies, and let there be concluded an international treaty which will guarantee reciprocal relations. Time, which is fertile in resources, will do the rest. . . . The establishment of a life government, or whatever form is desired, but always in conformity with public opinion, will be the other extreme that the Congress might adopt. . . . I know that the present Republic cannot be governed without the sword, while at the same time I cannot but agree that the military spirit is insupportable in the civil command. . . ."[1] The Congress will always have to return to the question of dividing the country, because, whatever may be done, the election of the President must be excluded."[2] How far this beautiful vision of a confederation of America has fallen, which yesterday was to have been the union of the Bolivarian nations and which to-day is a precarious defensive alliance between New Granada and Venezuela!

On the 22nd of September, Bolívar put an end to the tentative plan for a monarchy by ordering the Council of the Government to leave to the forthcoming Congress "all necessary freedom for the accomplishment of its high duties; and that the present Administration suspend all the proceedings which have to do with the success of the negotiations with the Governments of France and England."[3] This is what Restrepo called the "sharp official disapproval" of the Liberator. From Japio, on the 18th of December, Secretary Espinar likewise condemned the project in question. Bolívar[4] refused "to permit an implied consent which

---

[1]These words explain the apprehensions of Bolívar before the crisis occasioned by these elements and by the pretentions of the military. *Vide* Restrepo, IV, 242.

[2]*The Liberator to General O'Leary, Guayaquil, September 13*, 1829. This document has been published several times and in different forms. *Vide* the *Memoirs of O'Leary, Letters of the Liberator*, XXXI, 514, and the *Documents for the Public Life of the Liberator*, XIII, 629. In order to determine just what were the ideas of Bolívar on the monarchical attempt, consult, in addition, his instructions to Colonel Austria, his envoy near to . . . and the letter of Páezy to Don Joaquin Mosquera of September 3, 1829.

[3]*Note of the Secretary of the Liberator to the Minister of Foreign Relations*. The representatives of Colombia in Paris and London took up this matter with the respective governments. That of France refrained from considering it. The British Government declared that it did not find the principle unacceptable, provided, always, that a Spanish prince was under consideration, but that nothing could be done during the life time of Bolívar. Bresson, the French agent in Bogotá, was an enthusiastic supporter of the plan.

[4]*Espinar to the Minister of the Interior, Japio, December 18*, 1829. In order to conclude the debate, already tedious, on the aspirations of Bolívar for a crown, it may be useful to note the testimony of Doctor Alejandro Próspero Révérend, his last physician, although we do not know at what precise moment the manifestation of which this learned man presents were made. It is nevertheless of much importance concerning the condition of the Liberator in Perú. "Among the papers," declared Révérend, "which according to the testament of the Liberator

openly opposes his own honor and individual interest." For many months the members of the Cabinet had covered themselves with the skin of the old lion.

In Venezuela, the proposition of the Minister of War, presented in a form which suggested the authorization of Bolívar, and later the formal project of the Government was inimical to the Colombian unity and the prestige of the Liberator. According to General Soublette, this project drove the Venezuelans into the path of separation.[1] That is to say, the two forces which had allied themselves since 1826 for the purpose of bringing about the dissolution of Colombia, or to substitute a federal system for the centralism of Cúcuta, the military party and the civil oligarchy,[2] took advantage of the opportunity to aim new and mortal blows against the national organization. In July, 1829, the electoral college of Caracas had recommended to the future congress, the conservation of the popular representation in the government and the prolongation of the terms of office for the high functionaries. In Maracaibo there were manifestations in favor of the life presidency of Bolívar, but as the Minister of the Interior in a circular to the prefects had declared, on the 18th of October, that the Government desired to know the opinion of the people on the reforms which were to be submitted to the forthcoming assembly, affirming that "the Liberator had no personal view of the nature of the government and of the administration which should preside over it"; and as Bolívar, on his part, wrote to General Páez that he wished him to investigate the popular will, freely expressed,[3] the secessionists of Venezuela resolved to make use of these circumstances to realize their program. Páez tried to learn in the meanwhile if the Liberator really wanted the establishment of the monarchy, and requested definite information from the Government. "Not being able to give a positive answer to this question," declared Restrepo, "he sent First Commandant José Austria to Bolívar with orders to obtain precise instructions."[4] Briceño Méndez asked Bermúdez his

---

was given to me, there was one, the only one which Mr. Pavagean took with him, giving an account of various subjects, whose dates I remember very well and which was also known by the contemporaries of the epoch, if still living, in which was a suggestion to the Liberator that he crown himself. Bolívar refused the proposition in the following terms: 'To accept a crown would be to ruin my glory. I much prefer the title of the First Citizen of Colombia.' These words affirm as that of a man of honor who has seen the statements in this document, but which were not published because of the orders of the Liberator, and also because they should not compromise the signatures of the authors of the proposition." *Diary on the Illness of His Excellency the Liberator* (*Diario sobre la enfermedad que padece Su Excelencia el Libertador*). The ninth article of the testament of Bolívar reads: "I order that the papers which are in the possession of Mr. Pavagean be burned."

[1]*General Soublette to General José Tadeo Monagas, Caracas, December 18*, 1829.
[2]*Vide* Gil Fortoul. *Obra citada.*
[3]The letters of March 25 and September 13, 1829.
[4]This phrase of the Minister of the Interior is another proof that the Council did consult Bolívar on the matter. It would seem as if these horrible members of the Government staged a comedy ordered by the Liberator. IV, 206.

opinion of the question of a monarchy, believing confidently that
the resolution of the Liberator, who "is not posted on the project"
might subordinate itself to the desire of the great military chiefs.[1]
The men of Venezuela, without distinction of party or flag, were
in doubt about Bolívar's thoughts on the subject, or feigned to be
so. His friends feared to disturb him; his enemies predicted distrust. We should not fear the lion but the serpent, wrote Vicente
Azuero. Nobody believed that Bolívar had no desires, no projects, no strength. "The declining star" threw out the last sparkles
before sinking into the "living death, silent and portentous."[2]
His soul was invaded by bitterness and renunciation. He really
desired "license or liberty, like the soldiers and the slaves."[3]
He refused to write another constitution, because he knew that
it would meet the fate of the two which he had written in ten
years.[4] He proclaimed, with sad irony that it matter little to him
what the country did. He wrote:[5]

> "Federation may be one of the favorite systems of the people. Let them
> adopt it, then, and let us struggle no more. If they want the Constitution of
> Cúcuta, or the twenty departments with their departmental assemblies, nothing
> is easier, because there will be no work rewriting it. If they do not wish mon-
> archies or life offices, and even less aristocracies, why do they not immediately
> bury themselves in the noisy and happy ocean of anarchy? This is indeed popular,
> and accordingly should be the best, because according to my own maxim the
> *sovereign must be infallible.*"

The Spanish threat brought back to him, nevertheless, a little
energy in order to save the Republic and his glory.[6]

On the 13th of November a meeting of the citizens of Valencia,
in the presence of General Páez and his secretary, Doctor Miguel
Peña, voted in favor of the separation of Venezuela from the
Colombian State; on the 17th Puerto Cabello made a like pronouncement and on the 26th Caracas renounced the authoirty of
Bolívar, adhering to the resolution of Valencia and called Páez
to exercise the supreme command. This action of Caracas, in-
jurious to the Liberator, was signed by Lino de Clemente, prefect;
by Narvarte, Fortique, Alfonso, Mariño, Arismendi, Escalona,
Echezuría, Ayala, Lanz, Antonio Leocadio Guzmán, by four
hundred and more persons. At that moment the old enemies of
Páez took an active part alongside of Clemente, an old enemy
of Páez, and of that of Guzmán whose youth had been honored
by the great man, and General Juan de Escalona, and the patrician
Tovar. Soublette, leagued closely with the Superior Chief,
whom in reality he disdained, now used words which did not com-

[1]Briseño Méndez to General Bermúdez, Caracas, October 8, 1829.
[2]Gonzales, *On the Margin of the Epoyee, Declining Star.*
[3]*The Liberator to Doctor Alamo, Popayán, December 6, 1829.*
[4]*The Liberator to Doctor Vergara, Guayquil, August 31, 1829.*
[5]*The Liberator to Don Joaquin Mosquera, Guayaquil, September 3, 1829.*
[6]*The Liberator to General Alcántara Herrán, Garzal, October 3, 1829.*

fort with his illustrious career.   The union was possible through
the separatist cause.
    The circular of the Government opened the valves of anarchy.
In Manabí and Guayaquil the presidency of Bolívar was acclaimed.
Panama sought freedom of commerce and the opening of a canal.
The citizens of San Felipe voted for a confederation. The patriots
of Puerto Cabello desired that the name of the Liberator be consigned to oblivion. . . . .
    General Páez informed Bolívar of the events of Venezuela,
requesting him not to oppose the separatists, for it would throw
the country into civil war.[1]   The Minister of the Interior also
received official news of the events.[2]   Bolívar had taken the last
steps to keep Venezuela in obedience by offering his support to
General Páez by elevating him to the presidencia of Colombia.
He suggested through the medium of Señor Austria that it would
be proper for him to give up the command, although he would
retain that of the army.[3]   The Liberator forced himself to overcome the bad impression caused by unfortunate project of the
Government. He declared:[4]

> "If some persons interpret my mode of thinking and errors appear in it,
> I am sorry for it, but it was inevitable. People desire to do good and evil with
> my name in Colombia and many choose it as a subject of their disputes. There
> are not a few who have spoken to me of a monarchy, and at different periods,
> but I have always said frankly what I think on that subject. The nation may
> assume the form which it desires, the people have been asked in a thousand ways
> to express their will and it should be the only guide in the deliberations of the
> Congress. But be persuaded and let the whole world be persuaded that I shall
> never be king of Colombia, neither by an extraordinary event, nor will I make
> myself a creditor whereby posterity may despoil me of the title of Liberator
> which my fellow citizens gave me and which surpasses all my ambition."

    At the beginning of the following year he left the people of the
South, who had already begun to agitate, and returned to Bogotá,
where he changed the composition of the Cabinet. On the 20th
of January Bolívar installed the Model Congress.
    The Liberator refrained, because of fatigue and because he
wished to give a proof of his disinterestedness to the nation,
from recommending to the Assembly the bases of a new Constitution, and showed that he had no desire to influence it in its
deliberations. His hopes had vanished. He wrote:

> "Independence is the only good thing which we have acquired at the cost
> of everything else."

    He presented the renunciation of his powers, this time definite-
ly and irrevocably, in sad and eloquent terms, which resounded

---

[1]*General Páez to the Liberator, December 1, and 21, 1829.*
[2]*General Páez to the Minister of the Interior, December 8, 1829.*
[3]*The Liberator to General Páez, December 15, 1829.   Vide* also his letter to
Briceño Méndez, October 23, 1829.
[4]*The Liberator to Antonio Leocadio Guzmán, Popayán, December 6, 1829.   Vide*
also his letter of the same date to Doctor Alamo.

in the Congress and throughout America as a knell in the funeral
of our glory. He declared:[1]

> "Protect me, I beg you, from the insults which await me were I to con-
> tinue to occupy a position which never can shield me from the vituperation of
> ambition. Believe me, a new magistrate is now indispensible for the Republic.
> The people desire to know if the time has not come for me to cease governing.
> The American States look upon me with inquietude, which may some day
> bring about evils in Colombia like those of the war in Perú. Even in Europe
> there are not wanting those who fear that I may discredit with my conduct the
> beautiful cause of liberty. Ah! How many conspiracies and wars have we not
> suffered through attempts upon my authority and person. . . . The
> Republic will be happy if, on accepting my resignation, you will name as presi-
> dent a citizen beloved of the nation. It will succumb if you refuse them what I
> have ordered. Hear my supplications. Save the Republic. Save my glory,
> which is that of Colombia."

The proclamation of Bolívar to the people was a defence of
his acts and ideas against the calumnies which had depopularized
him. He affirmed with an imperious voice before the nation and
before history the purity of his republican sentiments: "Never,
never, I swear to you, has my mind entertained any desire to
be king, which my enemies have artfully charged to lower me in
your opinion." And he made even then a desperate effort for
fraternity and for obedience to Congress, which is "the national
wisdom, the legitimate hope of the people and ultimate bond of
union of all the patriots."[2]

The dismemberment of Colombia was completed. The efforts
of the Congress to make an agreement with the separatists of
Venezuela failed in the crash. Marshal Sucre and the members
of his commission did not succeed in having the Venezuelans
accept the bases of the agreement that Bogotá proposed, namely,
the integrity of Colombia; popular government, representative
and elective; establishment of legislatures for the districts, with
power to deliberate and resolve local questions, and to represent
them in matters of general interest to the Republic; irresponsibility
of the chief of the State, except in case of high treason; Roman
Catholicism as the national religion, with the exclusion of every
other cult. The Congress of Valencia was already preparing a
special Constitution for Venezuela.[3] The policy and the name of
the Liberator were buried in a bewilderment of unpopularity,
dragging with it the future of Colombia and the most beautiful
ideals of our history.[4]

---

[1] *The Liberator to the Constituent Congress, January 20,* 1830.
[2] *The Liberator to the Colombians, January 20,* 1830.
[3] The Constituent Congress of Valencia convened on May 6, and proclaimed
the Venezuelan Constitution on September 22nd.
[4] The Marshal of Ayacucho, Bishop Esteves and Aranda entered into, on
approaching the frontier of Táchira, a discussion with the governor of Mérida,
who showed the sentiments of the Venezuelans who were either Bolivarians or
supporters of the Government. General Piñango states that the commissioners
did not enter the territory of Venezuela, nor he in "scientific controversies" in
order to settle the differences which existed between the Congress and the Govern-

From the 15th of April General Domingo Caicedo, to whom as president of the Council of State, Bolívar had yielded the command, suggested to the Congress of Bogotá, the need of convoking a Granadian Convention, in view ot the futility of all attempts to maintain the Colombian unity.[1] The Congress preferred to draft a new code, which was to be offered to Venezuela, on the bases agreed upon. In reality, this statute was a triumph of the Santanderians and it might have been wiser to have accepted their program at Ocaña, and thereby to have avoided the dictatorship of Bolívar. Passions attained an incredible degree of violence. In Caracas the Liberator and the Congress were insulted. In Bogotá, in the heart of the Assembly, voices were raised calling Páez and the Venezuelans scoundrels and robbers. The Constituent Convention of Valencia soon decreed that the relations of Venezuela with New Granada could not be renewed so long as there remained in the territory of the latter. . . . the Liberator of America. The anti-Bolivarian reaction grew stronger with the election of Joaquin Mosquera to the presidency, who yielded the power to the liberals. In the meanwhile, Quito pronounced for separation and General Juan José Flores convoked, on the 31st of May, a Constituent Convention in the city of Riobamba. The assassination of the Marshal of Ayacucho, the first captain of the Revolution, the most illustrious man of the Continent after Bolívar, raised to the limit this barbarous and bloody anarchy.

The Liberator was now become only the plaything of dishonor and misfortune.[2] Sick and desperate, he took refuge on the coast of Granada, on the way to Europe, where he wished to go to die of sadness and misery. He carried with him the glory of America.[3] There still came to him those who seek the fidelity of his last moments, helpers to offer his dying hand an illusory and usurpatious power. We take part, in this sad hour, in the final struggle which is taking place in the depths of his immense soul. One moment he appears to have decided to go to die in foreign lands, and a little later he refuses to leave the country, not desiring that "they eject him" because Colombia and Venezuela would dishonor themselves in doing so. "I am dying," he declared, according to Posada Gutiérrez, "my time has come. God calls me. I must prepare to give Him an account, a terrible account, of the conduct of my life. And I desire to yield up my last breath in the arms of my old companions, surrounded by Christian priests of my country

---

ment or Bolívar. The Marshal, on this occasion, was irritated to the point of committing sacrilige and insults.

[1]Restrepo declares that the Liberator desired to be elected constitutional president once more, maintaining that if he surrendered power he would be the laughing stock of his enemies. This is merely a matter of opinion, which Bolívar settled quickly before the adverse opinion of his counsellors. IV, 309.

[2]*The Liberator to General Justo Briceño, Fucha, March 8,* 1830

[3]*The Liberator to Don Joaquin Mosquera, Fucha, March 8,* 1830.

and with a crucifix in my hands. I shall not go."[1] Urdaneta, master of the Government, has him acclaimed in the capital. Bolívar answered in equivocal language which lent itself to any interpretation.[2] He promised to march to Bogotá but refused the command of the army because it was useless, because he did not wish to finish the ruin of his reputation.[3] He did not accept power because he had no hope for the country, because not having authorized this movement, if he accepted the fruit of its insurrection, he would be responsible for it. He declared that he was asked by Urdaneta to go to Bogotá because "Santa María made me see that you would divide yourself into a thousand parties and ruin the country completely if I answered that I would not accept. I offered then vaguely to serve as a citizen and a soldier." But "everything is lost forever," and his friends whom he pities cannot count on his assistance. In addition, he was proscribed, "the tyrants of my country have taken it away from me. Therefore, I have no country to which I can make the sacrifice."[4]

The last sacrifice of the Liberator shall be that of his resentments. His last proclamation to the Colombians was a word of pardon for his adversaries and an appeal for harmony among the parties.

---

[1]Letter to General Urdaneta. Proclamation to the Colombians. *Cartagena, September 18*, 1830.
[2]*The Liberator to General Justo Briscéño, Cartagena, September 4*, 1830.
[3]*The Liberator to Doctor Vergara. Cartagena, September 25*, 1830.
[4]*The Liberator to Doctor Vergara, Cartagena, September 25*, 1930.